THE
GOLDEN AGE
RECORDED

New and Revised Edition

P. G. HURST

THE OAKWOOD PRESS

1963

The Publishers wish to thank the Proprietors of "Punch" for their kindness in allowing a number of contemporary cartoons from its pages to be reproduced here.

Printed by R. C. Stephens, 1 Belgrave Terrace, Woodford Wells, Essex

CONTENTS

PART I

A COLLECTOR'S SURVEY

PART II

THE ARTISTS AND THEIR WORK

No tongue have I, no hands, nor yet a voice,
Yet talk, or sing, or play, which is your choice?
There is no instrument that you can name
I am not mistress of; 'tis all the same.
With song I sing untiring with the purest tone,
Soprano, alto, bass or baritone.
All languages are mine, with wondrous skill
I talk, weep, laugh, and will your senses thrill
With stirring scenes from playwrites, comic, tragic,
All bow in turn to my resistless magic.
Music and song my captives, sound my throne,
I reign supreme, their Queen,
                    THE GRAMOPHONE
                                        ANON.

From a "Berliner" catalogue dated January 1901.

The author hopes that the omission of all accentation throughout this book has removed fruitful causes of error besides tidying his pages.
He has not adopted strict uniformity in the matter of opera titles except in a preference for the language of their origin. This is sometimes to preserve the character of the catalogues of the period, sometimes to avoid monotony, and occasionally to indulge his own fancy.

INTRODUCTION TO SECOND EDITION

SIXTEEN years have passed since I launched the "G.A.R.", as it is now generally known, at my own expense and acting as my own publisher. Despite its manifest shortcomings it can at least claim to have gone out of print before demand became exhausted; and in the belief that the great expansion of the numbers of collectors of rare and historical records that has taken place since those days, as well as the fact that to the best of my belief that it is still favourably regarded as the only serious attempt to codify the subject, I am offering a much revised edition in a more permanent form.

I might add another reason, namely that at my advancing age I may be the last to be able to speak coherently of personal experiences of times and events which already are growing misty and conjectural—the last to testify to the actual beginnings of a gramophone industry and to the lost art of truly great singing. I shall carry the reader back as far as 1900, when I first felt the quickening of interest in these events which in sixty-three years has never diminished but has continued to increase, and of which I hope I have conveyed something in the pages which follow.

I find that what I wrote in 1946 calls for little revision in principle. But I have seized this opportunity for improvement (as I hope), for pruning of dead wood, the correction of those slips and errors which so pertinaciously intrude themselves, and for developing the old material and introducing new, while the fundamental truths and basic structure remain.

Although I must deal with several artists whom I never heard in person, the focus on the Covent Garden of the Edwardian decade as my spiritual home of singing is not likely to pass unnoticed, for its prestige was still unlimited at the beginnings of the recording industry, and New York talent-spotters looked there for their lead. To have sung with success at a Syndicate season was the crown on a career, and would open all doors. Mistakes were made, of course, and we had much tribulation at times, but it was not until the inter-war seasons that an infiltration became formidable, particularly a crop of baritones which caused us grievous distress. The old dress tradition was still precariously maintained, but the opera made its first fatal sideways slip in accepting the baleful interference of *quasi*-politicians and other weird characters as the price of a government subsidy, and thereafter the "Royal Opera" became in fact if not in name the State Opera. *Sic transit.*

In the belief that it will please my old friends of the G.A.R., it has been my aim to retain the amateur status of the old book, striving to avoid cliches and their offshoots, and to speak my mind. I cling obstinately to such authentic English usages as the plurality of "none", to a constitutional abhorrence of such unnecessary innovations as the adjectival "nearby", and seeing no reason to sidestep the good old English "got". In giving precedence to the "Princess" over the "Marschallin" I follow Strauss, Hofmannsthal, their publisher Furstner, and the early usage of Covent Garden until somebody at a later date decided otherwise. The Princess' rueful reference to herself as *die alte marschallin* carries its own meaning, for she was "Her Highness" in her own right before being the mere Field-Marshal's lady. Among other foibles I have collected over the years is an aversion which I think is not pedantic to hearing a long o in "opus"—a gaffe which in the days of classical precision was very properly a caning matter; but any doubts on this point may be settled by consulting a Latin dictionary. This is only one of the pseudo-educational preciosities which emanate from some of our great pseudo-educational institutions.

*   *   *   *

What will follow in this book is intended to interest and perhaps help those who, while possessing a keen musical sense and a desire to understand and to preserve the highest traditions of the vocal art, have felt the urge to seek out recorded examples of the Golden Age.

All collectors must have felt in some degree the vein of sentiment that runs through all forms of collecting, and which defies cool reason. It is intangible and vague, but it is there, and it is felt by young collectors who "knew not Joseph", and this susceptibility in the younger generation has been one of the most unexpected and pleasing features of our fellowship, for it has flattered us elders with the thought that our impressions were not based merely upon the traditional admiration for the things of our youth, as is the perennial complaint of the young against the old. Few indeed among collectors are there who can claim to retain vivid memories of the events which led up to the advance of the "talking machine" into the realm of art; but the writer, who remembers the issue of each and all of the records which will be mentioned or tabulated herein, was a faithful witness of all of them. He hopes therefore to be able to suggest in the written word some part at least of that recurring excitement which so stirred him as these wonderful discs successively appeared.

A QUICK REVIEW

SERIOUS recording for the gramophone indeed began just as truly great singing was on the point of beginning its decline. This is no controversial statement. It is a matter of history how the Covent Garden triumphs of the 'nineties did not long survive the death of that *entrepreneur* of genius, Augustus Harris. He had put Jean de Reszke into his dominant place, and with that supreme artist's departure in 1900 the break came with some precipitancy. The influence of his art, by example and by precept, contributed to build up that higher standard of artistic endeavour which resulted in the thrilling *crescendo* of excellence which marked the progress of opera throughout his period, and if this is accepted as true, it would seem that the effect of his departure was inevitable. With the passing of the century, of Queen Victoria and of Jean de Reszke the great stars began one by one to disappear from the London operatic stage. Within the space of only three or four seasons we may write *finis* to the Covent Garden careers of Tamagno, de Lussan, Eames, Alvarez, Saleza, Salignac, Plancon, Calve, de Lucia and Ancona, leaving the short and lustrous years of the Edwardian epoch, so aptly described by the critic Klein as *operdammerung*, to use what material was left over and to find its own. The twilight, however, was a warm and genial one, and indeed the two seasons of 1904 produced a truly vintage crop of superb singers. But in retrospect it was not for long. Covent Garden became an increasingly close preserve as Melba's ascendency reached its peak. Sad as I am to relate it, many first-rate sopranos either sang only once or twice or never at all, and the inevitable consequence was that this starving of the life-blood of opera resulted, following the halcyon season of 1908, in a hard and cold competence while performers of real brilliance tended to become exceptional, and this state of affairs continued until the war in 1914.

The gramophone, as we have seen, came just in time, but only just. Some of the greatest voices of the 'nineties were recorded not unsuccessfully while still in their prime, as well as those of a few who were actually flourishing as leading singers in the 'seventies and early 'eighties, and whose day had naturally passed, but whose records are none the less historical documents of the first importance.

It is now generally recognised that there was something ironical in the pioneer struggle to improve recording technique without giving thought to the crude and inefficient apparatus which was then the gramophone. It was a matter of twenty years before this truth was realised and acted upon, and was celebrated by the appearance of the first really revolutionary change in

9

gramophone design. This was, as I recollect, more stereophonic in character than what we now accept as stereophonic sound, and on account of its succession of sound chambers was called the Re-Entrant Gramophone. This important development demanded the "loud" steel needles to bring forth its full sonorous effect, but was too soon superseded by the still more exciting discovery of electrical reproduction with all that it implied. It has now landed us into the position of having to sit through thirty minutes or so solid listening to records of which we may be growing weary, or worse still to compositions which we once admired and are now, through overmuch repetition, heartily sick of. The "78s" were too short to get tired of in the same degree. But I will not labour this point: the LP records produce glorious synthetic sounds, which, with the usual cabinet resonances are about as unlike a living voice or orchestra as they can be. The absence of surface noise is an advantage which cannot be denied, but I remember with pleasure the occasion of a visit by two young members of the New Opera Group who wished to hear some examples of the Golden Age recorded. I explained, or began to explain, how a certain amount of scratch would have to be endured, only to be assured that they had brought with them scratch filters of complete efficiency—their ears. In other words, these enlightened musicians were able to concentrate on what they wished to hear and to disregard what they did not, which in my view is a better approach than a concentration on surface faults and disregard of the more aesthetic values.

Let us now turn to the practical side. As most collectors know, the Berliner phase of recording left little that was memorable except itself, but I will deal with it in greater detail later. It just overlapped the beginnings of the "Gramophone and Typewriter" epoch, which I named "G&T", and which raised its sights somewhat higher than the Berliner output. G&T records went into production in 1900 in London, Paris, Moscow and St. Petersburg and probably elsewhere, and in 1902 and 1903 the London recording studio made an artistic and meritorious step forward by recording the voices of concert artists of high standing for the popular market. It was not altogether successful, either commercially or technically, being before its time, since it is likely that buyers of gramophones were hardly numbered among serious concert goers. Fred Gaisberg used to say that the best singers made the best records, but this was to over-simplify a complex problem. So, many of the better artists were quickly withdrawn and their places taken by selected singers whose voices were judged to have been better suited to the purpose, and whose reputations were less brittle.

We shall find, after a brief survey of the recording done during the "collector's period", that the year 1907 offers such palpable advantages for ending a recording era that it would be difficult to find another equally logical. In the eight years from 1900 to 1907 all the singers, one might say, of immortal renown made their first recordings; and that period was distinguished by a well-defined characteristic in recording generally, and put a term to a rather happy-go-lucky, hit-or-miss approach. Also, it marked the end of the G&T period; and this, by fateful coincidence, applied the datum line to Fonotipia also. After that year G&T seemed to confine themselves to a straight line of policy rather than branching out into something fresh, especially into greater enterprise in combinations of top-ranking stars. Except for the solitary duet by Boninsegna and de Lucia there were no such combinations. Every credit must be given to the Gaisbergs for their unique pioneer work, but they lacked the wider vision. G&T recording began to suffer from a lack of realism in the search for smoother surfaces, and Fonotipia thought it a progressive policy to re-record much of their previous work with orchestral accompaniments. We certainly thought so at the time, but it is a curious fact that many of the earliest such accompaniments were better than many that followed. It is impossible even to attempt to convey to present-day collectors what we thought about the gramophone at that time: there was so much that was intangible, ephemeral and imponderable; the too rapid deterioration, the scratch problem and our clumsy attempt to mitigate it, and always the hope that *our* gramophone and *our* records would win the admiration of our friends.

The first G&T catalogue, as such, was undated, but was issued in November 1901, but it is certain that G&T records had been on sale earlier, and probably appended to the Berliner catalogue.

More interesting, perhaps, is the early history of the red label, which put celebrity artists into the recording picture. At double the standard price I rather naively supposed that they would play for double as long, but in fact they were exactly the same.

Here again the very earliest specimens of this historic series nearly merge into the mists of obscurity. The pioneers of the red label issue were made, neither in London nor in Milan, but in St. Petersburg and Moscow, in the year 1900. So the first "celebrities" were Russian, and were recorded under the aegis of Mr. Michaelis, to whom is ascribed the original idea for the use of red labels for the celebrities.[1] With Mr. Michaelis was A. T. Lack, who recorded Boronat in 1904, and Fred Gaisberg did much of the recording of Michailowa. In March 1902 Gaisberg recorded the first G&Ts by Caruso, and thus was history made.

From 1902 onwards and for the next four or five years, each year produced its batch of new recordings by international artists of the highest standing, and it is a fortunate coincidence for collectors that in each of these years certain small but significant changes were made which enable collectors to fix with almost complete accuracy the year of any G&T disc, whether red or black, as will be seen in its place. The first 12-inch records were made in

London in 1903, but after that year the centre of gravity for the production of celebrity records, excepting those of Melba and Patti, settled down in Milan and with the associated Victor company in the U.S.A. So far Europe had had the monopoly of the red label issues, but at the latter end of 1903, the Victor company took over this sideline and developed it into a major part of the rapidly growing industry. The Victor celebrity records were issued in Europe under the aegis of the G&T company, with a caption added to the European red label. These I christened "Victor-G&T", to keep it in the family, so to speak. They had characteristics of their own, advantageous as regarded smoothness and durability (an important asset in those days), but somewhat lacking in the spontaneous "nearness" of the voice, until this was more fully revealed by highly specialised modern methods. In the final phase of the G&T period the "Victor-G&T" caption was dropped, and some New York recordings are found with the plain G&T label.

While the Victor company was busy with its red label issues, Fred Gaisberg in London was occupied with the absorbing and exciting experience of recording Melba, an experience to which none other than himself could do full justice.[1] In these London issues of 1904–5–6 the G&T methods were employed with the advantages and drawbacks already mentioned fully in evidence. Melba was not, in fact, an ideal recorder, having regard to the only method of reproduction open to the industry of those days, but given fine copies and modern reproducing apparatus and a tolerant ear, the voice of Melba is fully revealed in all its beauty in a manner and with a vocal fidelity never again to be quite the same. Nearly all these titles were re-recorded by Victor in 1907 and many again later, with better surfaces but less fidelity and life, although unmistakably Melba to those who had heard her in person. With this American issue all those titles which it replaced were withdrawn, again with the losses and gains peculiar to the respective methods, and thereafter for a matter of twenty years Melba recorded exclusively in America, until at the age of sixty-three she recorded her last in London.

Soon after Melba's debut as a recorder for the gramophone its instant success induced Patti to break her silence, although, like Melba in the first place, she insisted upon playing the mountain to the gramophone's Mahomet; and accordingly Mr. Gaisberg and his myrmidons, who included Landon Ronald to act as accompanist, betook themselves to the castle in Wales where in a leisurely and spacious manner the first session was held.

---

[1] Gaisberg in his book *The Music goes Round* ascribed the red label to one Rappaport, a dealer in Moscow, and makes no mention of Michaelis being in Russia (he was in Milan in 1902). It seems likely that this Rappaport made the suggestion to Michaelis who forwarded it to his superiors in London. I corrected a good many errors of fact in this book for the American edition *Music on Record*.

After 1907 the G&T company embarked upon a scheme for regrouping their celebrity artists. The honoured red label was downgraded to second place, with a pink label, hitherto sacred to Patti, allotted to the senior group. Nothing, however, could be clearer than the need for avoiding any conclusion that this new demarcation signified any comparison of merit, which becomes very evident when we find among the new-style reds the names of Ancona, de Lucia, Boronat, Kurz, Boninsegna and Journet. We may suppose that they had exhausted their selling power, and so were put into the bargain basement.

For the duration of the G&T period Melba 12-inch records with a lilac label sold at a guinea, and a few 10-inch at twelve-and-sixpence and poorly recorded; Patti's and Tamagno's at £1, 12-inch red label (including Victor-G&T) at fifteen shillings, 10-inch at ten shillings. Black label 12-inch were seven-and-sixpence and 10-inch were five shillings. At the time of the regrouping just referred to all these prices were reduced excepting Tamagno. By that time Melba had come under the control of the Victor company and doubtless with a different contract.

At a date which is still under discussion, as will appear in its place, the Fonotipia company of Milan—later to be known as of Milan, Paris and London—(although where London came into the picture is something which I have never understood), startled gramophone circles with their astonishingly brilliant issue first of single-sided 10¾-inch discs soon followed by double-sided records, which now rank with G&T as collectors' specimens. They were limited to renderings of the finest vocal music, except for some highly popular items by the famous violinist Kubelik, who, with several other G&T artists, had walked over to the new company, leaving G&T in a state of some disgruntlement which expressed itself generally in the withdrawal of the records by the defaulting artists. They will be described in a special section, where I shall deal particularly with the numbering and dating of this interesting series.

There were also a very few Columbia, Beka and Odeon records which had the merit of standing alone and were not repetitions of earlier recordings by artists of our period.

PART ONE

A Collector's Survey

CHAPTER ONE

ORIGINS

HOW IT BEGAN

COMPARED with the number of collectors who owe their beginnings directly or indirectly to the author's early writings in *The Gramophone* magazine, a far greater number nowadays will never have heard of them, but who may none the less care to know how it was that the beginnings came about.

There had been a few collectors—perhaps three or four—before my own part in the more extended history of record-collecting was thrust upon me, and this arose out of a feature in *The Gramophone* called "Collectors' Corner", which handled anything of a curious nature among gramophone records. It was in these notes and in the year 1929, that I read a suggestion that it might be quite a good idea to try for a small collection of *early* records, a suggestion which struck so powerful a chord in my memory that I immediately sensed the possibilities that I thought might lie ahead. The idea gathered impetus from contributions to this Collectors' Corner from the owners of the initials R.E.G. (London) and M.H. (Thirsk), with whom I soon got into touch, finding their identities as Robert Garnett and Malcolm Hurtley—both to be my friends for many years—when they became reconciled to the idea that their esoteric cult was to be made public. Through Robert Garnett I met Eric Bernard, another ardent and highly knowledgeable collector who also was to become a close and much valued friend.

I had some background both from the curious interest I had while still in schooldays in the doings at the opera, and even so early the names of Eames, Melba, de Reszke and Schumann-Heink were familiar to me, and from the immediate fascination which the first red label celebrity records exercised over me. This would have been in 1902, when I already knew by heart the contents of the celebrity catalogue of records and greatly longed to possess them.

As a modest customer of Messrs. Alfred Hays when opposite the London Royal Exchange I would often slip down into their gramophone department in the hope of hearing some of the much-coveted "reds", and it was by these means that I got my first initiation in the cult of great singing. Through the kindly offices of Messrs. Hays' assistants, who doubtless regarded me as something of a curiosity, I was sometimes able to salvage, very much *sub rosa*, many expensive records in varying degrees of decrepitude which had been turned in for exchange at the generous break-up value which was then offered, and this gave me a liberal education which was to serve me well later.

But now, jumping the intervening years, I return to the beginnings of my own "Collectors' Corner" in 1931, for without entering into further detail, the editor of *The Gramophone*, Mr. Compton Mackenzie, offered me the job of trying my hand at reviving this moribund feature. (It had in fact then ceased to appear.)

I liked the idea, and hoped that I might be able to concoct two or perhaps three single-column articles from my own recollections of the early days of recording. In fact it took four such articles before anything really happened, and then quite suddenly everything seemed to happen at once. Enquiries began to arrive in steadily increasing numbers and within a matter of weeks my column became two columns and then four. I was soon in touch with correspondents as far away as Bombay, Tokyo, and even Norfolk Island, and made many contacts some of which I am happy to say continue cordially to this day. Robert Bauer of Milan, Professor Wilhelm (as he later became, and a most courageous anti-Nazi), of Saxony, Lenti of Leningrad, Aleman of Havana, Cara Hartwell of Toronto, my cherished lady collector: too many in the U.S.A. to mention by name, and much the same must be said of Australia, except that Laurie Root of Melbourne has never ceased to exchange letters with me since the early 'thirties. All these and countless others contributed generously to the success of "C.C.", and I am grateful to them all, whether named or unnamed. Through "C.C." I knew Fred Gaisberg (of whom more anon), Cecil Pollard of *The Gramophone*, always and still a loyal friend; Anna Instone of the B.B.C. and pleasant memories; Fred Grisewood of occasional encounter; Zelie de Lussan of whom I have written much; Agnes Nicholls (Lady Hamilton Harty), who, like Zelie, was a friend of twenty years standing; Blanche Marchesi, unique, and indirectly how many more. Some of these are already a distant memory: I have unconventional recordings of the voices of some, and the clearest mental pictures of all. They are very much in my mind as I revise this book.

*   *   *   *

In the six years of "Collectors' Corner", an enormous expansion had taken place, and a number of splinter-groups had emerged. This was quite natural and healthy, and a proof of the vigour and virility of the cult; but what was not quite so good was that the old spirit was less in evidence and a new spirit of antagonisms had replaced it. I could not understand this, and still do not. "C.C." served a definite purpose and never wavered from it; nor did it criticise other groups, but continued on its way without altering its policy or its trend. Admittedly it had the strategical advantage of occupying the pulpit, from which it preached the only doctrine it understood, but the end was ignominious and I was unceremoniously flung out. But I consoled myself with the thought that a creation for which I had foreseen a life of two or three months had grown and expanded for six years, which, in the days of the Decline and Fall, was quite a respectable period for the reign of a Roman Emperor.

*   *   *   *

Linked with the rise of record-collecting was the interest it was creating within the B.B.C., where "C.C." had its personal adherents; and having arranged a programme for Christopher Stone from my own embryo collection with my own script, it was not a far remove that I should put over a programme myself. Christopher Stone's programme opened a crack in the door to an entirely new policy for the B.B.C. and I was enabled to walk through it. This was in 1934, and the B.B.C. certainly did me well, with forty minutes to myself at the peak hour of the evening, and with the Chief Announcer, Stuart Hibberd, to speak a special introduction which certainly put me on my mettle. This was before the days of the mechanisation of broadcasting, and the announcer spoke into the microphone over my shoulder—Hibberd, as was his custom, wearing a dinner jacket. Many years later I persuaded him to record this announcement for me, and this record ranks as one of my super-rarities. It was certainly an occasion, and produced much flattering comment in the announcers' common-room after it was over, and such a "fan mail" as brought about several repetitions. I gladly attribute this success to the expert coaching of E. J. King-Bull of the B.B.C. Broadcasting in those days was great fun and a very friendly business; but later, as when the announcers became invisible and the announcement merely a sound in the studio speaker and nobody seemed to be around, it lost its novelty, for me, at any rate, although there was no lack of volunteers to make their broadcasting debut through this medium.

My programmes received acknowledgements from Suzanne Adams, Zelie de Lussan, Blanche Marchesi, Emma Nevada, Susan Strong, Herbert Heyner, Ben Davies, Redvers Llewellyn, and many who were unknown to me who wrote very pleasantly, and whose letters and postcards I carefully preserve to this day.

CHAPTER TWO

THE EARLY GRAMOPHONE

"In the thirteenth century a certain Albert Magnus constructed a piece of mechanism which sent forth distinct vocal sounds, by which Thomas Aquinas was so greatly terrified that he struck at it with his staff, and to the mortificaion of Albert, annihilated the curious labour of thirty years."

[1] The above reference is taken from Isaac D'Israeli's *Curiosities of Literature*, 1859.

THE earliest commercial gramophone is still happily a familiar object to us, through the famous "Dog" trademark. I sometimes wonder whether any collector save myself has seen the original of this most remarkable painting. The artist, Barraud, had painted it in the hope of disposing of it to a talking-machine company, and trying first the Columbia or Edison-Bell, I forget which, had depicted a cylinder machine otherwise identical with the gramophone. The offer was refused and the artist went to G&T who at once accepted it on condition that a disc turntable was substituted for the cylinder mounting. This was quite successfully accomplished, though the outline of the cylinder can still be detected under close scrutiny. The picture became perhaps the best known in the world. If my memory serves I was told on the occasion of a luncheon in the E.M.I. board room that the fortunate (or unfortunate) artist was commissioned to duplicate this painting until some 400 copies had been made for distribution to G&T's branches throughout the world, and that each copy was so perfect as to be indistinguishable from the original, the over-painting of course excepted. Very roughly, and again speaking from memory, it may measure 30 ins. by 25 ins., and it hangs over the mantel of the E.M.I. boardroom.

Few today would realise how fearsome a thing this gramophone was for the work it was expected to do. The little horn was joined directly to the soundbox by means of a leather elbow, so that horn, soundbox and supporting bar came up together in one movement when changing a needle or a record. The turntable was of 7 ins. diameter intended for Berliner records, though the later G&T "Concert" 10-in. records could be played, if not too long, by removing the winding handle. The speed regulator was not calibrated, and offered no indication of how it was set. Although the soundbox was a crude contraption with a mica diaphragm attached by a blob of beeswax to a

20

stylus, its inventor had hit upon the right idea, and the principle it embodied remained unchanged for as long as acoustical reproduction survived. The same may be said of the rest of this gramophone, for although its successors passed through stages of various modification and refinement, they remained virtually and basically unchanged for over twenty years. It passed through such phases as the "gooseneck" attached to a tapered arm—a patented sound conduit to which G&T attached prime importance—and so excellent was their workmanship and so clever their publicity that none of their near-imitators made any deep appeal to the true gramophonist. Next came the built-in horn hidden discreetly behind two doors, and with the turntable enclosed. This was largely non-metal and so had a damping effect which reduced scratch. The mistake they made was in using this device on very small portable machines which were little better than toys, until they in their turn were greatly improved by hidden sound chambers. This development embodied the principles used in the "Re-Entrant" which was the first major advance in the history of the gramophone, and so soon to be lost sight of in the discovery of electrical reproduction. This machine greatly extended the musical range both ways, but especially in the bass, and "listen to the bass" became the popular appeal, until it slowly dawned upon us that what we were listening to was something quite unlike reality, although highly stimulating. From that time (roughly 1924) the H.M.V. gramophone passed, and electrical devices took its place, passing through a teething stage of sheer horror to something capable of reproducing reality in the hands of a tactful operator.

*   *   *   *

Two freak machines were constructed by G&T in the quite early days which are worthy a place in this note. The first, in about 1904, had three turntables vertically ganged and worked by a single motor with a separate horn and soundbox for each. Three identical records were adjusted by marks, the soundboxes placed, and the spring released. What happened next I cannot relate, for although I saw the thing I never heard it, but evidently it was hoped that the adjustments would synchronise and that a three-power record would result.

The other was named the "Auxetophone" and was the pioneer of artificial amplification. It was a big gramophone with a longish horn, but the new principle lay in its soundbox, which was activated by a stream of compressed air. Heard at close quarters the Auxetophone had little if anything to recommend it, for the hiss of the compressed air, reinforced by record scratch of the same audio-frequency, was painfully apparent, while the weight of the soundbox with its compressed air attachment was death and destruction to records.

However, it possessed a definite virtue, for its carrying power was extraordinary, and G&T used this for a giant demonstration in the Albert Hall in 1907 on an occasion at which the writer was present. So interesting was this demonstration, when the Albert Hall was packed to the ceiling with an invited audience, that some account of it may be given.

The Gramophone and Typewriter Company had engaged for the occasion three artists who had recorded with conspicuous fidelity—Amy Castles, John Harrison and the 'cellist W. H. Squire—each of whom gave selections which were immediately repeated on the Auxetophone, except that the instrument was accompanied by a living pianist on the platform. Everybody present was genuinely astonished, even the non-gramophonist who accompanied me. No hiss or scratch penetrated the vast interior and both voices and 'cello were indistinguishable from the living performances. I forget the order of the programme, but Squire gave *Simple Aveu*, and later played the obligato with Amy Castles in the beautiful *To the Angels* which they had lately recorded. Mme Adami successfully covered up the weak piano recording, and nothing more completely successful could have been imagined or wished for. Harrison, who was loudly acclaimed by the gramophonists present, sang *Tis the Day*, the English version of Leoncavallo's *Mattinata*, and Richardson's *Mary*, which were repeated on the Auxetophone. Included in the programme were several records without the living exponent, and it was then that I heard for the first time Melba's first *Mi chiamano Mimi*, most beautifully accompanied and quite movingly beautiful. We heard Caruso's new records *Che gelida manina* and *Spirito Gentil*, and with Scotti in *Solenne in quest'ora*; but perhaps the biggest surprise of all was to hear Gogorza's rather commonplace recording of Dubois' *God my Father* accompanied by the great organ rising to a climax at which the voice easily soared above the full weight of this massive instrument. We also heard, before its publication, Evan Williams' stupendous *Sound an Alarm*, which in fact opened the concert.

Evidently the demonstration was as successful commercially as it certainly was artistically, for a second recital, also at the Albert Hall, was given by invitation some months later, when the living artists were Susan Strong, John Coates and Robert Radford, and much superb singing was heard. Coates sang *Cielo e mar* in the grandest of grand manners; Susan Strong, a little past her best, gave *Plus grande dans sa obscurite* and *Mary Grey of Allendale*. Mme Adami again accompanied; and I have heard that she was still with us a few years ago, and yet her recording memories have never been tapped. I have a reproduced photo showing Edward Lloyd in the act of recording *The Fleeting Years* which he did at the request of Queen Alexandra, with Whitehouse playing the 'cello obligato and Mme Adami at the piano. This interesting relic came to me, like so much else which was rare, esoteric and difficult to get, from my ineffable, reliable and utterly knowledgeable friend, the sage of Melbourne, Laurie Root.

I never heard whether the Auxetophone was used again. It was the invention of Parsons, the world-famous inventor of the turbine engine and of so much else, including what was probably a spare-time job, a device for amplifying the big brass, and which Henry Wood tried out during a season of promenade concerts. I heard this also, choosing a Wagner night.

The last word in acoustical reproduction lay with the E.M.G. hand-made gramophone, which scientifically corrected every major fault of the earlier machines. It used an immense horn of heavy *papier-mache*, a tuned (but too heavy) soundbox and proper track alignment.

CHAPTER THREE

THE ANTIQUARIAN ASPECT

SOME AIMS AND OBJECTS

A WORD of comment may be appropriate here regarding the dual nature of the historical record, which perhaps more than anything else has been the cause of confusion in the minds of those collectors who differ in their opinions of each other's aims.

There seems always to have been something vaguely provocative to the non-antiquarian collector that a disc might have a museum interest as a rare specimen, apart from, as well as because of, the voice that it carried. To some, a record of whatever age or period, is merely a device for reproducing an admired voice and has no greater interest in itself. The collector exercises his undisputed right to make his own selection in his choice of voices—perhaps to match his individual taste at its present stage of development, or else to study within known and defined limits the technicalities of the singing art, and to form a gallery of its most famous professors within such period of recording as he may choose. Those who collect along such lines are usually harmonious and not aggravating to each other; but they will generally combine against those other collectors who have discovered as collectors will a reverence for what is rare and antique. In this they show some lack of understanding, for they are leaving their own territory and encroaching upon that of others on which they are at some disadvantage. To the point of tedium and to the exhaustion of patience have I quoted the cases of highly respected collectors of rare books and rarer stamps—objects which may be quite devoid of artistic, literary or even instructive interest—and yet escape criticism and ridicule. But where a record is rarer than any stamp or book, and which in addition possesses both virtue and merit besides its rarity, many otherwise perfectly well-ordered minds become muddled and confused, and enquire wherein lies the merit of a mere label!

I need not enlarge upon the defective nature of this reasoning, but it amply demonstrates what I have described as the dual nature of the historical record. This happy duality gives collectors both a choice and a combination which they are free to follow, and neither group need exercise themselves unduly over the activities, aims and objects of the other.

A significant reflection on the above remarks, which I have lifted intact from the previous edition, is that the devotion of collectors to the rare and historical has been in no way damped or affected by the wholesale dubbing of their most cherished specimens for exploitation on L.P. I remember the most grievous forebodings that for this cause the vested interest in rarities would vanish overnight—a dismal view which I have invariably dismissed as quite absurd, pointing out that the value of priceless books, paintings, etc. has never suffered from cheap reproduction. I never have believed that collectors had been paying ten, twenty, fifty pounds and even more merely for the pleasure of hearing them; but *possessing* them—that is quite another matter. And so events are proving themselves.

(a) *Berliner Records*

The first Berliners to arrive in England were those made in New York by Emil Berliner himself assisted by his ubiquitous factotum "Professor Gaisberg". The early struggle to get the enterprise on its feet makes quite a story in itself, but is outside our scope. They made 5-in. and 7-in. records, exporting only the latter. They reached us in 1895 if not earlier—I have two of this date and have never seen an earlier one. It was in 1898 that Berliner despatched William Barry Owen to London accompanied by Fred Gaisberg to be followed by his brother William, where he formed The Gramophone Company Ltd., and did such good business that in 1900 they added the typewriter to their activities. The typewriter, however, was a failure, and so it was that the G&T period ended, for in 1908 the title reverted to The Gramophone Company as before.

The American discs were crude in the extreme. The titles and names of singers or other performers were scratched lightly and roughly—apparently each one by hand; but it was not long before tidier methods were used, and an embossing process and neatly etched handwriting became incorporated in the master. The London Berliners contain much historical material, and from 1898 there was a steady stream of the popular musical comedy music of that day, neatly sung by Miss Marsden, Florence de Vere and some male singers who were not unpleasant to hear. We can still hear through their shallow grooves charming echoes of *The Geisha, Floradora,* and *San Toy*—perhaps the richest and best of Sidney Jones' work—and—perhaps the best of all for sheer opulence of deathless melody—*The Belle of New York* by the greatly gifted American Gustav Kerker. Fred Gaisberg spotted the violinist Jacobs while playing at the Trocadero restaurant, London, and enlisted him to make some records. The Berliner I most greatly value is of an elaborate piano transcription of Leslie Stuart's immortal *Soldiers of the Queen,* arranged and played by the composer himself. Other names well known at the time included the tenor Wills Page (whom I heard in my first *Messiah*), the great actress Marie Tempest, then a musical comedy queen and a very good singer, the Savoyard Henry Lytton, the inimitable Maurice Faroka, the serio-soubrette Lil Hawthorne, Ada Reeve and Connie Ediss, Edna May (the Belle of New York and the most beautiful actress of her time) and that prince of coon singers Eugene Stratton. To our virgin ears

they sounded marvellous, and even today they are well worth listening to.
I would like to mention especially Marie Tempest's rendering in its
original French of Gounod's *Jewel Song*, which we played and played until
the needle nearly appeared through the back: also a Madame Roma who
sang operatic arias in good style.

Landon Ronald, who had in 1900 made a reputation for his playing in
Wormser's *L'Infant Prodigue*, recorded a transcription of Isolde's *Liebestod*
on a 7-in. Berliner; and very shortly before his death in 1938 I ventured to
chaff him with having recorded this passage, not sung, but on the piano!
Sir Landon was only moderately amused.

Before leaving the Berliners I would like to recall a few of their natural
successors the 7-in. G&Ts, for on some of these we can hear still more of
the tuneful musical comedy music of the most prolific tune-writing period
of the last hundred years. With such composers as Sidney Jones, Lionel
Monckton, Ivan Caryll and Paul Rubens, every first night was a certain
success; and of all the succession of epoch-making productions at the old
and new Gaiety, Daly's, Prince of Wales' and Adelphi, it is strange that the
finest musical score of any, Ivan Caryll's *The Earl and the Girl*, remains
deeply buried and forgotten. From this, Henry Lytton recorded *By the
Shore of the Mediterranean* on a 7-in. G&T, and *The Cosy Corner Girl* on a
10-in. Paul Rubens' enchanting *Three Little Maids* is recalled by Florence
de Vere's archly tuneful *The Miller's Daughter* with its saucy innuendo,
and Monckton's *A Country Girl* by the same singer in *Try again, Johnny*
and *Molly the Marchioness*. *A Country Girl* was produced in the autumn of
1901, after which the Berliners were no longer dated. *Try again, Johnny*,
sung by Florence de Vere, was on a Berliner which may be dated as 1902,
and her *Molly the Marchioness* (both from *A Country Girl*) on a 7-in. G&T;
so we may deduce that 1902 was the Berliners' last year of manufacture.

Their grooves were narrower and shallower than those of G&T, and they
actually played for longer than a similar width of 10-in. G&T grooves.

(b) *G&T Records*

In the same year (1900) that the Gramophone Company incorporated
the typewriter, the manufacture of "Gramophone Concert Records" began.

The energetic Owen had established a pressing plant in Hanover, and
all our records up to 1907 bear the legend on their backs "Reproduced in
Hanover". A few are found to have been pressed in Warsaw, but I cannot
suggest how this came about. The English issues of Victor company recordings were also pressed in Hanover, clearly indicating the matrices only
were sent overseas, and in this connection it is noteworthy that American-
pressed and labelled records were sent out with very much better surfaces;
the American factory having evidently surpassed the methods of Hanover
as early as 1904 or 1905. This arrangement ended when G&T opened their

own factory and offices on their present site at Hayes, Middlesex, in 1908. The classification of G&Ts by date is not difficult when once the method is understood, for, as has already been explained, the physical signs and marks by which this may be done happened to coincide with each of the years which falls within our period. The collector is guided largely by that much-abused object, the label, and to some extent by the style of the disc itself. The first G&T discs, which *may* have dated from as far back as 1899, had a perfectly plain reverse side, except for the legend "Reproduced in Hanover", which about two years later carried the "Angel" trademark: the label was flush, and larger than that which afterwards became standard. The catalogue numbers, those above the label, were neatly etched and close together, and the matrix numbers, where shown, were deeply and roughly etched under-neath the label and showing through. The catalogue numbers unfortunately are of limited use for placing the date, since it quite frequently happened that re-recordings or even other records were given the numbers of withdrawn titles.

It should be noticed that these deeply etched matrix numbers and a flush label continued in use to some extent into 1902 with standard labels, though such examples are rare. Up to that year the practice was to press directly from the original master, and in the case of the first red label series some two or three thousand copies could thus be reproduced before duplicate matrices were introduced. This would account for the speedy re-recording of many popular items, as well as for the marked deterioration in later pressings from the hard-worked master. Thus the term "original" is used with some elasticity where two such distinguishable types evidently ran concurrently.

The first change became noticeable in 1902, and it is likely that the occasion for this was the debut of the red label or celebrity series in England, although French as well as Russian red labels retained in their beginnings their original large size. The new label for all G&Ts was neatly mounted on a raised boss, and the matrix numbers were roughly etched below it, though this latter was replaced in 1904 by an embossing process, both sets of figures often being found on the same disc. In some cases the embossing is found on original 1902 copies, probably because the etching had failed.

Presumably because this method of mounting the label was found to cause rubbing and damage, it was fixed flush to the disc but surrounded by a raised protective ring. This was in 1904; and in 1905, as a further measure of protection, the label was sunk below the surrounding surface. In exact step with the label alterations there were concurrent changes in the numeral types. The catalogue numbers accompanying the 1902 labels were embossed instead of etched, although in the same manner. With the raised ring label of 1904 the numbers became more spread out and more boldly embossed, and in 1905 they were sharply reduced in size. All were marked as "Reproduced in Hanover" until the new factory was completed and the "Typewriter" was dropped, and "G&T" in our jargon became "Pre-Dog", for reasons which will immediately appear. In 1909 the company were deprived by a long legal suit of their monopoly of the term "Gramophone" which they had hitherto jealously guarded. "There are many kinds of talking machines," they used to say, "but only one *gramophone.*" But the court upset this—rather arbitrarily as I thought—and in consequence "Gramophone Concert (or Monarch) Record" became "His Master's Voice" with the "Dog" appearing for the first time on the label.

The general re-shuffle of celebrity labels in 1908 resulted in a brilliant and bewildering array of labels for all sorts of purposes—pink, green, buff, blue, white—with the red demoted to a more lowly position, but all intended to represent various degrees of super-excellence.

The experimental stage had been passed, and record making had become a grimly serious business.

The G&T and Victor-G&T catalogue numbers repay examination for the rather unexpected code which they reveal, and which may be explained as follows: take as an example number 052125; the 0 is simply a prefix which tells us that the record is 12-in., and where there is no such prefix the record is 10-in. Next to the prefix 0, where used we have a language pointer, which operates like this: 1, Hebrew; 2, Russian; 3, French; 4, German; 5, Italian; 6, Spanish; 7, middle European; 8, all Scandinavian languages including Finnish; 9, Dutch.

For some 12-in. records, especially though not exclusively those sung in English, the language pointer is omitted; and where numbers are preceded by a numeral followed by a dash, thus—3–2938, a repetition of the series is indicated.

So much for the first two figures. The third, which tells us the style of performance, goes as follows: 1 is for speaking, 2 denotes a male singer, 3 a female singer, 4 is for concerted singers, 5 for pianoforte, 6 for violoncello, 7 for violin (sometimes, probably in error, for 'cello also), 8 for concerted instruments. The remaining figures show the actual sequence of catalogue numbers beginning, in defiance of mathematics, with 000.[1] Our example is now revealed as a 12-in. record, sung in Italian by a male singer, and the hundred and twenty-fifth of the series. There is nothing there to indicate the type of voice, nor to offer any reliable clue to the date of recording; nor is there any distinction between red and black label.

[1] It is amusing to notice that it was customary to start record series at zero instead of at 1, thus somehow squeezing eleven titles into the first ten. Was it possibly an echo of the strange controversy whether the twentieth century opened in 1900 or in 1901?

It has happened, however, that this code has been violated, as in the case 032034, *Vi ravviso*, by Plancon, which indicates the French instead of the Italian language; the reason being that the proper number had already been appropriated for Didur's *Ave Signor*, and the makeshift 032 preserved the numerical catalogue sequence. The same thing happened with Clara Butt's *Il Segreto*, the correct Italian number having been used for Farrar's first *Un bel di*.

There is probably a hidden dating code in the matrix numbers, but that is for the future despite much agonising research.*

¹ But now see Mr. J. Ward's masterly analysis in *The Record Collector*.

The early recording in London was done by the brothers Fred and William Gaisberg, each of whom had his code letter. Thus, Fred's recordings carry the letters a, b, and c for 7-in., 10-in., and 12-in. records respectively and William's e, d, and f. Sometimes William gave his initials in script, as on Santley's records, and as some records show neither letter nor initial we may conclude that another operative was at work.

It may be of sufficient interest to note some first titles in their respective series, and here are some of them. The first 12-in. record to be sung in Italian by a male singer was of *Non piu andrai* sung by Santley, and therefore 052000, and the first by a woman was 053000 of *Ernani involami* by Mme Sobrino. Both were recorded in London. Litvinne was responsible for 033000, Sedlmair for 043000. The French tenor of the Opera Affre had 032000, and the Russian Figner 022000. Ben Davies had 02000, and Ellaline Terriss 03000. Dan Leno made the first 12-in. speaking record 01000; Eames and de Gogorza made 034000, and the first 10-in. of that series was by Lafitte and Paty, 34000.

The matrix numbers of the early Melba records were given a private series of their own, beginning with I for *Mattinata*, but, while the catalogue numbers run consecutively, the matrix numbers show gaps for unpublished records which of course had no catalogue numbers.

Collectors of Victor-G&T records will have found a distinct deterioration where the matrix duplications run high, and especially where red label records have been graded to pink. Greater surface noise and a muddy quality is often noticed in some of these. On the other hand great improvement took place when the pressing plant at Hayes was opened in 1908, with results similar to those previously obtained in U.S.A. This is yet another milestone at the year 1907, which closed not only the G&T epoch but also the right to the term "Gramophone", as well as the Hanover factory.

(c) *Fonotipia Records*

Some mention of this remarkable issue has been made in the introduction, and it is necessary to refer here particularly to the confusions which have arisen in the dating of the entire 39000 series. I have myself clung to Bauer's original dating as derived from the code supplied to him by an ex-employee of the company, the key to which Bauer sent me, and even after this lapse of time I remain in ignorance of his reasons for his later rejection of it. Three separate dates struggle for recognition—1903 (the Fonotipia operative), 1904 (Bennett) and 1905 (Bauer). It would be useless to add my own testimony except to say that it was later than 1903 that Fono records reached England.

Mr. J. R. Bennett, in preparing his discology "Dischi Fonotipia", was given every facility for his diligent researches, and claims to have discovered that Fonotipia began recording in October 1904. Although not to be disputed, this date does not nevertheless accord either with the highly circumstantial dating code of the Fonotipia operative or with Bauer's own dating, but stands somewhere between the two, and although undeniably authoritative it does not altogether remove the impression left by the operative's code, which I feel is worth preserving in a historical survey on account of its detailed and meticulous nature.

Unlike the G&T, the Fonotipia numbering was chronological throughout each series, the first beginning with 39000. The label for the first few months was gold on white, and the artists identified with this very rare label during the time of its currency were Barrientos, Russ, Petri, Burzio, Stehle; Parsi-Pettinella: Garbin, Sammarco, G. Pacini, Maurel, and Bonini (all but two). These were single-sided discs, and the numberings were retained when the recordings were coupled in 1904 and the label altered to green and red on white ground, which is found also on a few single-sided discs.

It is not necessarily to be supposed that the company consciously changed the series at fixed intervals, but as with G&T the changes do seem to fit into such a plan happily enough for us to accept it as a workable if rough-and-ready hypothesis.

The code now standing its trial is this: records numbered from 39000 to 39099 were ascribed to the year 1903; those from 39100 to 39599 to 1904; 39600 to 39699 to 1905; and in 1907 the 39000 series was completed, curiously analogous to the end of the G&T era. So there is our perplexity. Is it possible to reconcile the dates given respectively by Bauer, Bennett, and the Fono operative? I see only one way, but it may work. Let us assume that the original company of 1903 ran into difficulties and had found it necessary to reconstruct. A new company was formed introducing new money, new blood, and new ideas. The new management abolished the single-sided gold label issue, and put out the more attractive double-sided records with red and green labels. It pushed a more vigorous export trade, one result of which was that we in England saw Fonotipia records for the first time. We next assume that the old company's books have not survived, but that its matrices and catalogue numbers were taken over. All we have to do now is to say that October 1904 (i.e. Bennett's date) was the date of the new company's beginnings, turn the handle, and everything clicks into place. Bauer, in his introduction, although nowhere else, had given the opening year as 1904, which tallies with Bennett, leaving the operative's highly circumstantial code to draw the original company's issues into the picture. I believe that this hypothesis will have to stand, since material to refute it seems to be lacking, and it looks watertight to me.

The new company—if such it was—advertised in England with the issue of a specially coupled record carrying Bonci (*La donna e mobile*) and Kubelik (Souvenir); and a little later with another of Zenatello (*Vesti la giubba*) and the *Trovatore* duet by Talexis and Longobardi.

From the end of 1907 appeared the first orchestrally-accompanied records numbered 92000, in which form many artists repeated their previous recordings, and although the orchestra was better than the G&T combination, it was still lacking strings. All these numberings apply only to the 10¾-in. discs. The 74000 group were 12-in., beginning perhaps in 1905-6.

The 13¾-in. piano accompanied discs may be dated 1905 and their number group is 69000. These comprise solo and *ensemble* items by Bonci, Russ, Luppi, Garbin, Giuseppe Pacini, Sammarco, Pinkert, Stehle, Longobardi and Magini-Coletti. Also violin records by Kubelik.

Although the handsome labels retained their graceful design, they underwent certain small changes, chiefly in giving more detailed titles. The soft green and red became noticeably harder, and the Fonotipia recording angel suffered in re-engraving. During the first war the Germans impounded the H.M.V. and Fono records under their control and crudely imitated the Fono label, introducing a violet tint.

It will almost certainly remain true to say that in the fulness of time those artists who left their voices for posterity on Fonotipia records may be regarded as the most fortunate, for there was in the early days a fidelity, volume and clarity, and freedom from surface troubles and flaws, which was remarkable in comparison with other makes. Fonotipia never passed for sale a record that was not technically flawless, even on the plea of its artistic or personal value. It was their misfortune that there were few machines then invented which were capable of handling the immense volumes of sound their records sometimes emitted, with the result that possessors of less efficient apparatus took a dislike to them which some never overcame. The playing speeds were generally higher than was usual with G&T, reaching sometimes up to 85 r.p.m., and the gramophonist should need little reminding how easily the ear accommodates itself to a wrong speed and in consequence to a wrong pitch, and how necessary it is when acquiring new specimens of early recording to test them carefully.

Fonotipia also showed originality and artistic sense, under the guidance of its musical adviser, the composer Giordano, in devoting entire sides to the recitatives preceding the better-knowns arias. Even though we may find that well-used copies suggest which side was the more popular, the uses of recitative on the gramophone are no less than on the stage, which is to say that they are of the greatest possible use, and the finished art of the great singers in handling these passages does not suggest that they were in any way ungrateful to sing. The recitative in these cases is nearly always of the declamatory or dramatic character rather than the *recitativo secco*, which latter was an art wholly confined to Italian singers of the old school, and it is a misfortune and a loss that we can so seldom point to recorded examples of one of the most delightful experiences in opera, which on untrained lips is so tuneless and tedious. The passages recorded by Fonotipia are most revealing, exhibiting a type of singing calling for talents and training of the highest order, and, which is the important thing, serving as the proper introduction to the air which may sound bald and bereft without it.

All vocal Fonotipia records of the standard size were introduced into England at the price of twelve shillings, which, being double-sided, compared favourably with that of celebrity G&Ts. Like G&T, however, Fonotipia entered upon a process of regrading and repricing, at a date which may have been in line with the introduction of the orchestrally-accompanied records. We may again assume that the process of selection was prompted by the sales returns, for we find such shattering examples as the total expulsion from later catalogues of no less an artist than Maurel, whose records were exceptionally historic, and the masters, as we have good reason to know, were well preserved. However, to understand is to forgive, and we do know that Maurel was difficult at times.

By the beginning of 1912 the only survivors from this stricken field were Anselmi, Bonci, Vignas and Zenatello, whose titles remained untouched and prices inviolate, also Barrientos and Regina Pacini. Litvinne was reduced to Odeon status, and Bonini (one of their best singers) as a soloist disappeared. Ernest Van Dyck's name had appeared, but the recording, for some reason, was entirely unsatisfactory, and a later attempt to reproduce from surviving matrices was hastily abandoned and forgotten by its horrified sponsor. Other names appearing in early prospectuses but not as yet otherwise traced included Jean and Marie de Reszke, Bellincioni and Caron. A single record by Victor Capoul exists, and represents the famous tenor thirty years after his retirement singing in a tired and worn voice Godard's *Berceuse*, but in immaculate style.

The large number of recorded *ensembles* was noteworthy, and these showed, as perhaps might be expected, a wider enterprise in selection than anything attempted by G&T with its relatively parochial outlook, and to Fonotipia we owe a knowledge of many operatic passages of which we might otherwise have remained in ignorance, including, perhaps not surprisingly, a rather big proportion by the artistic director himself.

(d) *International Zonophone Records*

Probably synchronising with the formation of G&T was the International Zonophone Company of Milan, apparently a subsidiary of the Anglo-Italian Commerce Company. In the early days of "C.C." we knew nothing about this concern as a separate entity, but only in so far as it became in some way connected, in a quite junior capacity, with G&T.

This "International" company carried on independently for about three years, and was then absorbed into G&T; but previously to this it had paved the way, if somewhat tentatively, for G&T's activities in celebrity recording. It had recorded Caruso, Magini-Coletti, Caron, Calve, Plancon, Luisa Tetrazzini, Wermez and Torressella, of whom we know examples, although probably incompletely. It worked in Paris as well as in Milan, and evidently had invented a clearly defined hierarchy of labels, the black label being apparently the basic colour, working up to orange, dark blue, and light blue: one by Plancon that I am able to record was successively issued as black, orange and light blue. A large number of black label artists covered an extensive field of operatic and other serious music by artists of whose status and quality I must admit to complete ignorance; but among the light blues I' recall a superb record by Giovanni de Negri whose *Morte d'Otello* puts this tenor in a very high place, and reminiscent of Tamagno himself.

There is a great scarcity of International Zonophone records, as well as of information concerning them.

c

CHAPTER FOUR

RELATIVE VALUES

No more perplexing or embarrassing aspect of the collecting field could be approached by an indiscreet commentator than that of the money value of rare discs; and yet, it must be touched upon if only as a basis for academic reflection. It may be taken as certain that, whatever our present ideas may be, they will be subjected to much change with passing years, an extended interest, and a proper perspective of the whole question.

In the beginnings of the second-hand record trade, which was first brought to my notice by a roughly printed leaflet thrust into my hand opposite the Royal Exchange in about 1909, used records were priced on the assumption that those which were most recently issued would command the highest price. Instead of proceeding to catch my evening train I walked the short distance to the address given, and found myself climbing precariously up a definitely dangerous stairway in a side street off Cheapside, long since demolished, to premises rented by Messrs. Holt, Lees & Co. It was a scruffy outfit, but they had a few records and I took a few home. It was here as I learnt from later visits that it was possible to buy the pirated pressings made from actual records of many of H.M.V.'s highest priced discs, which Gaisberg describes in his book as originating from Russia. They were not worth having, as the reproduction was faint and the surface scratch appalling.

About half the retail price would have been the charge for a current record, and about a quarter for a withdrawn one; but while used copies of Carusos of 1909 were not uncommon, the old G&Ts were very seldom seen, and would not have been very saleable except to some of those early collectors whom I have mentioned, and who did, in fact, pick them up. The principal reason for this scarcity was the allowance against new purchase of one-third of the price of a new black label record, that is, tenpence, one shilling and eightpence, and half a crown for 7-in., 10-in., and 12-in. discs respectively, the bulky and expensive material being bought back for re-use. This was a consideration, and caused many customers, when tempted by new issues, to weed out their collections to avail themselves of this liberal concession. I have already related how I systematically benefited from this arrangement, not as a collector, but as a means of acquiring expensive red label and Melba records at a price I could better afford, and—always of a bartering disposition—with the certainty of passing them on at a profit! One may ponder upon the number of tons of G&Ts that were immolated in the cause of the economy in this way.

This procedure undoubtedly disposed of the great bulk of the earliest and most interesting issues, but those who preserved them with artistic foresight are much in credit to posterity.

As prices of records were lowered, and doubtless with economies in the use of material, these allowances fell to a negligible figure, which certainly played into the hands of a second-hand trade, which relied, as just stated, upon records as new as possible. No special value was then placed by dealers upon records which today are actually costly, but when, many years later, and thanks or no thanks to "Collectors' Corner", a selective trend in values began to emerge, it was not surprising that a good deal of confusion resulted.

How important it becomes to us to understand accurately what it is that is desirable to collect and what to reject needs no emphasis, for it may be said that all records falling within our dates are rare, so rare that there may not be one which we may set out to buy and succeed in finding, but by no means all are of value. So rarity alone is not enough—there must also be merit; but as merit is a relative term it is necessary to give it a definition which will fit our case. But this cannot easily be done until we have immersed ourselves pretty deeply in the history of the world's opera of the last hundred years and the singers who have served in it, and have informed ourselves how to tell good singing when we hear it, and not allowing ourselves to be fobbed off with the second best. Let great art, then, be the aim of our definition, with all that that portenous expresstion implies.

But to be able to agree upon what it is that constitutes great art is not as simple for some as it is for others. It should be independent of personal considerations and prejudices, and with due regard to the medium in which it is offered to us. Those of us who have known artists personally may be inclined too much in their favour, and others less privileged than ourselves may perforce have had to listen to eulogies not wholly deserved. Retired singers of our period have felt a great interest in our pursuit, and with one exception only in my own experience have been more than ready to assist in placing correct assessments; and even where those others were not (by any means) personal friends of the subject of enquiry, I have never encountered any lack of generosity towards their art.

How often have I been assured in books and articles that no truly great singing could be heard outside the walls of the Vienna State Opera in the days of Mahler—many of them singers who had never ventured beyond those walls. Of those who did drift into our orbit some were first class, but others who evidently gave satisfaction in Vienna seemed to us to be very ordinary, and I will say nothing about a tenor of vast stature except that he wrote a comic book of reminiscence. Anyhow, the proposition is inherently unlikely, despite the great influence of the elder Marchesi: but when this great teacher moved to Paris the centre of gravity moved with her.

A great artist must be one who is recognised as great by the best judges, and the value of his records must depend upon this in relation to the availability of his recorded work. Every credit is due to the immediate recognition of the worth of the first record to be discovered of Anna von Mildenberg, one of the greatest of the Vienna school, and there is a special reference to this record in the artists' section of this book. It is also listed in the Appendix, for although it is reputed to have been unpublished it was given a catalogue number and therefore intended for issue.

The two greatest-of-all artists of the recording epoch will generally be agreed as Jean de Reszke and Milka Ternina, and although it is certain that the former recorded—probably for three companies—one copy only has been credibly reported, and its present whereabouts are unknown. Ternina never recorded. She was a shy and retiring woman, and made no concession to publicity. I have tried to say something about her in *The Age of Jean de Reszke*, for she was my first and greatest Isolde.

For our purposes, then, a great artist must have international fame, which is surely a prerequisite to greatness (or is it the other way round?), and whose records would reflect this greatness, for no collector would willingly acquire anything, however meritorious he may believe it to be, that would not reflect credit upon him as a collector. (There are some, it is true, who pin their faith to second-rate singers in the belief that they are showing a liberal spirit of enlightenment, but there is no real future for these.)

The question of the great artist's personality as the original collectors knew or imagined it, as well as the circumstances surrounding the issue of his records, is in its nature an ephemeral one. It dies out with the passing of old collectors, and a new set of values insensibly grows which must of necessity exclude the inestimable value of first-hand experience. The aim of "Collectors' Corner" was largely to give a touch of reality to what were otherwise mere names to a younger generation, but one result of this was to leave an impression that singers less heavily underlined in this way were less worthy of their attention, and so was the law of supply and demand to some extent falsified. This influence, naturally enough, has passed without trace, and what it is that fixes the higher values today is beyond my understanding and the shaping of events in the commercial field today suggests a tendency for record prices to move in an inverse ratio to values. The dealers (whom "C.C." tactfully ignored) are bound by these laws of supply and demand in much the same way that dealers in the upper strata of art and *vertu* are likewise bound, but we are seeing under our incredulous eyes such erratic changes in values, both up and down, that we may be permitted to wonder whence comes the lead in such matters, is it amateur or commercial enterprise or a mixture of each? The seasonal changes in the trends of fashion in the arts are doubtless contrived with no less forethought than changes in costume, the secret in each being the recognition of the psychological moment for launching them. What could be more natural in our own circles than to utilise a similar technique, and, when the supply or demand for rare G&Ts shows signs of abating, gently to lead informed opinion into fresh woods where may be gathered the once despised Zonophones, and a sprinkling of ambiguous early Russian singers and doubtless other attractive allurements? The parcelling up into a sort of picnic hamper of cherished collectors' specimens in the shape of long-playing records is characteristic of an age of packaging, and if the idea is an artistic one it will probably endure. Time will prove whether these phenomena are natural developments of an artistic cult or malignant excrescences calling for the remedy of balanced opinion and the processes leading to maturity.

The seventeen years during which the G.A.R. suffered some criticism for what was thought in some quarters to have been its too limited outlook have not uncovered any substantial swing away from its reflections of the feelings of the majority; and still, as then, this writer has no wish except to foster an enjoyment of record-collecting in its real sense with all its offshoots and temporary aberrations.

There is a fairly accurate evaluation of the artists of the G&T celebrity period, and of those who may be readily referred to in biographical works, but the law of supply and demand should, if it is to work logically, presuppose a reasonably free market, which is exactly what has never existed in rare records. The average prices asked do not reflect true value for that reason, and the trade perforce fixes what can only be described as provisional prices such as it finds a sufficient number of its customers will pay. It would be fallacious to contend that an object's value is what it would fetch in an open market when no such thing as an open market exists. The expert in rare objects does not throw his treasures away in a period of stagnation; he knows their value. A collector should know what his records are worth, and a temporary lack of demand means nothing.

Collectors should realise that some of their specimens may be some of the rarest objects on earth, although I am often assured that such and such a specimen is "common", even when not a floating copy could be found, however diligently searched for. I speak entirely disinterestedly, my own collection having been reduced to a few token mementoes, and I have never speculated in the commodity. By common consent a small number of outstanding examples of historical rarities have been exalted to great heights of material value where such discrimination has been fully justified, which only tends to stress the inequalities suffered by others of no less importance. To attempt to assess the actual and relative values of the records of Albani, Bellincioni, Fabbri, the 12-in. records of Santley, and the red G&Ts of Maurel and Litvinne would call for a very precise appreciation of all the factors governing a calculation of this kind—all the more difficult because it is so seldom tested. I have indeed seen a record priced at 8 guineas for which I would not pay eight pence.

Let us be content, therefore, to hasten slowly in this matter of record values, for miscalculations have a way of begetting others. There can be no real standard of values, which must vary with each individual transaction, with the length of the buyer's purse and with the strength of the seller's nerve—both of which do in fact vary very considerably.

CHAPTER FIVE

SOME EARLY CATALOGUES

ON my first day as a gramophonist I enquired at one of the big London shops for a catalogue of records. It was then possible to get 7-in. Columbia records for a shilling; they made a gratifying noise but little more. But not at this shop; I was handed first a catalogue of records priced at ten shillings each, which rather daunted me. Anyway, I took it home and studied it. At any idle moment I brought it out and studied it afresh, until I knew the titles under the names of every singer. Need I add that this was the first and original catalogue of red G&Ts of 1902? In course of time it got swept up as rubbish, but it had laid a firm foundation. I got to know the names of all the standard operatic titles long before I heard the music of them, and was to some extent prepared to hear them when the opportunities came. Years later I had the good fortune to replace this catalogue by a fine copy of the 1903 edition, which, like its predecessor, was fully illustrated with portraits of the artists with notes on their work, but with several important additions of 1903 recordings added. The portraits, some in character costume, were of Suzanne Adams, Calve, Caruso, de Lucia, Renaud, Plancon, Van Rooy, Scotti, Battistini, de Luca, Valero, Santley, Figner, Mey-Figner, Vialtzeva and Schaliapine. Those without portraits were Maurel, Gravina, Giraldoni and Garbin. There were others of "Carmen Sylva" the *nom de plume* of the poetess Queen of Roumania, Joachim, and Kubelik; and on the back cover page and surmounted by the ecclesiastical Cross were the records taken in the Palace of the Archbishop of Rome by the singers of the Sistine Chapel, and of Professor Moreschi, perhaps the last of the *castrati.*

On the front cover, printed in red and black, is Caruso's record of *E lucean le stelle,* evidently already recognised for its superlative merit; and a sticker added to warn us to use only genuine gramophone needles, which was the outcome of what I may claim as my first impact with the gramophone world, having reported a very palpable retailing deception, for which I received a letter of thanks and two boxes of "genuine" needles!

The catalogue of 1904 which I also possess was of half the superficial area but with more pages, with the issues of 1903 deleted, due to the defection of the artists to Fonotipia. The Foreword to this catalogue emphasises that the records should not be played faster than 72 r.p.m.—a vital piece of advice that was lost sight of for a matter of twenty years or more. To the earlier portraits were added those of Albani, Melba, Tamagno, Boronat, Ancona, Sobinoff and Sammarco. (Sammarco had figured in the 1902 catalogue but was evidently overlooked in 1903.) Without portraits were

Bellincioni, Boninsegna, Campanari, Marconi, Kashmann and Fabbri. The injunction as to genuine needles was incorporated.

A later catalogue of the same year had added Pinto, Carelli, Angelica Pandolfini, Kruszelnicka and Storchio, all to become Fono artists, and after a few months celebrity items appeared in red print at the end of the general catalogues with the increasing number of Victor-G&Ts until 1910, when a new type of celebrity catalogue appeared with Melba's portrait outside and a large number of miniature portraits within, and was inclusive of the *Faust* green label set. And I find another, apparently of the same year, but of solo records only, with a long introduction which mourned (in 1910) the deterioration in singing, and how the old singers were not being replaced. The anonymous writer was writing just after the opening of the 1910 season, when Donalda had replaced Tetrazzini on the opening night, but before Melba's *rentrée* after a year's absence (not two years as there stated): and he does no justice to Donalda in commending the *Boheme* and *Faust* records. This catalogue includes a number of black label artists, and was evidently planned to synchronise with the opening of the opera season; it was a "preliminary puff" for the season with the true emphasis on the gramophone.

I have a stout catalogue dated January 1914 which comprehensively sets out all singers and instrumentalists of celebrity status, although not necessarily red label artists. It runs to 175 pages and is fully documented with well produced portraits and not unnaturally contains a few errors beside those detailed in the errata slip. This was the last H.M.V. catalogue in which celebrity singers were presented as such.

*   *   *   *

Reference to the Fonotipia catalogue dated January 1907 shows that it contains every record issued to that date excepting Jean and Marie de Reszke and those artists who had been transferred to Odeon, among whom Destinn and Litvinne were casualties. This collector's prize, which came to me rebound in stiff boards, is a large and slender volume measuring 12 ins. by 7 ins. and is number 10 of its series. It is printed in Italian and fully illustrated by very high-class photo reproductions of great interest and it conveniently carries us to the end of the 39000 series with which we are concerned here. It prints several appreciative letters from satisfied artists who have recorded for Fonotipia, including most significantly one from Jean de Reszke saying how after having refused to record his voice for other companies he had decided, after hearing the remarkable discs of the Fonotipia company, to accord them *definitement la concession exclusive de reproduire ma voix.* Unlike other letters, this is undated, or the date is omitted in reproduction, but Bauer enters the date of two recordings as 22nd April, 1905, the titles being from *Romeo et Juliette* (Gounod) and

Le Cid (Massenet). The numbers being 69000 and 69001 they were pressed as 13¾-in. discs. The date accords with those of letters from the dramatist Sardou, Maurel and Kubelik.

I have also seen a H.M.V. brochure of 1908 giving portraits of their leading artists, among which was that of Jean de Reszke but without comment attached to it.

CHAPTER SIX

STRANGE INTERLUDE

FOR some few years prior to 1950 I had been puzzled by the appearance of a number of rare G&T records, many of which had never been on sale in England, and all in perfectly mint condition. I cannot at this date say whether I had suspected any possibility that these had made an appearance through the wrong door, but it was in that year that something happened to focus my attention on that possibility.

What brought the matter to a head was the appearance of a very curious object—what should have been a G&T red label of 1902, but with the obverse side unlabelled and the reverse side bearing a *black* label of unusual design. This was something I had never seen or heard of, and although I do not claim any particular perspicacity for having instantly placed it as a private "library" specimen evidently belonging to the late H.M.V. company, what has mystified me from that day to this is why nobody else who had handled this specimen as well as others like it had not been drawn to the same conclusion. That there are several examples of these now lurking in private collections there can be little doubt, if only from the negative premise that relatively so few of them came to light in the investigation that followed. Only a handful of library copies of that period were labelled in this curious way, the rest being as normally prepared for sale.

Such black label records as figured in the proceedings had been selected with expert care, and included super-rarities of the earliest continental recordings by artists such as Russ, Zenatello and Vignas (see Appendix).

The criminal proceedings in which the Crown undertook the prosecution and I testified for the Crown were not pressed very far, and nothing of them appeared in the newspapers; and although I was shadowed by reporters it was understood that silence was to be the rule. Nobody emerged from the affair with any particular credit, and the least said was soonest mended. I quite enjoyed my long and meticulous cross-examination, which was aimed at upsetting the credibility of the "expert witness", and besprinkled with rather too-obvious traps, but nothing emerged except a compliment from the judge, who was probably completely mystified by the entire proceeding. A satisfactory point was that my evaluation of the salvaged records was practically identical with that of the other side.

A touch of comedy was, however, given to the matter by what must have been the oddest record recital in the annals of the gramophone. Part of the function which I was invited to undertake was the evaluation of the large number of valuable records which were exhibits in the case, and this took place in the disturbed atmosphere of the detectives' common-room at Scotland Yard, amid the clicking of typewriters, long-range conversations and a good deal of free and easy chaff. For I had been provided with a portable gramophone which enabled me to hear a good number of most interesting and possibly unique records, which added to the general air of unrest.

Few, I fear, appreciated the treat they were being given, but one of the 'tecs asked me if I had *Mattinata*: "A beautiful morning is breaking"? I asked. "Yes, that's it; I was working for the company when they made it, (he meant John Harrison's record) and I reckoned it was the best they ever made." I said, "Yes, and it still is".

The salvaged records were only a small number of those raped from the library, and as soon as the news broke, a large proportion of them were hastily shipped abroad where no questions were asked, and others went to earth in this country. As soon as I had been convinced that the original and rightful owners wished for nothing better than that the matter should be dead and buried, I procured from overseas and elsewhere some of the most interesting of them, but because they gave me little satisfaction to possess I let them go to the B.B.C. where they will remain frozen and lost for ever. Anyway the transfer from E.M.I. to B.B.C. is not a matter of great public concern. The only ones in which it was not possible to make this vicarious restitution were some of the early Russians, which went securely to earth.

There is much that is unique in record-collecting, but perhaps one of the strangest things about it is that whereas any other art treasure of whatever kind can be convincingly forged, I believe that the possibility of a forged G&T lies very far ahead.

CHAPTER SEVEN

FRED GAISBERG

IF the triumph of the gramophone could be ascribed to any one cause, those who know most about it would have no hesitation in making the award to Alfred Clark, who ran the business side, and to Fred Gaisberg who made a business side possible. In fact Gaisberg was exactly suited to the job, as he possessed the asset of his unique personality and his flair for handling artists and enticing them to record. When he joined G&T no artists of standing had made records, and within a year or so he had, with the help of the young accompanist, Landon Ronald, who was *repetiteur* at Covent Garden, lured the pick of the international operatic singers of Europe to make the very records which form the hard core of the collector's ambitions. He was already exercising his talent in this direction when he first met Caruso in Milan in 1902, and was certainly apprised of the tenor's forthcoming debut at Covent Garden in May of that year. Caruso's fame was already very great, which certainly gave him the courage necessary to demand a fee of one hundred pounds for making ten records, the time for which was to be squeezed in between his many engagements. Fred, somewhat appalled, telegraphed to London for permission to accept this unheard-of proposition, and as it was flatly refused—presumably by the aforesaid Alfred Clark— he took the matter into his own hands to the extreme displeasure of his directors. Never was there a better investment, for it could hardly be called a gamble by those who understood, and since the records were on sale in May it need not be doubted that they exercised a strong influence on that wonderful bunch of singers who had gathered at Covent Garden. The prestige value of the "London Reds" as they are now known must have been incalculable, and in those months the gramophone was made.

I had the pleasure and privilege in later years of knowing Gaisberg well, and every meeting with him was something to be eagerly anticipated and pleasurably remembered. He was short in stature, with an intensely expressive countenance, whimsical, and the very prince of raconteurs. His eyes gleamed and beamed and glinted behind his glasses and radiated kindliness and humour. Behind his merry exterior, however, he was self-contained, and seldom spoke about himself unless systematically pumped, when he would relate how as a boy of seventeen working on the embryo gramophone under Emile Berliner his job was to scout for such talent as could be induced to come and make records, with himself as accompanist, and described on the record as "Professor Gaisberg", besides countless other episodes which escape both my memory and my skill to reproduce. I met him first in the early 'thirties when I was engaged in searching for material for "Collector's Corner", in the company's library, and was carried off by him to lunch in the canteen, where I also met Louis Sterling of Columbia, Rex Palmer, and several unidentified "high-ups". Greatly did Fred entertain us all with stories that his colleagues must have heard pretty frequently, but evidently with unabated enjoyment. I kept in touch with him on gramophone matters but it was many years before I met him again, the occasion then being a H.M.V. committee convened to discuss the re-issue of early recordings. This committee accomplished little, although we sat weekly for some time, but the meetings served as wonderful occasions to draw Fred and make him talk of old times and old artists. Just at that time the English edition of his book had appeared, in which was a lively snapshot of himself at lunch with the famous tenor Marconi, and pledging each other in glasses of red wine. I had chaffed him about this, and when the name of Marconi came up in the course of business, Fred looked across to me and raised his hand as though holding a glass. When the great and aloof Melba was finally prevailed upon to record of course it was Fred who had the job, for if anyone could make Melba laugh outside her own circle, he was the one. The recording was done through a horn projecting through a partition behind which the operator worked, having a peephole built in for him to receive the word to set the machinery in motion. Melba was all set, when Fred's face unexpectedly appeared in the window. "Take your ugly face away, you little imp; how can I sing with a thing like that staring at me?" By some standards this would be merely rude, but the apparition disappeared from sight and the angelic voice was recorded. Peter Dawson also was at the receiving end when he and two other trembling singers were making ready to act as "chorus" in some plantation songs. Dawson, never one to be put down, boldly claimed also to have come from Melbourne, to receive the withering retort: "That's nothing to be proud of; a city of pimps, parsons and prostitutes!"

Fred was absolutely fascinating to hear and to watch, his charm being much too elusive to set down on paper. He exuded merriment and kindliness, and kept one on tenterhooks waiting for a coming indiscretion. He enjoyed relating Calve's tremulous forebodings when being driven in a four-wheeled cab to the studio, a euphony for a rather squalid upper room, and became convinced by the surroundings to which she was being taken that she was being abducted for immoral purposes, and stubbornly refused to disembark from the vehicle until—so Fred averred—he had to go in and fetch the cheque to convince her of the bona fides of the proceedings. One is left to picture the famous prima donna torn between cupidity and fears for her virtue being propelled up the dirty staircase, and her agitated state may clearly be traced in the resulting records if we choose to think it so.

My dedication to him of this book pleased him greatly, and I received in return a generously inscribed copy of his own, in regard to which I have to add that with the connivance of his secretary I felt constrained to make several corrections for the American edition.

On his official retirement Fred retained a lively interest in the artistic side of E.M.I., and continued to take charge of celebrity recordings. At one of these sessions he introduced me to Gigli, on the rather ludicrous occasion when after frantic efforts to induce the imperturbable tenor to pronounce "worship". He had recorded the air in *La Juive*—in my judgment a few years too late—followed by an admirably balanced performance of Lalo's *Aubade*. After this he was induced, or wished, to record Tosti's *Parted*, and *I'll walk beside you*. Both these were tried over with the piano as a preliminary, when it became painfully evident that in the former ballad the often-repeated "worship" was sung broadly as "worsheep". Fred did his best, but although Gigli pushed his spectacles up to his forehead and carefully marked his music, the next try-over was no more successful. Finally the ballad was sung with the orchestra for balance, after which the recording engineer strode out from his hideout, clapped the mystified tenor on the shoulder, and began it all afresh! At this point I remarked *sotto voce* that Gigli was singing "years" as "yerhers". "Oh for God's sake don't you start on him too or we shall never get through!" was Fred's rather testy rejoinder. As all know who have the record, both the flock of "sheep" and the "hempty yerhers" were enshrined for posterity. Gigli knew no English to speak of, so on leaving at the end of the session I gave him all the Italian I was capable of—"Mille grazie, signore, bella voce, bravissimo," which produced a wintry smile and "grazie, grazie".

Fred Gaisberg died, irreplaceable, about two years later, in 1952.

CHAPTER EIGHT

SOME REFLECTIONS

WHEN all is said and done, wherein is this subtle attraction which the early records have for so many of us? We have to admit that their contribution to music in the abstract is small, but as that is not what we seek in them, this deficiency may be overlooked; if it is purely musical interest we want, we must, and can, and do, look for it elsewhere. No; the true value to us of these records is their power to demonstrate the individual art of great singers who still flourished at the end of the age of great singing, and the way in which this art was applied to the music to which it properly belonged. And this brings us to the reflection which seldom fails to provoke discussion, that nearly all music of the classical operatic period is incomplete unless rendered with the highest possible degree of vocal accomplishment. Not even the most erudite musical scholar who prefers to read his own scores rather than to entrust them to the possible faults and failings of the interpretations of others could succeed in phrasing and understanding vocal music unless he also possessed a working knowledge of singing. Despite this most undoubted truth, are we not often enough afflicted with attempts to perform music of this kind without the training necessary to understand what it requires and the ability to execute it? If great singing has died in our time for lack of the incentive to accomplish it, may it not be accepted as an encouraging sign that the pre-condition of revival is already apparent in the enthusiasm for performances of such inadequacy as to cause us little except amazement that such things should be so lightly attempted? The authorities at the Covent Garden we used to know always pursued the policy of leaving unperformed such operas as they could not present with suitable singers, instead of forcing upon a complacent public works palpably intended to feed the star system but minus the stars, whom the present opera pundits affect to despise. We are, so much the worse for ourselves, allowing and even encouraging ourselves to become acquiescent towards the second- and third-rate in operatic performance, according to a system which requires singers to open and shut their mouths at the right places provided that they do not attract too much attention to themselves, for they are certain of delirious applause whatever they do.

We can usually find, in refutation of the champions of former days, probably in all periods of decline, whether of music or any other art, that the complaint of deterioration can be traced back *ad infinitum*—that the present is always inferior to the past. It is a comfortable and specious form of casuistry, especially as it contains a germ of truth, and if not pressed too far may even succeed in whole or in part in concealing its own negative quality.

But it should not too tamely be accepted, or revival will be impeded. Judgments of this kind have too often depended upon the output of microphones and loudspeakers, where the possibility of exaggeration and ill-balance (*always* ill-balance) must be present.

We know that fine singing is not an art to be acquired by the mere accident of good fortune, although many "born singers" can give pleasure to the uninitiated for a short time, and there's the rub; a short time—as we see on the stricken field of once fine voices.

Adelina Patti wrote "a beautiful voice is a gift of God", which is true enough, but a gift that is not cultivated and cherished is wasted and will wither, for a perfect singer such as she was is the very excellent work of man, the product of years of hard work and self denial, such as could hardly be contemplated by the aspirant to fame of our day.

We should, I think, all be on our guard against too receptive an attitude to the opinions of others. Listen to them, of course, and compound them with our own, but never allow ourselves to be persuaded that our grandfathers and great-grandfathers, who studied these matters certainly no less carefully than we do, were destitute of musical taste and understanding simply because they saw beauty in works that make no particular appeal to us. The link is that their generations appreciated vocal art, which alone could give life to some of these works, and ours does not. The wheel of fashion revolves, often strangely; but by its nature, and without too greatly begging the question, it returns to its starting point sooner or later. Let us recollect that early in the present century the great Hans Richter epigrammatically remarked that "there was a future for Mozart", but the poor man hardly foresaw what that future would be. I had heard his *Don Giovanni*—before the German re-wrote it—which brings me from the general to the particular.

It is natural that in a time when fine singing is so little cared for, vocal conventions and traditions should be cast aside, often enough on the specious plea that the composer left no record of them. As to what a singer may or may not do in interpreting the work of the classical masters of the Italian school, much self-evident nonsense has been heard, and when musical purists insist that the composer's intentions, whether rightly interpreted or not, should be rigidly obeyed, it is strange to find these same experts traversing both the spirit and the letter of the same composers' markings in ways to which I shall refer.

There is, I believe, a letter still extant written by Mozart to his father on the day following the production of *Il Seraglio*, in which he ruefully lamented that owing to organised opposition *no encores were possible*. And yet the modern Mozartian regards the merest suggestion of an encore with unconcealed horror; which shows how dangerous a thing a little knowledge can be. Mozart liked encores, and wished for them; but the more dedicated of his disciples today at all costs protect his memory from such an insult!

It is a historical fact and beyond dispute that composers of classical opera and oratorio did not consider that their singers were in need of instruction in the singing conventions which were then *de rigueur* and which were therefore part of their compositions. They knew, for example, that it was part of the education of a finished singer to know where to place an *appoggiatura* or an ornament, and that it was no more their business to presume to indicate them in their scores than it was to mark the places where breaths should be taken. The *appoggiatura* was in the tradition of the day, and convention ruled that it should remain unwritten. The same principle applied to flourishes and finishes, and therefore when we hear from our records that singers of high repute would if they felt that way finish Don Giovanni's *Serenade* on a high F sharp, instead of looking pained we should endeavour to discover the reason. I adhere very forcibly to the belief that a composer of vocal music would never quarrel with a singer for imparting to it all the beauty at his command, and would be more likely to feel aggrieved to hear it given with no more imagination than cold print could suggest. Musical notation is at best a makeshift device, and relies on the musicianship and intelligence of its interpreters to bring out all that is hidden in it. Otherwise, of what does interpretation consist?

Ornament, *appoggiatura*, *mordente*, *acciaccatura*, *rubato*, *con espressione*—all these and more besides are at the disposal of the finished singer or instrumentalist to add lustre to a composer's work—sometimes built up on the stark framework of the score, and sometimes written in in whole or in part, depending upon the usage of any particular period. A composer may justly complain of vulgarity in treatment, and this he cannot control, but we are considering artists, which rules out any such possibility.

There is no dispute that in the early days of opera the composers relied on their singers to fill in the details of their arias, which naturally left them a good deal of latitude against which no complaint would be valid, although such complaints are now in fact of frequent occurrence. They are used to belittle the great singers of the Golden Age, and to charge them with lack of musicianship, when in truth they possessed it to a very high degree. The Mapleson cylinders, mere whispers though they are, do great service in proving this, for in the excitement of actual performance is the real truth apparent, for they reveal instances of very high musicianship both in improvisation and attack, as well as an evident desire to extract from the music the fullest beauty that lay in it.

Until the present wave of uneasy professorship (is it already in decline?) it was, to quote a single example, universal practice to use the unwritten flourish at *Ah quel amor* in *Ah, fors' e lui* in *La Traviata*: and it would seem that it was never sung otherwise. It almost certainly had Verdi's approbation and possibly even his authorship—which places the onus on later editors; but that is a point that could be settled.

D

On the other hand it was a common practice in the highest singing circles to divide a note purely for vocal effect, often following a turn, but I have yet to hear of any grumbling at this deviation from the exact reading (ref. *bel canto*). Consider Santley's singing of *Non piu andrai* as recorded by him, where every unwritten *appoggiatura* is meticulously placed and with a bold flourish added for good measure. And Santley, as I need hardly add, was very much of a purist.

This holier-than-thou attitude was aimed at curbing the prominence that singers had acquired in stage performance, forgetting that opera owed its very survival to its interpreters who gave life to the printed page. We have to endure the vagaries of musical fashion, but certain fundamental truths must be preserved, and the primary importance of the singer in the operatic scheme is one of them.

Since this matter was first touched on in the first edition of this book, the wheels have been slowly, very slowly, grinding; and I am glad now to thank whoever it is that I have to thank for much return to sanity; and there is good hope that the perfect reading of that quaintly miscalled "*opera giocoso*" *Don Giovanni*, so nearly achieved in the London Festival Hall in 1961, may be round only the next corner.

Those who held the now exploded view that an eighteenth-century printed score necessarily had said the last word of the composer's conception have looked again and discovered that by practice and custom it was considered untidy and tasteless, as well as slightly impertinent, for him to write meticulous directions which trained musicians did not require and might even resent, especially since there was always so much more that no such directions would cover (e.g. *rubato, con expressione*, etc.) and without which his music would sound as dead as a German reading of *Don Giovanni*. Likewise, *L'istesso tempo* is at length recognised as governing the beat and not an editor's marking. As I have indicated, we are progressing nicely backwards.

*   *   *   *

The question of correct pitch in playing early records has already been touched upon, and out of this there naturally arises that of *tempi* generally. To assume that all pre-electric "78s" play at 78 r.p.m. would distort our sense of pitch and the proper *tempo*. The current craze for speed and greater speed can be most irritating to those whose only wish is to enjoy the music rather than to worship the conductor's back, and there are many striking examples to be found among records of fifty and sixty years ago which reveal better than any printed score what the composer's intentions really were, and while his writ still ran.

These *tempi* can always be arrived at by playing the records at the proper pitch. Melba's records of 1904, and especially the March issue, were almost invariably played too fast, giving the impression of a thin and pinched voice in a hurry. The correct speeds for these and many others will be found in the Appendix, or may be arrived at by noting the key as shown on each label. Special note should be taken of the exceptional speed of Patti's *Batti, batti*— which at 81 r.p.m. exactly catches its key of F—the contrasted speeds of the Caruso's 1902 and 1903 issues, and the marked difference between the 10-in. and 12-in. records of Tamagno. But most if not all of my readers will possess ears of such accuracy that they will need no guidance, but should some of the *tempi* seem disconcertingly slow, let them take heart, for it will be likely that they are hearing them correctly for the first time.

Hitherto, all our natural curiosities about qualities and performances of artists of the far distant past have been frustrated at the point of conjecture. We are encouraged to believe that the great singers of the late eighteenth century were so greatly endowed both by nature and by training, as to have been superior to those of our own Golden Age. Perhaps they were. In the nineteenth century singers had the assistance of more or less dramatic subjects with some movement of action, and every singer knows the advantage of this compared with the static conditions of the platform. But in the previous century, when opera took the form of a sort of dressed-up concert, the singers had no such aids, and yet they maintained a very high standard of interest in their work. The operas of Handel provide a case in point, requiring as they did the highest imaginable singing qualities combined with the minimum need for acting ability. Although it is likely that the artist of each epoch had got something that the other had not, we must in fairness be prepared to give the fullest credit where there is evidence of the deepest study. Tastes, and ears, change with passing epochs, and we cannot without confusion draw exact analogies between past and present. To speculate on the past must be unprofitable until the gramophone comes to our help. Looking very far ahead, the lost years (i.e. pre-gramophone years), may seem very few indeed, when we have captured impressions of the veritable Golden Age of the 'nineties, which can be compared in another hundred years with the diversities of styles and fashions which will have supervened.

Already this Golden Age is widely and thankfully acknowledged, and what will be the potentialities for purposes of comparison in generations to come?

We say, and I think rightly, that Handel's *Messiah* is man's sublimest flight into the realm of music, but what are we to think when we find to our consternation that this mighty work as we know it would hardly be recognised by its own composer? Only a musicologist (what a word!) could tell us what rearrangements and transformations *The Messiah* has suffered, and as to the music itself we have to face the unpalatable fact that what so greatly moves us is not so much Handel's music as what various hands have made of it. If somebody over-persuades us to listen to it as Handel wrote it, with the orchestration then available to him, our adapted ears are tolerably certain to find it thin and tiresome—interesting only to "musicologists". Which prompts the thought whether Handel would have used what modern orchestral development has brought about. Can it be doubted? Although progress is not necessarily improvement, modern orchestration in itself is a great advance, although lacking as it does the melting, liquid and most moving quality of the old French horns, unmanageable as they were: I think Handel would have insisted on their retention, and Beethoven also. Taking a reverse view, would Bach have preferred his jangling harpsicord to a modern grand piano? I hardly think it. The well-worn cliche about putting the clock back has never been more aptly illustrated than in the plugging of this obsolete and irritating instrument in the name cf historical truth. There are also the recorder, the viola da gamba, the bass viol, to say nothing of the psaltery, lute, sackbut and dulcimer whose turn will come if this trend continues.

The original orchestration of *The Messiah* is for the archives and not for the concert hall—if the concert hall is to be filled; it is certainly "putting the clock back" to attempt its reintroduction.

Serious music as we understand it is an art form of comparatively recent growth, and being circumscribed by the permutations of the octave [1] it must tend, as it approaches the end of its cycle, to become either imitative or revolutionary. For myself, opera is inseparable from singing, and although the best of singing will not create life in a bad opera, inferior singing kills the best of operas. Leaving opera aside, I think I now find the purest pleasure in Elgar, meaning the violin concerto, the symphonies and symphonic pieces, notwithstanding that the much admired melody in the concerto is lifted practically intact from *The Mikado*. But how many melodies, folk tunes and the like, now go under the names of famous composers? Not being a Brahmsian I generally identify Brahms' unaided work by its dullness: but I suppose it is unbecoming in us to complain when the only alternative to natural harmony and inspiration becomes unnatural discord and a problem in mathematics, and it is useless to tell me the old story that Mozart in his time was found dissonant and revolutionary because I don't believe it.

[1] *Cf.* under Maurice Renaud.

If in this section I have unwittingly created confusion by the uses that I have made of the terms "tradition" and "convention" I have used them on the assumption that we are discussing music and not logic, since, in music at any rate convention is or should be the forerunner of tradition; so if tradition is a good thing, as we may suppose, it would follow that the convention that brought it about must be a good thing also. If, however, it should be insisted that convention is in itself a bad thing, then let us beware of confusing the issue by seeking to discredit tradition by dubbing it as convention, which is a thing very easily done.

(1) The *appoggiaturas* referred to in the course of this section signify the raising of the penultimate note in a musical phrase either in recitative or aria in proper and appropriate places.

(2) Reference to *The Interpretation of Music of the Seventeenth and Eighteenth Centuries* by Arnold Dolmetsch will cover contingent points.

(3) *Attempt at the true manner of Keyboard Playing* by C. P. E. Bach, 1753, supplies contemporary authority for the *necessity* of ornamentation by performers.

PART TWO

Artists and their Work

In this revised edition the author has deleted a number of references to singers who have not, he thinks, made good with the majority of collectors, and has added a number of others whose claims for inclusion are indisputable. The aim is to place emphasis on singers of international repute whose names carry the highest vocal, historical and romantic interest and to avoid as far as possible anomalies and inconsistencies. Despite this laudable aim, it may be that certain readers will discover omissions which they will regret, but I can only assure any such that this will not be due to oversight. There are indeed a negligible number of red G&T artists who did not make the grade either then or later, and there were others who made a very decided grade, but in directions where I could not follow them.

It will be natural therefore that the comments which will accompany my final selection will be uniformly eulogistic, and if any should find that uninterrupted eulogy can become tedious, I should have to reply that it was one of the main objects in writing the book. I am not here as a critic but as a fervent admirer—in fact, I come to praise Caesar, not to bury him.

SOPRANOS

AINO ACKTE

AINO ACKTE'S records will be acceptable to many collectors. She was well known in Paris, where she sang Nedda with Jean de Reszke's Canio, also in London and New York in periods ranging from 1904 to 1913, and in roles as different as Micaela in *Carmen* to Strauss' Salome. She had a voice of power and purity, and a sense of style in roles that combined vocal and dramatic qualities, and thus was highly successful as Elizabeth in *Tannhauser* and Elsa in *Lohengrin*. In London her first appearance was in 1907 when she sang Elsa with the great Danish tenor Herold with Marie Brema as Ortud; and in 1910 her Senta added to her reputation. It was as Salome, however, in the same year that she attracted the greatest public attention, the occasion being the London *premiere* of Strauss' notorious work. Witnessing this, one was tempted to regret her departure from more lyrical roles, though her performance was a clever one.

Records

The records made by this Finnish soprano were some French G&Ts in 1903, 1904 and 1905; some light blue Zonophones in 1902, and Finnish Zonophone in 1905. The French Odeons which are dated by Bauer as 1906 are probably a transferred issue by Fonotipia of the previous year.

SUZANNE ADAMS

SUZANNE ADAMS was a greatly gifted Irish lyric soprano, born in U.S.A. She was blessed with the beauty of her race and was a most popular figure both on and off the stage in London which she made her home until her death in 1953. Studied in Paris with Jacques Bouhy and Marchesi, making her debut there in 1894. Her London debut was in 1898 as Juliette with Saleza as her Romeo, following which the name of Suzanne Adams was on the lips of every opera-goer, for her voice and style perfectly reproduced the Marchesi method, having that delicious limpidity and bird-like ease so much appreciated by London audiences. She gave dignity and disdain to Donna Elvira, an *ingenue* charm to Marguerite, Nedda and Micaela, and was the ideal Gilda. When, as often happened, she alternated with Melba in the latter's favourite roles, no disappointment was felt, for in the vocal sense the two had remarkably much in common.

Adams sang as Marguerite in a Command Performance of *Faust* at Windsor with Jean de Reszke, Plancon and Scotti; and received the *cachet* of another Command for a State Concert at Buckingham Palace.

To the general regret, ill-health compelled her early retirement following the autumn season of 1907.

Records

Adams' red label records are numbered among the "London Reds", and they remained as red label for two years only, after which some were re-labelled in black, and for another brief spell appeared in the general catalogue. It is rarely that a black label copy is seen, although the reds are fairly widely distributed, and they are very delightful echoes of Adams' very charming style. Good copies are essential to bring out the butterfly lightness of her delivery, and good reproducing also. Her *Jewel Song* is a triumph, and the critic Herman Klein described this rendering as a model of Gounodian style. In the airy and melodious waltz *Coquette* by her first husband Leo Stern, a 'cellist of repute, Suzanne Adams sings with a spontaneity and joyousness quite wonderful to hear, with a clearly cut *coloratura* of Marchesi's method.

In 1903 while touring in the U.S.A. Adams repeated her previous titles for Columbia (thereby falling foul of G&T), but like all Columbia records of that period, the tonal quality was shrill, and for one reason or another Adams' singing fell much below her own best, and these records are best destroyed when found.

SALEZA-ROMÉO BETWEEN JULIETTE MELBA AND JULIETTE ADAMS.
" How happy could I be with either ! "

Punch, May 18, 1904
(Melba, Adams, Saleza, Journet)

EMMA ALBANI

The name of EMMA ALBANI is one of the most illustrious in the Golden Age, and her London career continued with hardly a break from 1872 when she was engaged by Gye for Covent Garden until 1896, when she celebrated her retirement from the opera by appearing for the first time in London as Donna Anna. Running the whole gamut of operatic heroines, she made her debut in the conventional manner as Amina in the *Sonnambula*, and created for Londoners the roles of Elsa (1875), Elizabeth (1876) and Tamara in Rubinstein's *Demon* (1881), and doubling the roles of Marguerita and Elena in Boito's *Mefistofele*. Albani was especially successful as Elvira in the *Puritani*, as Lucia and as Desdemona, and set the crown on her career as Isolde. When she retired from the opera she devoted herself to oratorio for which she had a special aptitude, and for years was the leading soprano at the great Handel Festivals at the Crystal Palace. Her great gifts combined with her sympathetic nature endeared her to Queen Victoria, for whom she sang frequently in private as well as in the State Concerts, which the Queen did not herself attend.

Records

Her voice had a silvery and celestial quality comparable with what we hear of her great contemporary Christine Nilsson, as is clearly shown in her slight recording output. In Handel's *Angels ever bright and fair* both the quality of her voice and her marvellous breath control are displayed to admiration, and will give unalloyed pleasure to those who wish to hear Albani's great vocal accomplishment, and will acquiesce for once in allowing Handel to take second place. In the *Ombra mai fu* there are passages of almost unearthly beauty, and a shake which, if unduly prolonged, of a heavenly quality. The two ballads are less important and less successful.

TERESA ARKEL

TERESA ARKEL had a successful European and American career, and recorded for G&T on black label in 1903 and for Fonotipia in 1904/5. Arkel's records show a voice of power and quality and a high technique although there is some suggestion of an overstrained mechanism in a tendency to avoid a *mezza voce*. The difficulties of *D'Amor sull'ali rosee* are overcome with sufficient ease and all the resources of a dramatic soprano, and in *Siccome un di* she adds, with the reservation mentioned, the finishing touches to lyrico-dramatic accomplishment.

SIGRID ARNOLDSON

SIGRID ARNOLDSON, the brilliant Swedish soprano, made her London debut at an unusually interesting moment in the history of London opera. She was, in fact, one of the most successful of the new importations with which Augustus Harris made his bow as an *entrepreneur* of opera in 1887, which courageous venture saved the opera houses of the capital from complete disintegration, which years of disastrous competition had brought almost to the pitch of certainty. Her debut was at Drury Lane in *Il Barbiere*, in company with de Lucia, Battistini and Edouard de Reszke, and so great was her success that Harris re-engaged her for Covent Garden in 1888, and again from 1892 till 1894.

Arnoldson's other roles while in London were Mozart's Zerlina, Cherubino, Papagena, Baucis, Marguerite de Valois, and Sophie in the two melancholy performances of Massenet's deplorable *Werther* in which Jean de Reszke scored his only failure. The artist's success in these roles may be better appreciated when it is understood that she sang them in direct competition with such renowned singers as Ella Russell, Minnie Hauk and Zelie de Lussan.

Arnoldson made a number of red label records in Berlin from 1906 till 1910, her *Ah fors'e lui* being outstandingly successful.

MARIA BARRIENTOS

MARIA BARRIENTOS was a Spanish *soprano leggiero* who began a distinguished career while still under twenty years of age. Her appearance in 1903 at Covent Garden in *Il Barbiere* coincided with the debut in London of Titta Ruffo. Ruffo made no impression, but it can hardly be doubted that Barrientos was one of the victims of Melba's pathological jealousy, as she never re-appeared. She had unbounded success at the Metropolitan, and was leading soprano with Caruso in his much-publicised visit to Havana.

Her high soprano was limpid and fluent, the tone colour admirably blended and the execution superb. At the age of only fourteen she actually sang the role of the Queen in *Les Huguenots* at Barcelona.

Records

Barrientos was one of the original Fonotipia recorders, and her records were beautiful and uniformly successful. The purity of her *legato* was remarkable by any standard, and the bell-like voice was produced with an ease and fluency hardly credible in so young a singer. The two sides of the cavatina in *La Sonnambula* show her in this debutante's role to perfection, and a very attractive coupling was made of the *Voci di primervera* with the first recording of *A te o cara* by Bonci.

GEMMA BELLINCIONI

GEMMA BELLINCIONI was a very famous singing actress, and in Rome in 1890 created the role of Santuzza, and in Milan that of Fedora with Caruso. Her Carmen was considered remarkable, for Bellincioni was an artist of outstanding personality and distinction. In 1895 she sang her Santuzza and Carmen at Covent Garden.

Records

Bellincioni's records represent some of the collector's highest hopes both for their extreme rarity and for their historical interest. She made four red labels for G&T of which two appeared briefly in the English catalogue of celebrity records for 1905—the *Mefistofele* and *Cavalleria* airs, the remaining two being *Ah! fors' e lui* and the rather dull air in *Fedora*. The records suggest skill rather than charm, and doubtless her genius as an actress carried her voice with it.

CELESTINA BONINSEGNA

CELESTINA BONINSEGNA. It is hardly possible to mention the name of this famous dramatic soprano without raising a dust. For no reason that is clear to me, a great amount of material has been unearthed to debunk the great reputation of this great artist. Apparently the case against her rests chiefly on the ascertained fact that Boninsegna had only one season at the Scala (Melba had only one), and that her *first* American engagement was only moderately successful. As to the latter point, this really boils down to a preference by some individual critics for Russ who was singing in New York at the same time—which was fair enough, but did not detract from Boninsegna's excellence. It happened at the time of the fierce competition between Hammerstein and the Met., and one may guess without too much stretch of imagination the sort of lobbying that went on. On one date *Aida* was given simultaneously with Russ singing for Hammerstein and Boninsegna for the Met., and needless to say Hammerstein managed to secure the bigger audience. Without suggesting that he did so, Hammerstein was fully capable of buying up the entire New York press for the occasion, but I do feel quite certain that he did not sit quietly in his office reading the newspaper.

I heard Boninsegna in London in 1905 twice as Aida and once as Amelia, and perhaps it will suffice to say that, having heard Aidas in plenty including Destinn, when I think of Aida I think of Boninsegna. I have read also that she did not sing in company with the top artists, and that her career was undistinguished, and much trouble has been taken to demonstrate this. In an exhaustive survey of Boninsegna's career of twenty years in an admirable article in *The Record Collector* for January 1958, I find that among a host of others she sang with Vignas, Amato, Stracciari, Arimondi, Sammarco, de Marchi, Zenatello, Didur, Caruso, Lunn, Plancon, Baklanoff, Fabbri, Gay, Alda, Battistini.

Her "undistinguished" career carried her besides all over Italy including Rome, to London (Covent Garden), Madrid, New York, Boston, Philadelphia, Pittsburg, Chicago, Montevideo, Buenos Aires, Rio, Sao Paulo, St. Petersburg, Odessa, Havana—is it necessary to continue?

My own conclusion from the mass of contradictory opinion that has been collated is that for some reason out of a dozen possible ones Boninsegna found the doors of La Scala closed to her after one season, and that in the rivalry with Russ her press agents were less skilful. Anyway, neither Russ nor Boninsegna established a footing at Covent Garden, Boninsegna scoring two seasons to Russ' one, which only adds to the confusion. Twenty years of continuous work seems a long time for an unsuccessful artist: but of all those who have sat in judgment none have heard her in person excepting myself, and although I was obviously very immature at the time, I remember her well.

Records

It has even been suggested that the magnificence of Boninsegna's records was due to the fortuitous circumstance that she possessed a "recording voice", which is neither generous nor true. I can recall many voices which recorded better than hers, but the records did show the grandeur of style, the richness of *timbre* and the complete command of an exceptional range— the purity and ease of her climb to the top C in *O patria mia* surpassing any other I can recall, and she carries the sweeping phrases of the *Forza* arias to sheer triumph.

The first series had the advantage of piano accompaniment which for the period was good, the *Suicidio* being an excellent example in every way. In the historic *Faust* duet with de Lucia Boninsegna is hardly at her best, but in the scene from *Aida* with Vals she dominates by the advantage given to her by her position *vis-a-vis* the recording horn, for poor Vals was not the *tenorino* that he was made to appear. Unfortunately too many of the later records suffer from "hurdy-gurdy" accompaniments which make them difficult to listen to with appropriate gravity, but the odd thing was that anything with orchestral accompaniment was considered superior, and so much was this the case that these hybrid orchestras were frequently employed even for simple ballads where the pianoforte was obviously required. I suspect that the purpose was to cover up to some extent the noise of the steel needle.

OLIMPIA BORONAT

OLIMPIA BORONAT. It is usual to show some reserve in tracing the origins of Mme Boronat and even in the pronunciation of her name, but from A. T. Lack who recorded her in St. Petersburg in 1904 I culled the information that she was of Spanish-Italian birth and derived her professional name from her husband the Polish count Boronatski, and that her name was correctly pronounced to rhyme with tabby-cat. She studied in Milan under Leoni, and made her debut at the Bellini Theatre, Naples, with enormous success, afterwards singing in Madrid, Lisbon and in America. Her main career, however, was in Russia, where she became prima donna at the Imperial Opera House, St. Petersburg, where up to 1914 (my information ends there) she continued to sing annually, also appearing in all the large towns of Russia and abroad during two or three months of each year, from which we may infer that she did not believe in overworking her delicate voice.

As an exponent of the purest *bel canto* this exquisite singer occupies a place apart. Having acquired the highest possible technique wedded to a great depth of temperament, Boronat irresistibly suggests to the opera historian the style of a bygone age with its celestial and ineffable beauty. Her singing had that quality of appeal in the most delicate shades of expression in *mezza voce* and *rubato* which places her with the tenor de Lucia as a pattern of those achievements so much admired by our forebears—something that blossomed and faded under the fierce light of competition. What a misfortune that we did not hear her in London.

Records

Boronat's red label issue of 1904 were veritable gems, and G&T must be complimented on having secured them and on having introduced them to England. The *Qui la voce* in *Puritani* will remain a classic example of the true way to sing Bellini where the ability to do so is present. But in this as in all her records of this series there is something of herself that would defy imitation, for her rendering is deeply felt besides being exquisitely sung. *The Last Rose of Summer* is something different again, and is an astonishing feat of long phrasing—so much so that one verse only occupies the 10-in. disc. Alabieff's *Nightingale* and Ivanow's *Zabava* are given with moving intensity, and the *Caro Nome* with brilliance and pathos. A 12-in. set made in Milan in 1908 prove that the great success of the Petersburg issue was no lucky accident, and notwithstanding some inferior pressings on an "Archive" series of which I have heard reports, fine original copies which I have heard leave no doubt of this.

EUGENIA BURZIO

EUGENIA BURZIO was a Fonotipia artist, whose contribution to the 39 series was small but its quality great. She was a dramatic soprano in the truest sense of the word, for her singing was dramatic, not to say emotional, in the extreme. But she sang in the grand manner, and, like Boninsegna, was heard to great advantage in Verdi of the middle period. In the big solo in *Un Ballo in maschera* and in the following duet with Zenatello she sings with an intensity of passion hardly to be matched; and in the *duo* with Magini-Coletti in the *Trovatore* Burzio expresses with startling vividness the pleadings and rejoicings of the unhappy Leonora. Another artist we could have welcomed in London, but so content were we with Destinn that neither Boninsegna nor Russ nor Burzio were necessary!

EMMA CALVE

EMMA CALVE'S name will live for ever in opera history as the last, or last but one (reserving Maria Gay) of the truly great Carmens. Emphasis is given to this claim by the fact that she came within the living memory of those who could recall Minnie Hauk, Trebelli, Pauline Lucca and Zelie de Lussan—all ladies of outstanding force of character such as the role requires. Perhaps the secret shared by all these great Carmens was their thorough understanding of the character of the gipsy, and that none of them were under the misapprehension that the simple flamboyance of a queen of musical comedy sufficed to put the role over the footlights. I never saw Calve, but I saw de Lussan's Carmen, Gianoli's and Maria Gay's, but no other who has made any impact on my memory. These Carmens were not mere flighty girls, but were introspective, haunted creatures, afraid of themselves and dreading the outcome. That Calve was in the direct line is attested by all commentators, but she had numerous other claims to fame. She claimed to have three voices, and the variety of her roles lends colour to this. She could produce a high soprano perfectly adapted for the Ophelia of Thomas's *Hamlet*, and could sing and act a wonderful Santuzza in which she made her London debut in 1892, when the *furore* created by Mascagni's masterpiece was at its height. With de Lucia she sang in the London *premiere* of the same composer's lovely *L'Amico Fritz* (unaccountably neglected by the gramophone industry). A black-haired Marguerite in *Faust* and *Mefistofele*, a picturesque Messaline in de Lara's opera and a vivid Salome in Massenet's *Herodiade*. Besides these roles which Calve sang in London, she sang Amy Robsart in de Lara's less successful work of that name with Alvarez and Lassalle.

I have listened to the delightful story of how Emma Calve and Zelie de Lussan, lunching at the latter's flat, and warming under the influence of Zelie's burgundy, assured each other that of course the real Carmen was—the other!

Records

    The Calve London red label records were the first of this historic series, and a reference to them will be found under the note on Fred Gaisberg. The *Carmen* items were inevitable and are very well done, and the *Voi lo sapete* also. The *Zanetto* is little but a trifle, and its rather abrupt ending gives the impression of some misunderstanding, but I am assured that this was as written. The *Enchantement* by Massenet gives the singer great opportunity for intensity of expression, and for once the recording apparatus caught the tones of the accompanying piano with a near approximation to realism. But the gem of the series is the *Magali*—a Provencal song practically unaccompanied and sung with a pure brightness of tone in a high *tessitura* which displays her versatility as well as her breath control. Her *"ecoutez, maintenant"*, just before a very long-sustained note is clearly audible.

EMMA CARELLI

EMMA CARELLI was a G&T celebrity soprano who recorded in 1904 but survived in the catalogue only for a matter of months. The extremely limited opportunities one gets of hearing her recorded voice suggest that the gramophone was not her medium, while leaving the impression that as a tragic or emotional actress Carelli was impressive. Whether her G&T records were unsuccessful, or whether their quick withdrawal was due to the artist's move over to Fonotipia cannot be asserted, but the results obtained by the latter company were good examples of a passionate and dramatic singing actress.

HARICLEA DARCLEE

The illustrious HARICLEA DARCLEE, who created in Rome the roles of Iris (1898) and Tosca (1900) recorded for Fonotipia in 1904/5. It seems that none of her records have come to light.

ZELIE DE LUSSAN

ZELIE DE LUSSAN. Surely one of fortune's greatest favourites, for seldom has so dazzling and brilliant a personality been endowed with so lovely a voice and with such musical gifts. She was introduced by Mapleson to Harris who engaged her for the last night of the season of 1888 to sing Carmen. Despite that Minnie Hauk had been repeating her triumphs, de Lussan scored the victory that Mapleson had foretold for her. Zelie de Lussan, who was American born but of purely French descent from de Lussans of mediaeval times, had received her training and had acquired much experience in Chicago, where Mapleson had noted her talents and urged her to come to London immediately where he hoped to do something for her. It is hardly possible to speak or write for long about de Lussan without using the term "vivid"; she had lustrous black eyes which she could use with devastating effect, and a deep contralto speaking voice, although she sang soprano. Her Carmen became and has remained historic, and she used to say that she had been slain by no fewer than fifty-six different Don Joses and was none the worse for it. But like her colleague Calve, Carmen was not her only role, for she had thirty-one others, singing with Maurel, Tamagno, de Lucia, and with Melba as the first Musetta in *La Bohème* at Covent Garden. She sang *Carmen* at Windsor Castle and various Command Performances in opera and concert and became a favourite with the Queen.

Her voice deserted her in middle-age, but her looks, her vivacity, her neat figure and girlish ankles, and above all her unfailing cheerfulness both at home and abroad, kept her a young woman. Either as hostess or guest her social charm and cheerful wit, while never raising her voice, would keep the party on tenterhooks, hoping for something revealing—which, if it came, was very *sotto voce*. Zelie never said an unkind thing; and I will venture to repeat the conclusion of an appreciation I wrote at her death in 1949: "In the final count, what Zelie had was faith, hope and charity, and therefore she was unconquerable".

Records
    Zelie de Lussan did little recording, and her most interesting series was for the Beka company, and a few for Victor, but none were issued in England.

EMMA DESTINN

EMMA DESTINN was a Czech dramatic soprano who came to London in the fruitful season of 1904, making an instant success as Donna Anna, a role in which she has never been approached, for she sang it in the Italian manner and in such a way that the critics saw in her the true successor to Titjiens, whose mantle had been unclaimed since that great singer's retirement in 1877. Destinn was a singer of real distinction with a voice to match her presence, and nothing came amiss to her. She was the last great exponent of the exacting role of Valentine in *Les Huguenots* in which her physical beauty showed to great advantage and her impassioned singing with Caruso in the final act left an unforgettable memory. It must surely be due to a tradition left by her beautiful singing in *Madama Butterfly* that the merits of this work seem to be taken for granted. Destinn seldom missed a season at Covent Garden until the outbreak of the first war, and reappeared singing if possible more beautifully than ever in 1919 when as Amelia in the *Ballo in maschera* her duet with Martinelli received an ovation. She died in 1930, the same year as Albani, Sammarco and Kirkby Lunn.

Records
    The story of Destinn's recording is of one long series of muddles. Her first records were for Fonotipia, but requiring to be played at about 84 r.p.m., they evidently were not appreciated, as refinements of this kind were unthought of. Consequently these records were transferred to the associated Odeon company, which occasioned a definite loss of prestige, and with the voice showing a strongly contralto *timbre*, this admirer at least found little virtue in them. (Later, of course, he knew better.) When in 1906 she came to G&T her gramophonic reputation was not remarkable, but instead of celebrating in a worthy manner their success in having secured the world's finest dramatic soprano, G&T timidly produced her on 10-in. black label, and—as with Fonotipia—in German! When it was much too late, the Gramophone company raised her long list of black label records to red label status, but of these I have never seen a copy. She also recorded part of the Aida-Amneris duet with Kirkby Lunn, which has historical associations, a copy of which recently fell into my hands, after eluding me for so many years, but in this, Destinn was overshadowed by Lunn's opulent phrases and the rather muddy recording.

PAULINE DONALDA

PAULINE DONALDA may in this year of 1963 claim to be the *doyenne* of English-speaking singers of the later Golden Age. She seems not to have been feared by Melba, and in fact the writer heard her singing as her substitute as Mimi, with Caruso, Scotti and Parkina. He thought her better suited in *Faust*, the opera in which she made her London debut in 1905, following which she was re-engaged. Ironically, her first records, which were red G&T, and were of the *Jewel Song* and *Mi chiamano Mimi* were poor both in recording and in performance, but some of the later ones were pleasing. Donalda made her debut in Nice in 1904.

EMMA EAMES

EMMA EAMES (incorrectly pronounced "Aympz" by some) was one of Marchesi's finest pupils. She passed through the Paris Opera to Covent Garden in 1891. Thus she sang contemporaneously with Melba throughout the 'nineties, sharing the roles which were common to both. Coming from the same school there was little to choose between Eames and Melba, although the hypercritical might claim to detect a greater purity of style in the singing of Melba; and those who were critical without knowledge found that both Melba and Eames lacked warmth, so we will leave them there. Emma Eames retired in her prime in 1909, but twenty-five years later I met her for a chat, and oh dear, what opportunities I lost! But she left me a much-prized memory of a gracious and lovely woman; she had corresponded with me with great cordiality and gave amusing accounts of her recording sessions, of which her recollections were by no means favourable, nor did she consider that her records were true reproductions of her voice; however, perhaps she was not the best judge of that, since nobody accepts their recorded voice as approximating to their own.

Records

Eames' records are among those which repay for modern reproduction, some of them being thinly recorded, but the style and technique of this great singer make them historic. It is hardly necessary to call attention to specific items, but her first *Ave Maria* by Gounod without the obligato may be mentioned as illustrating the great reserves of breath and the sheer weight of the chest notes. Try supplying the obligato yourself, and you will see what I mean better than I could explain it!

At the end of the G&T period Eames recorded the *Faust* finale with Dalmores and Plancon, the result of which was less excellent than might have been hoped owing to some bungling in the studio. This was done at or nearly the same time as the Melba-Caruso duet which also suffered in some degree from lack of balance, and both, it may be noticed, were issued as "Gramophone and Typewriter" records, with the Victor caption dropped.

Human nature being what it is, Eames' flatness on the final note arouses more comment than the magnificence of the rest of her singing: Plancon is barely audible. Collectors have wondered why this recording was not rectified, but in those days it was not possible to "play back" without ruining the "master", and by the time its defects were discovered the three world-famous artists were probably widely separated; it might have been consigned to the "great unpublished", but those of us who have fine copies and suitable equipment are grateful for a truly exciting record. Bauer fixes 1911 as the year of Eames' last records, and J. M. Moses in his *Collectors Guide to American Recordings* extends the date to 1913 for each or some of the three final titles.

ALICE ESTY

ALICE ESTY was a leading American-born English singer at the turn of the century, and is remembered as the first Mimi in *La Boheme* in England, for the Carl Rosa company. I met her also, and although I longed to tell her that she was my first Marguerite with the Moody-Manners company, and how vividly I remembered the final tableau, with herself bathed in a golden light, Francis Maclennan in mauve, and Charles Manners in satanic red, I was too young and bashful to open my heart, finding her a rather severe lady.

Records

The 12-in. records were fine examples of their period, and Alice Esty's easy mastery of the testing aria from the *Trovatore*, *Breeze of the Night*, fixes her quality.

GERALDINE FARRAR

GERALDINE FARRAR, before leaving Berlin for New York, made some black label G&Ts in Berlin and London from 1904 to 1906, the London titles (concerning which there has been fierce controversy) coinciding with her appearance at the London Albert Hall in the latter year. Although there were some nice records among them they were not outstanding, and were quite swamped by her copious and distinguished output which were issued in Europe on pink and green labels, the latter with Caruso generally as her partner. The first of her green labels was the *Butterfly* duet with Caruso, which also has aroused sharp differences of opinion. Although Miss Farrar has forgotten the incident, and the Victor company had expunged it from their archives, there was evidently some high-spirited play in the studio, for *Si per la vita* became transformed with startling clarity and gusto, aspirates and all, into "He's had a highball". Otherwise the record was immaculate. This, of course, would not do, and another was made, this time with *Si per la vita* sung with undistorted purity, *and* with a *mordente* ornament near the end. But it blasted rather badly, and was quietly replaced by the first record on the same numbers and green pre-dog label. I was one of the first to possess this first issue, and Laurie Root has it to this day. A report of yet a third recording in which Caruso made a suitable repartee in English sounds a bit too god to be true.

CESIRA FERRANI

CESIRA FERRANI belongs to history as the creator of the role of Mimi at the world *premiere* of *La Boheme* at Turin, having already won Puccini's approval for her creation of Manon Lescaut. That she was not definitely in the first rank appears from a letter from the publisher Ricordi to the composer to the effect that Angelica Pandolfini greatly surpassed her, and an interesting 10-in. record of *Mi chiamano Mimi* lends some colour to this opinion, for it is acceptable without challenging Melba's rendering. And while on the subject I would like to offer an *amende* by saying here that the only record or live singing that I have ever heard that does compare with Melba in this aria is a record by—Maria Callas! Never having been subdued by this *diva's* conceptions of how to sing, I can now appreciate what she can do when she tries.

EVANGELINE FLORENCE

EVANGELINE FLORENCE is sure of her place in gramophone history, being one of the first-class British artists to be rounded up by Fred Gaisberg in 1903. As a concert singer she invariably headed the bill, having a high soprano of limpid flexibility easily reaching to E and F, but full of colour and of a pleasantly mellow *timbre*. Her records display her as a finished *leggiero* with a fine sense of line, and are listed in the appendix.

MARIA GALVANY

MARIA GALVANY was Spanish born and Spanish trained, and made her debut at Cartagena as Lucia in 1897, afterwards singing with total success in Madrid, Milan, Genoa, Nice, Parma, etc., etc. That she did not come to Covent Garden will be no surprise to readers of this book, although she appeared in provincial cities in England in 1909, as well as in a curious assignment at Messrs. Harrods in London where no charge was made to her audiences. With her on these occasions was "Signor Tamini" introduced as one of the new Carusos, who was in truth a German of limited talents. Galvany sang the full repertoire of a *soprano leggiero* with the utmost ease and fluency, and although not gifted with beauty, she possessed what was of more solid value, a great charm of personality and a lightness and precision in her wonderful *coloratura* which she delivered with a delightful inconsequence of manner.

Records

Galvany made her first records for G&T in Milan in 1903 on black label, and these can be accounted as special rarities. Indeed none of her earlier G&Ts, including the red labels, seem to have reached these shores in any appreciable numbers. Of her pre-dogs *L'Incantatrice* by Arditi is probably most often heard, and it is *tour de force* of flexibility, purity and neatness of execution. Galvany also recorded in duets, most notably with Marconi and de Lucia.

MARY GARDEN

MARY GARDEN had made a great reputation in Paris before coming to London in 1903, when she sang with great success the roles of Juliette, Marguerite and Massenet's Manon. But the greater part of her career was in America, where she also displayed great enterprise as a manager of opera. She was much admired in Charpentier's *Louise*, and made the first record of the air *Depuis le jour* for Victor. This record lacks the imagination of Edwina's poetic rendering which may be said to reflect the training of her teacher Jean de Reszke in an extraordinary degree. This fine artist and singer may be written down as another who failed to conquer Melba's opposition.

Records

Of particular value are the four excellent records made by Mary Garden for G&T (black label) in 1903 in Paris. These were three *Ariettes* by Debussy, and a short passage from the opera *Pelleas et Melisande*, in which opera Debussy greatly admired her. All have the unique distinction of the composer's own accompaniment.

SALOMEA KRUSCHELNIKA

SALOMEA KRUSCHELNIKA was a Polish soprano approaching the dramatic of quite exceptional gifts. Her voice was of velvety intensity and delivered in a charming and gracious manner. Her G&T records were taken at Warsaw in 1903, and so have some affinity with the beautiful "Warsaw Batts", and one of these was included in my much regretted "Collector's Choice" LP. Her later Fonotipias were of higher recording merit, and are valuable examples of one of those too-many singers who were lost to us in London through what seems in retrospect to have been our over-addiction to Melba and Destinn.

SELMA KURZ

SELMA KURZ was perhaps one of the most attractive and accomplished of *leggiero* sopranos to come to London. Her debut at Covent Garden was in 1904 as Gilda. I had the pleasure of being present on that occasion which was a triumph for her, when the cast was Kurz, Caruso, Renaud and Journet and later as the Queen in *Les Huguenots* and as the Page in the *Ballo*. She was another of Marchesi's most brilliant pupils, with that free and spontaneous delivery which was so characteristic of them. Besides her gifts and achievements, Selma Kurz had great beauty of person, supreme grace of movement, graciousness of deportment, and a lady as we used to understand the word. Her wonderful trill became and has remained a legend, ending her aria *Saper vorreste* in the *Ballo*. It was a trill such as only the Marchesi school accomplished, so pure and so clear was it: it seemed unending as she carried it leisurely across the length of the stage, the conductor (it was said—

I didn't notice) having laid down his baton, until it seemed that everything that was capable of vibrating was put into movement. But besides this special accomplishment, Selma Kurz was a great singer in a variety of roles, and was chosen to create the role of the Princess in the *Rosenkavalier*, but owing to some dispute this happy thought did not materialise. To have heard her was one of the great experiences of an opera-goer, and even when in company with the brilliant casts in which it was my privilege to hear her, it was Kurz who shone with the purest radiance.

Dainty Miss Elisabeth (Fräulein Selma Kurz),
a drawn Bet on first Ascot day, and no better
to be found anywhere!   *Punch*, June 22, 1904

Records

A few of the earliest records by Selma Kurz were 7-in. black G&Ts made in Vienna in 1902, evidently while singing at the Imperial Opera under Mahler in the second stage of her career. In fact all her recording was done in that city, her red G&Ts coming in 1906 when she was a world star. This was a misfortune in that she used German to an undue extent, even for the most Italian of music, and in concerted pieces with heavily Germanic colleagues. The *Lakme* Bell Song, despite its German form is almost certainly the best ever recorded, and two Italian renderings—*Caro Nome* and *Ah, non giunge*—might make the same claim. For those who might enquire how Kurz compared with Melba, I should, after deprecating comparison in any form between two such superlative singers, hazard the opinion that

Kurz was fully Melba's equal, after taking account of the handicap of thirteen years difference in age. That Melba did nothing to encourage more frequent engagements can hardly be doubted.

LILLI LEHMANN

LILLI LEHMANN did not record until 1907, by which time she was fifty-nine, but being the great singer she was, age affected her very little. But she, like Selma Kurz, sang overmuch in German in the long list of impressive titles she has left us. She sang only for Odeon, and covered everything from *Fidelio* to *Traviata*—and in Mozart showed a *coloratura* that would have been more credible at half her age. She came to London in 1880, appearing as Violetta, a role for which she evidently kept an affection, for she remembered it in her recording, and in the following year as Filina in *Mignon*. In 1884 she astonished the critics by appearing as Isolde, only two years after *Tristan* had first been heard in London, and in 1887 she had the misfortune to be associated with Mapleson's last heroic but ineffectual venture which finished his operatic career, singing her superb Fidelio to half-filled houses. I am not sufficiently familiar with Lehmann's records to offer comment on them.

FELIA LITVINNE

FELIA LITVINNE (*nee* Schutz) had much success as a dramatic soprano, and being a kinswoman to the de Reszkes, found ample opportunity. Her London debut was in 1899 as Isolde, singing with Jean de Reszke, afterwards appearing at Covent Garden over a period of ten years in *Aida*, *Don Giovanni* (Anna), *Gioconda*, and *The Ring*. Her most striking successes, however, were neither in England nor in the United States, but her career on the Continent was an important one. In 1884 she sang in Paris with Maurel in *Simon Boccanegra* and *Ernani*. Litvinne was perhaps the most "operatic" of all operatic heroines, both on and off the stage, for she had the artistic temperament to the last degree.

Records

Litvinne recorded for G&T in Paris in 1903 on red label, all being accompanied by Alfred Cortot, whose name appeared on each label. At some date between 1903 and the latter end of 1904 all or part of this issue were re-recorded, with the original numbering preserved, and the same label being used. It has come to light, however, that with the re-recording a lady accompanist officiated under Cortot's name. Then from January 1905 the series was transferred to the black label catalogue. It would seem, therefore, that only copies having the clear 1903 form (see p. 000) could undoubtedly be classified as genuine Cortot recordings, since red labels of 1904 would show their label and other characteristics.

There were four French Fonotipias of 1904/5, and in 1907 came some recordings for Odeon.

BLANCHE MARCHESI

The records of BLANCHE MARCHESI were made in Berlin in 1906, and were not issued in England. Her fame as an interpreter of *lieder* and music of a strongly characterised kind placed her in the front rank of singing artists, but it was her tragedy that her vocal equipment never matched her superb artistic resources, and thus was a supreme operatic heroine lost, although she sang on occasion in opera with passionate fervour. I recall Isolda and Verdi's Leonora. As daughter and assistant to the greatest singing teacher since the younger Garcia, Blanche lived her youth in an atmosphere surely unique for a student, and absorbed her mother's methods through her pupils' courses.

Her recital in London in celebration of her seventy-fifth birthday, which was attended by a crowded and delighted audience in which every noted singer in London could be seen, was the musical highlight of the season of 1938, and provided a monument for all time to the correct methods of voice production. Marchesi sang unassisted throughout an arduous programme, seated like an empress, and without faltering. The writer found her in good spirits a few days later. She died in 1940.

NELLIE MELBA

NELLIE MELBA stands in the dead centre of the operatic universe of our epoch, and so highly have her gifts and attainments been acknowledged in her time that there can be little of originality to add. Her voice defied description or comparison—it was Melba's. Being Marchesi's most illustrious pupil, and having enjoyed robust health throughout her life, it was natural that she should still have been singing until the year of her death: but it was not natural—it was miraculous—that the voice retained to the end that ineffable quality of childlike purity that was unlike the voice of any other.

We have already noticed that Melba was by nature inclined to jealousy, and kept Covent Garden as her own close preserve; but nobody thought of what they might have been missing, since it was taken as an article of faith that any other would have been her inferior—as doubtless they would have been.

It was Melba who prevailed upon the opera management against their own judgment to produce *La Bohème*, and it almost seems as though she foresaw the great future that this work was to have for her. Her Mimi remains unique, and the role fitted her so perfectly in the vocal sense that it became her own in her own inimitable fashion. The accentation, the pointing of the phrases and the unaffected simplicity which so exactly matched her voice made Melba's rendering impossible of imitation and the despair of all who would seek to emulate her. Her acting in this role, moreover, was faultless, with no attempt to force drama into situations which were merely pathetic, which was too often the trap for some of the unwary Mimis that followed her.

The fact that Melba was not a great tragedienne was no reason for dismissing her as an actress. She knew to a hair what to do on the stage, and—especially—what not to do; and she remained strictly in the picture and part of it, which, as I believe, could not be said of a bad actress.

All the above could with equal justice be written of her Juliette, to which she gave the same personal touches which made Gounod's work a great opera, and one that might have been written for her. Attempts to follow her produced nothing but nostalgic memories.

Her farewell to Covent Garden, of which I still have the programme, consisted of the Balcony Scene in *Romeo*, the third and fourth acts of *La Boheme* and Desdemona's closing scene in *Otello*, and on this testing and emotional occasion Melba did not falter. In compliment to her country she chose as nearly as possible an all-Australian cast, with Charles Hackett, John Brownlee and Browning Mummery, and this was, I believe, the first occasion on which an opera performance was recorded.

Violetta Melba—costume 1904.   Germont Scotti—costume 1675.
Ce cher petit enfant Alfred Caruso—costume 1675.

Punch June 22, 1904
(Melba, Scotti, Caruso)

Records

The advent of the Melba records was perhaps the greatest and most significant event in our survey, and without question they gave the final cachet of prestige to the G&T company. At the price of a guinea each they sold by thousands, and they brought great credit to the gramophonist who had one or more in his collection.

The first recordings were done at Melba's residence in Great Cumberland Place, Hyde Park, and although these were believed to have been scrapped *en masse* and the project transferred bodily to the G&T studio, I have a strong feeling that this is only partially true, and that the piano-accompanied titles from *Mattinata* to *Lucia di Lammermoor* were salvaged from the private session. There is a special kind of crudity about these (as well as a great deal of beauty), which suggests this, and is not found elsewhere either in the Melba set or in any other. The accompanist was Landon Ronald, who had been Melba's indefatigable coach for many years, and he did not seem able at once to accommodate his touch to the doubtless awkward acoustics of Melba's drawing-room, which, in the prevailing fashion of the period, was much overfurnished; and a percussive wiriness was painfully apparent. The extent to which this was toned down and indeed overcome in the subsequent sessions suggests that the matter was given full attention, when it was realised that what would suit the human ear did not necessarily suit the early gramophone.

Another pointer in the same direction is the low speeds of the first seven, followed by an even 75 r.p.m. thereafter for both the years 1904 and 1905.

There is a subtle charm about Melba's record number 1—Tosti's *Mattinata*—for it patters along without pauses or expression, and, until the end, none of those *rallentandos* which caused Tosti so much annoyance. It sounds youthful and unsophisticated, and is probably inimitable. Melba used it in the Lesson Scene in the *Barbiere*, playing her own accompaniment, as she did in a later American recording.

In Bemberg's *Nymphes et Sylvains*, although some of the recording was faulty, especially where the piano was concerned, her personal touches abound, and no singer I can recall could express with her voice such lightness and gaiety—excepting Blanche Marchesi, when singing *Der Nussbaum*. Blanche, who detested Melba, considered this to be the best example of Melba's *coloratura*; but although there were other records of this period for which such a claim could be made, there were none excepting *Se Saran Rose* which had the sunlit sparkle of *Nymphes et Silvains*. *Se Saran Rose* just missed the bulls-eye owing to minor blasts when the recording machine failed to cope with the accompanist's exuberance, even in a good copy.

One could dwell upon the serene beauty of the *coloratura* in the *Lucia* Mad Scene cadenza or in the classical perfection of Handel's *Sweet Bird*, but in none, I think, did Melba exceed her own performance in the two sides of the *Hamlet* Mad Scene, and I recommend this as a corrective to anyone who is completely satisfied with any other rendering.

The *Addio* in *La Boheme* again is Melba's very self, and it seems to be impossible to approach it; for having low notes as well as high, she could sing all of it with equal ease—which, if you notice attentively, is not always the case. In Bemberg's *Chant Hindu* the simple phrases are so formed as to sound almost easy, which, of course, was exactly Melba's way—and yet nobody else could do it. This slow lament gives one ample time to take in and enjoy the purity and steadiness of her singing, and her marvellous sense of climax sinking to sad despair. For a record of the Melba voice, as a voice, this one is unsurpassed. Tosti's *La Serenata* is sung in a manner reminiscent of the same composer's *Mattinata*, and was a great favourite of mine from the earliest days. *Caro Nome* was the first Melba record I heard, shortly after hearing her sing it, sung with a girlish delicacy and birdlike ease again unsurpassable. For those I have not mentioned I could only repeat what I have said, for all are lovely, and most especially the shortened version of *Mi chiamano Mimi*, with its little bit of *recitativo secco* which would be the sheer despair of any would-be imitator.

In my complete set in original form of the London records are four which Melba herself gave to her teacher, Mathilde Marchesi, from whom they came to her daughter, Blanche, and so to me—records handled but seldom played by Melba and the Marchesis, although it may be doubted whether the austere Mathilde would have wished to countenance anything so modern and mechanical as a gramophone.

"Fortunate the generation that heard her," as *The New York Times* wrote on her death, "for we shall never hear her like again".

Punch, June 8, 1904   Dudley Hardy.

MEDEA MEY-FIGNER

MEDEA MEY-FIGNER, formerly Medea Mey until she married the tenor, Figner, and joined him in Russia, appeared at Covent Garden under Lago's management in 1887. She was prima donna at the Imperial Opera at St. Petersburg, and, like her husband, Court Singer to the Czar. She is often written of as a contralto, but apparently without greater justification than that she had a full and powerful lower register. She evidently was a dramatic soprano able to sing *mezzo* roles such as Leonora in the *Favorita* which she sang in London.

Records

These were made in St. Petersburg in 1900 and so were the greater part of the first and original red labels. They are among the greatest rarities and are readily sold to collectors at high prices, for they were practically unknown in England although included in the celebrity catalogues for 1902 and 1903. Her *Chanson Boheme* in *Carmen* might well have caused Bizet to remark "What a charming thing—who is the composer?" All are of great beauty, well recorded and most exquisitely sung, and when the H.M.V. library was ransacked not a single one of these remained!

MARIA MICHAILOWA

MARIA MICHAILOWA, a lesser Russian prima donna, first recorded on Berliners in 1900, and thereafter became a regular and prolific recorder who gave the less wealthy gramophonists the opportunity of acquiring a wide range of opera and opera-type music at a popular price. For this reason her records had a big sale in England, and her new recordings were a regular feature of the catalogue supplements. I am not proposing to give a list of her titles, since present-day collectors refuse to interest themselves in them; but from a historical angle they play their part.

ANNA VON MILDENBURG

ANNA VON MILDENBURG's solitary record was made in Vienna in 1903, and, until Jean de Reszke's record or records are authenticated, may rank as a collector's most valuable specimen. It gives us a unique example of great merit combined with great rarity, and its performance upholds the highest standards even of this great artist. Many of us are grateful to that big-hearted Californian collector, George T. Keating, for giving us the opportunity to hear, on a private issue, this magnificent record.

Von Mildenburg was a dramatic soprano of the Vienna Opera, whose Isolde was much admired in London as everywhere for its tenderness and its beauty—qualities which added to our admiration when in 1910 she startled us with her Klytemnestra in *Electra*—an uncanny study in human depravity. I heard this performance of hers three times, and I am convinced that like so many "creations" it has never been challenged—unless the critics have failed to notice it. Von Mildenburg had a powerful voice (which this role did nothing to improve), a majestic presence and a dominating personality. She was comparable with Ternina, with a voice more powerful and somewhat less sweet, and neither were of the kind which needed or tolerated direction from "producers", and truly Von Mildenburg's performance was Greek tragedy at its highest.

AGNES NICHOLLS

AGNES NICHOLLS (Lady Hamilton Harty) was perhaps the greatest of British singers of our period. She succeeded Albani as the leading festival soprano, and she was one of those who were fully able to cope with the immense spaces of the Crystal Palace. She herself disclaimed a big voice, saying that its carrying power was due to its poise. However this may be, she sang the Brunnhildes of *Die Walkure* and *Siegfried* magnificently, for her voice had a sweetness of quality not often heard in the bigger roles. Agnes Nicholls truly sang in the grand manner, and her serene confidence on the platform endeared her to her audiences—Rossini's *Inflammatus* being one of their favourites. When reminded of this she laughed merrily and said, "they liked waiting for the high Cs!", and truly they were worth waiting for.

In 1901 Agnes Nicholls began a highly successful career at Covent Garden, appearing first in lesser roles like the Dewman in *Hansel und Gretel* and the waiting-maid in *Messaline* in the same cast as Calvé and Tamagno; she was also employed to understudy the roles of Beatrice and Hero in *Much Ado about Nothing* for Marie Brema and Suzanne Adams. She sang Venus and Elizabeth in *Tannhauser* and *Elsa* in Lohengrin, and the Countess in *Figaro*. She was expected to be ready to sing almost any role at a moment's notice, and was given a regular contract with the Opera Syndicate until 1911.

Records

It was not until 1910 that Agnes Nicholls was prevailed upon to record for H.M.V., which was in an unfortunate period, and the results, although pleasing in themselves, gave little impression of the majestic breadth and sweep of her delivery.

The writer performed the pleasant ceremony of introducing Lady Harty to a meeting of the Recorded Vocal Art Society of London in 1959, to whom, at the age of eighty, she gave a two-hour talk on her career before a crowded audience. In that same year she died, having by her great courage and cheerfulness overcome much serious illness, and thus passed the last link with the great prima donnas.

ALICE NIELSON

ALICE NIELSON. Although this highly successful American soprano made only two records for Victor-G&T, she was so great a favourite with Covent Garden audiences in 1904 and 1905 that her inclusion here is inevitable. In the summer (i.e. "grand") season of 1904 she was an important member of the highly selective casts for Richter's "special" uncut performances of *Don Giovanni* (with which the season opened) and *Le Nozze di Figaro*. She sang as Zerlina with Suzanne Adams and Destinn (her London debut), Renaud, Salignac and Journet; and as Susanna with Adams as the Countess and Scotti as the Count, and it became quite a social event to have heard and seen these three ladies in these brilliant performances. (And may I interpolate that with Richter in charge there was no monkeying with traditional *tempi* or ornamentation. Although so long ago I recall the details of this performance with absolute clearness as though turning the leaves of an album.) In an autumn season that year, Nielson was the first Micaela I was to hear, with Caruso as Don Jose. She pairs with Suzanne Adams as the most charming of them both vocally and histrionically, and she sang the big aria in the grand manner, with the graceful and rhythmic gestures which were characteristic of her. In that season she also sang Mimi, and Gilda with Maurel. I next heard her early in the following year when she "assisted"

How Susanna-Nielsen, with her striking melody, catches the ear of Figaro-Seveilhac. May 16.

Punch, May 25, 1904
(with Seveilhac)

Maurel at the first of his London recitals, when she gave Tosti's *Goodbye* and *Mi chiamano Mimi*, joining Maurel in *La ci darem* in traditional *tempo* as marked; and the last time and perhaps most striking of all was in that triumphant *Barbiere* at the Waldorf with that truly Golden Age cast of de Lucia, Ancona, Arimondi and Pini-Corsi, when she easily fitted in with her veteran and distinguished colleagues, and was never put out by Pini-Corsi's impromptus and asides. She re-appeared at Covent Garden, this time as Butterfly, in the *dammerung* of 1913.

Records

Alice Nielson's first records were for the Victor company of New York, of which two were issued in Europe as Victor-G&T. These are dated by J. M. Moses as 1907–8, and comprised a delightful list of titles, of which not even the Victor-G&Ts, I believe, were on sale in England. Columbia made greater use of her in 1911 in an extended repertoire, and some of these reached England but are rarely found.

LILLIAN NORDICA

One of the greatest of singers and most disappointing of recorders was surely LILLIAN NORDICA, who recorded only for Columbia.

It was the astute Mapleson who discovered her while touring with his opera company in the United States and enrolled her forthwith. She became his prima donna in his Covent Garden season of 1887, that fateful operatic year in which four seasons of grand opera were mounted in London—two by Mapleson, one by Lago and the new dawning under Harris. Although Mapleson had lost public support and was constantly embarrassed by financial difficulties, he still aimed high and gave of the best that was available to him. Nordica's debut was as Violetta, to which she added the roles of Gilda, Marguerite and Donna Elvira, and despite the lack of brilliance in the productions as a whole, her success was so marked that Harris immediately secured her for his opening and historic venture at Drury Lane, where she at once established herself, and for a matter of twelve years Nordica was one of London's leading sopranos, notable also in the greatest Wagnerian roles, and with parallel successes in America. The story is told of how she, with the de Reszkes and Klein, were dining together on the eve of Jean's debut as Tristan, at which Klein was not able to be present, when Nordica and Jean, still sitting at the table, sang for him the duet in the second act—a striking tribute to all three.

Records

The virtual failure of Nordica's records can only be ascribed to lack of skill or understanding on the part of the operatives, for of the first series of eight runs (in 1906–7) two only were passed for issue, and a mere eight out of twenty-four made in 1910–11, including a *Liebestod* utterly devoid of

F

merit. Of the entire series, two only are worthy of notice, namely, *Suicidio* in *La Gioconda* and *Hunyadi Laszlo* by Erkel. Four of the unpublished titles which will otherwise be ignored here and including another *Suicidio*, were exhumed and issued for the benefit of such collectors as cared for such curiosities.

REGINI PACINI

REGINI PACINI who was one of Fonotipia's most important light sopranos seems not to have established herself with the Covent Garden authorities of her day, for after appearing as far back as 1889 she did not re-appear until 1902, when she sang in *L'Elisir d'amore* with Caruso in his first London season, and herein again can the fatal hand of Melba be traced. Pacini's reputation in Italy and elsewhere was high, and her records attest this, being made in days when it had not become possible by technical manipulation to produce renderings of great length and of a very improbable degree of perfection. In this year of 1962 I hear that Regini Pacini is still living in comfortable retirement at the age of ninety-two, and thus is the *doyenne* of our Golden Age. She was another of the Marchesi school.

Records

Regina Pacini's records are fine examples of finished singing, especially in the *leggiero*, for she possessed that skill in *legato* by which she was able to infuse an interpretation of feeling into the most decorative passages—an accomplishment which, although so rare in our day, we believe to have been one of the principal objects of the infinitely more severe training of earlier times.

With such technical equipment therefore, we feel no surprise to find that Pacini could execute an *andante* such as the air of Proch's *Variations* with a perfection of *cantelina* as may well be the acid test of the finished singer. Nothing displays for us the interplay of *coloratura* and *legato* better than the record of *Caro Nome* or the waltz in *Mireille*, and collectors will cherish them accordingly. The *Qui la voce* is less convincing, and is not wholly free from the "intrusive h", (q.v.) but the 12-in. *Io son Titania* is not only faultless in this respect, but is one of the most brilliant renderings that has come down to us.

ESTHER PALLISER

ESTHER PALLISER claims a place in gramophone history as one of the distinguished English singers who had the courage to record their voices in 1903. She was originally a singer in light opera, and became a member of the distinguished double cast that performed Sullivan's *Ivanhoe*. In the sensationally successful season of 1892, when overflow performances at Drury

Lane supplemented those at the overcrowded Covent Garden, she sang as Santuzza, which she repeated in an autumn season. She appeared also as Micaela, Marguerite, and even as Brangane in *Tristan*. She was well known and much admired as a concert artist and a singer of ballads in the old tradition, of which Hawley's charming short lyric *The Sweetest Flower that blows* breathes the very atmosphere of the epoch in which the record was made.

ANGELICA PANDOLFINI

ANGELICA PANDOLFINI was a daughter of the famous baritone who created the role of Amonasro at the Milan *premiere* of *Aida*. She ranked very highly in the operatic hierarchy, and created the role of Adriana Lecouvreur. She made six red label records which are among the greater rarities, and her passage in *Adriana* is a model of fine dramatic singing with a smooth and luscious *timbre*. (See also under Cesira Ferrani.)

ELIZABETH PARKINA

ELIZABETH PARKINA was a young American soprano, a pupil of Marchesi, and actually a *protegee* of Melba, making her debut in Paris in 1902. Her voice was exceptionally flexible and the tone brilliant; and the writer has heard the younger Marchesi declare that Parkina was a model example of her mother's singing method. Her appearances at Covent Garden in the seasons of 1904-5-6 as Musetta, Venus in *Helene*, Siebel in *Faust* and Amor in *Orfeo* were always commented upon in the press notices, and an occasion in which she understudied Melba in *Faust* was a personal triumph for her.

The pathetic little story of Parkina's departure from Covent Garden is told in the writer's *The Age of Jean de Reszke*, and any belief that it was owing to failure in her voice may be dismissed by the fact that she was immediately engaged to head the bill in a West End production of *A Midsummer Night's Dream*, in which she sang Mendelssohn's music with the greatest acclaim.

Records

Parkina's records are miracles of youthful lightness and vocal freshness and purity, for the small voice had poise and style which carried it easily to the furthest recesses of an opera house. Added to her beautifully free delivery there was always a little touch of human pathos in her singing which most of her records reflect, and is well displayed in Guy d'Hardelot's ballad *I know a lovely Garden*. By contrast Parkina's complete mastery of *coloratura*, again with warmth and charm, and well interspersed with the famous Marchesi shake, is well shown in Bemberg's joyous *La fee aux Chansons*, her only 12-in. record, and made during her Shakespearean engagement.

She will be affectionately remembered by any readers who heard her as the sprightliest of Musettas and the most feminine of Siebels.

ADELINA PATTI

The sensation caused by the announcement in 1905 that ADELINA PATTI had consented to make a number of records for G&T, was somewhat dimmed by the fear that it had come too late, and by the fact that Melba, still in her prime, had been there before her. Nevertheless the interest shown was enormous, for Patti was still a household word. In the event, however, most of the records successfully displayed the inimitable voice of Patti, although the gramophones of that day were less than kind to her high notes, and we have had to wait until recent times before we could hear them with unalloyed pleasure. The *Pur dicesti* is in my opinion and that of most other collectors also the finest of all, for not only is it a triumph of interpretation in Patti's peculiarly charming manner, but is perfectly and flawlessly recorded. The *Batti, batti* has an especial value and interest as coming from one of the *diva's* favourite roles, and also as showing the correct *tempo* in the 6–8 section; exceptionally, it requires a speed of 81 r.p.m. to bring it to its proper key of F, when the tuneful archness of the erring Zerlina is delightful to hear. Her famous *Home Sweet Home*, which made her final encore number in the *Barbiere*, does not appeal today, and compares unfavourably with that of Melba, and with the exception of the very charming *Si vous n'avez rien a me dire*, the ballads seem less in her vein than the more operatic type of music. Her *Voi che sapete* does not fit in anywhere.

There was a record of *La Calescera* which was made in the second session in 1906 but was not put on sale, although copies were labelled and prepared. A few of these have leaked out, and several special pressings have been made to the order of collectors who found it interesting.

ELISA PETRI

ELISA PETRI was a Fonotipia artist who seems to have recorded first as a soprano and later as a mezzo or contralto, but it is with the soprano that we are concerned. Petri was magnificently versatile, with temperament and vocal opulence showing through her work with satisfying abundance. Her delicate comedy in the Falstaff-Quickly duet with Magini-Coletti, and the impassioned beauty of *Amore, amor* will combine to establish her as an artist to be remembered, and there was nothing from light opera to Wagner which was beyond her range or capacity.

REGINA PINKERT

REGINA PINKERT appeared in lesser roles at Covent Garden in 1890 and 1891; but Fonotipia recorded her in 1904 by which time she had established a solid reputation in the principal opera houses of Europe and South America. Her records are seldom seen, but the 13¾-in. *Rigoletto* quartet in which she takes part is a notable one. Pinkert was the Micaela when in 1890 Jean de Reszke sang Don Jose in *Carmen*.

GIANNINA RUSS

GIANNINA RUSS was a lyrico-dramatic soprano much admired in Italy and a prima donna at the Scala where her prestige was of the highest. She was contemporary with Boninsegna, and both excelled in the Verdi-Meyerbeer-Ponchielli type of opera. Her voice was of a more even quality than was Boninsegna's and its tone perhaps more beautiful; nevertheless, Russ' G&Ts were under black label, and Boninsegna's were red; but allowing for Russ' early defection to Fonotipia there is a possibility that her issue 1903–4 may have been red also, although no internal evidence of such a thing exists to our knowledge. The G&Ts are sufficiently rare to be accounted as almost non-existent in England, but the many fine Fonos to her name are among the best the company ever made, and a large number of them are of concerted pieces.

FRANCES SAVILLE

FRANCES SAVILLE was yet another of Marchesi's show pupils, and made a great reputation in Vienna. She came to London in 1897, singing with success as Juliette, Manon and Violetta. Evidently she had a contract for the following season also, but found herself restricted to the thankless role of Gutrune, and thereafter London heard her no more, which was so much the worse for London.

Records

These were black label G&Ts from Vienna, where they did not greatly concern themselves with red labels. They were made in 1902–3, and the only one I have seen and possessed was a folk song, *Dites-moi, maman,* which plays at about 84 r.p.m.

SOPHIE SEDLMAIR

SOPHIE SEDLMAIR was one of the great names in Wagner opera, and came to London with a Viennese reputation in 1897 singing with Jean de Reszke in *Tristan* and *Siegfried*. Among her black label records made in 1904 special interest attaches to 044039, part of the love duet in *Tristan* with Erik Schmedes, which may have been the first attempt to record this passage.

MARCELLA SEMBRICH

MARCELLA SEMBRICH's triumphant debut in *Lucia di Lammermoor* at Covent Garden in 1881 was one of the highlights of Victorian opera. The young singer was preceded by great expectations which were more than fulfilled, and the event was celebrated by *critiques* of two of the long columns of those days devoted to rapturous praise of the newcomer. We may believe that on this occasion the newspaper critics felt themselves in no danger of over-statement, and history has fully confirmed their judgment. She immediately invaded the territory of Patti, even to the role of Caterine in *L'Etoile du Nord*, of which Patti was understood to hold the monopoly, and she triumphed whenever she sang. Sembrich's great success continued for five successive seasons, afterwards to be continued in the U.S.A. until her retirement after the Metropolitan season of 1908–9. Throughout her great career Sembrich rivalled both Patti and Gerster.

Records

By her records, Sembrich carries us back, with one or two others, to the remotest operatic period that is accessible to us. They show us more of her clear-cut delivery than of the beauty that must have been in her voice, and they cannot altogether escape the stricture of lifelessness. They are somewhat remote in tone and quality, which can be ascribed to recording technique, as she seemed to be standing unduly far from the recording trumpet. But great pleasure may be derived from the sprightly lightness in her duet with Scotti in *Don Pasquale*—which incidentally was the first red label record I actually bought new.

LUISE SOBRINO

LUISE SOBRINO recorded in 1903 on black G&T, and made the first 12-in. by a woman singer in Italian—032000, *Ernani involami*. After singing minor roles at Covent Garden, she sang Elvira in *Don Giovanni* in 1901. But it was as a concert and festival singer that she was best known.

ADELINA STEHLE

ADELINA STEHLE was the original Nedda at the world *premiere* of *I Pagliacci*. She had a fine career in Italy, though her recording was of the slightest. This consisted of a duet from *Adriana Lecouvreur* with the tenor Garbin, whose wife she became, and on a 13¾-in. record as Mimi in the quartet in *La Boheme*. The voice, like her husband's, was too ultra-Italian to have pleased London audiences, and she never made the attempt.

ROSINA STORCHIO

ROSINA STORCHIO whom I have heard only on one of her rare discs was evidently a singer of the highest class. She had that ineffable quality that distinguishes the great singer from the merely fine—something distinct from voice or ability, which was inborn and not to be taught. She had a personal approach to her music to which she imparted a fastidious elegance of her own, with phrasing and accentation of delicate fragility. Storchio seems to be the only singer of our period to suggest Olimpia Boronat, and her absence from London is one of our regrets. It was she who sang *Butterfly* on its first presentation, when the audience got out of hand, and the tawdry work was withdrawn for revision, after which Kruschelnika carried it to success.

The Storchio records are shown in the Appendix.

SUSAN STRONG

SUSAN STRONG, another Marchesi pupil although a dramatic soprano, made her London debut under Grau in 1897 as the heroine of a particularly successful *Aida*. She was notable also as Sieglinde, Elizabeth, Venus and Donna Anna. Her records, dating from 1907 to 1909—the most unflattering period—suffer under the same handicaps as did those of Agnes Nicholls. I made her acquaintance at Broadcasting House, where we were taking part in a series, and soon afterwards made friends with her cat, which was the largest I have ever seen.

LUISA TETRAZZINI

LUISA TETRAZZINI, in the light of retrospect, may be described both by record collectors and opera-goers as a complete anomoly. Although standing very high in public regard in Latin America and generally in Italy, although she did not appear at the Scala, she was totally unheard-of in London and New York. So when she made her sensational London debut, in the autumn of 1907 as Violetta, she created headlines for the following morning which ecstatically hailed "the new Patti". The truth about this unheralded appearance will, like that of her Zonophone records, probably remain obscure, but one story was that H. V. Higgins, the Chairman of the Royal Opera, wished to cancel her contract, which does not sound in the least the kind of thing which Higgins would have done, and that the irate Luisa created such a storm that he had no option but to bow to it, but compromised with the forces opposing Tetrazzini by withholding publicity. Nor does this sound like Higgins either, so it must have been someone else who had belatedly heard of the arrangement.[1] Her triumph on that night is a matter of history, and I was one of those who diverted his morning walk to his office to see about booking a seat, only to find a queue stretching from the Opera House to the Strand, and I did not in fact hear her until the following summer.

"Tet", as she became known, was a true *coloratura* in the grand tradition with a voice of delicate and softly metallic beauty, and with a ravishing sense of line and *legato*. Nor was this a mere flash in the pan, for her popularity was enduring, and so great was the crush to hear her that two years later Melba actually absented herself for the only season of her association with Covent Garden.

Records

The strange anomoly of Tetrazzini extends emphatically to her records, for those which were hurriedly made by the Gramophone company following her London triumph were of very little account, and it was not known until more than thirty years later that she had recorded for "a" Zonophone

---

[1] In her autobiography "Tet" mentions this incident, and pleasantly glosses it over.

company in 1904. By that date she was already known and acclaimed in what seems to have been a sound-proof portion of the globe, so that one may wonder how it came about that so famous a singer consented to record for a company of obscure and still undiscovered origin. For this so-called Zonophone company had no connection either with International Zonophone or with its remnants after that company had been taken over by G&T. It seems to have been formed for no other purpose than to record Luisa. The records were 9-in. and 10¾-in. and were accompanied by her brother-in-law the conductor Cleofante Campanini. The place of their origin remains unknown but certainly out of hearing of New York—possibly Mexico or even San Francisco—and these collectors' pieces are rare prizes.

ELENA THEODORINI

ELENA THEODORINI was a Roumanian, and is remembered by opera historians as one of the great dramatic sopranos of the late nineteenth century, and was engaged by Lago for Covent Garden in 1886, when she sang Valentine in *Les Huguenots* and the name role in *La Gioconda*. Also, and rather unaccountably she seems to have sung Zerlina in *Don Giovanni*, which may have indicated a lack of suitable material at Lago's disposal.

FANY TORRESELLA

FANY TORRESELLA claims some of our attention chiefly through her three International Zonophone dark blue label records which are now largely preoccupying the attention of the collectors of the two hemispheres. Augustus Harris' talent spotters included Fany for his initial venture at Drury Lane in 1887, but her appearance was limited to a single performance of *Rigoletto* in which she met with so cool a reception that Harris did not take her with him to Covent Garden. She shows on her records a light soprano of average merit which might have been useful in an emergency, but the critics of 1887 detected a "wobble", which might have been due to an ill-advised forcing of the voice in a theatre where none was needed or desirable.

Having so frequently mentioned the name of Lago perhaps I should say a word about him. He had been for many years regisseur to Gye and had done various odd jobs about the opera until in 1886 he decided to enter into management. That he had excellent qualifications is not to be doubted, for his seasons never lacked interest, and he was directly responsible for introducing several really important singers to London, among whom may be mentioned Ella Russell, Mme Valda, d'Andrade, Vignas, Medea Mey-Figner, Fabbri, Prevost, Ravogli and Ancona, with several lesser lights. Although he was backed and advised by the retiring tenor Gayarre, the timing of his venture was most unfortunate for him, for although the entry of a new impresario of knowledge and experience was already overdue, he happened to clash with Harris who had got what Lago lacked, which was capital: and the consequence was that as soon as Lago recruited an important new artist that artist was promptly and regularly lured to Harris' management. It was also greatly to Lago's credit that it was he who introduced Cavalleria Rusticana *to London when it was already producing something approaching hysteria throughout the whole musical world, and under his management at the Shaftesbury Theatre it had a run of forty-five performances and a Royal Command to Windsor Castle: so the following season it served as Harris' trump card produced on a far more lavish scale and with a cast of Calve, de Lucia, Dufriche and Ravogli.*

CONTRALTOS

GUERRINA FABBRI

GUERRINA FABBRI has been one of those singers whose records have made a special appeal to collectors, and besides their great scarcity there is a good reason for this. Fabbri was one of that rare kind, a true *coloratura* contralto, besides which she appeared as the Amneris on the opening night of Augustus Harris' first and historic season—on the night, in fact, when Jean de Reszke first sang in London as a tenor. She had previously appeared under Lago five years earlier, during the season at the Shaftesbury Theatre when hastily contrived performances of Gluck's *Orfee* and of *La Cenerentola* were interspersed during the run of *Cavalleria Rusticana*, Fabbri singing the name roles in each.

Fabbri recorded for G&T red label in 1903–4, but two only of her titles appeared in the English catalogue, to be withdrawn after a few months.

NINI FRASCANI

NINI FRASCANI was born and trained in Naples, and made her debut in that city at the San Carlo in the *Favorita* singing with Bonci, and later as Amneris in *Aida* with Vignas, appearing at the Scala, Milan, in the following year.

The record with Zenatello of the Amneris-Radames scene on two sides of a "39" Fonotipia is a most notable one, and to be highly prized by collectors.

She is here seen at Covent Garden in 1904 in the *Ballo* with Caruso and Selma Kurz.

Punch, July 13, 1904
(Francani, Caruso, Kurz)

MARIA GAY

The omission of MARIA GAY from the first edition was one of those unaccountable *lacunae* that sometimes afflict the best of intentions. Her sensational unheralded appearance at Covent Garden in the autumn of 1906 as Carmen produced immediate headlines, and although the event did not take place until the season had only eleven more nights to run, ten performances of *Carmen*, inclusive of several matinees, caused disorganisation to other fixtures. In the summer of 1907, with Gay absent, two *Carmens* were found sufficient, but on her return in that autumn the tally rose to twelve.

Maria Gay's Carmen was something quite unlike the popular conception as handed down through a long line of successful and distinguished artists. This was a formidable little creature, rather short and heavily built, bursting with temperament and energy, ruthless and demanding. It was a thoroughly "back to earth" interpretation. She did not exploit grace or charm, but instead a dynamic forcefulness in improvisation which made it imperative to see her as often as opportunity offered. Her voice was a luscious contralto, as perfectly produced as her style was faultless, and never has even the shadow of such a Carmen since appeared to challenge her—if one may judge from what passes muster these days. Maria Gay's other roles included Azucena, Orfeo, which she sang at the Scala, and Amneris which she sang at Covent Garden. This last role she treated in her hell-cat manner—not as the regal princess of tradition.

She gravitated to the Met., and married Zenatello, who was also a worthy partner to her as Don Jose, and thereafter New York aspirants had the benefit of their teaching for several years.

Pedro Tillett (q.v.) relates in his unpublished memoirs how aptly she was named, and evidently greatly admired her vivacity and picquancy on the numerous occasions when she bounced in and out of his office, leaving laughter and gaiety behind her. Maria Gay was born at Barcelona in 1879, and was only sixty-four when she died.

Records

Maria Gay recorded for G&T in Paris in 1904 and 1905, and two years later for Favorite, also in Paris. I thank Robert Bauer for the details which will be found in the Appendix, for which I can offer in exchange the startling fact for which I can personally vouch of the discovery of a large number of *empty* 12-in. envelopes bearing titles sung by Maria Gay of Spanish songs of which I once had a complete list but have since lost. If my memory serves (and it generally does) the records were made in Barcelona. (See "Strange Interlude" within.)

In 1908 we had an issue on pink pre-Dog, and later a *Chanson Boema* in *Carmen* sung in Spanish, which I still cherish as a worthy remembrance of the most remarkable and unconventional Carmen of the twentieth century. And in about 1912 there were some excellent Columbias including some superb duets with Zenatello.

ALICE GOMEZ

ALICE GOMEZ was much admired in England as a concert and oratorio singer at the turn of the century, and sometimes sang at Patti's touring concerts. Goetz's popular ballad *Melisande in the Wood* owed much of its success to her, and this is certainly the best of Gomez's few and very rare recordings.

LOUISE KIRKBY LUNN

LOUISE KIRKBY LUNN was, with Schumann-Heink, the finest operatic contralto to sing in England until Ebe Stignani came many years later. While beginning her career with the Carl Rosa company she made two Berliner records in 1901, and three black G&Ts in 1901-2; but this was before the Gramophone company took full advantage of her great fame and exceptionally smooth and velvety recording voice, for it was not until 1908 that Kirkby Lunn's true recording history began. She had the highest conception of the "grand manner" and was a good enough actress. Her Fricka in *The Ring* was a noble rendering, and in her scenes with Van Rooy greatest of Wotans—this pair were unmatched. It was in *Tristan und Isolde* that Lunn and Van Rooy each showed a rare sense of intelligence in that both invested their respective roles of Brangane and Kurvenal with a distinction never since seen and apparently never re-discovered. She was the invariable Amneris to Destinn's Aida; and although she sang many Carmens before and after the advent of Maria Gay, it was her superb singing that provided the reason.

In the London *premiere* of *Samson et Dalila* in 1909 in an otherwise deplorable performance of a deplorable work, Kirkby Lunn scored her crowning triumph. On the concert and oratorio platforms she was equally successful, notwithstanding an unconquerable nervousness which she never overcame, but her true place was the opera stage.

ARMIDA PARSI-PETTINELLA

ARMIDA PARSI-PETTINELLA seems to have sung all over the operatic world with the exception of London and New York. These omissions were unfortunate for these cities, for she was, judging from her beautiful and excellent Fonotipia records, an unusually pleasing contralto. Her voice was of a brightly resonant quality, and entirely free from "chestiness", and her style was superb. The further we delve into the history of opera singers, the more we may wonder what exactly it was that determined their courses. There is nothing objective to say about her records except to refer the reader to the Appendix.

ERNESTINE SCHUMANN-HEINK

ERNESTINE SCHUMANN-HEINK was one of the great names in opera and gramophone history. Although not much heard in London following the 'nineties, her career in Germany and later in New York was a very full one. Not gifted by nature with beauty or with more than average charm, Schumann-Heink had a pleasantly forceful personality, and achieved her great position by extraordinary musicianship, a magnificent voice, a rare intelligence, and an unlimited capacity for work. In slow music she displayed a command of tone production, breath control and interpretation that one looks for in an artist of renown, but with that little something added which might be genius. She would occasionally oblige by singing and recording trifling stuff when required, but in all the long list of her records over a very long period which display her versatility in every guise, it may be doubted whether in her own recorded work or in that of any other singer could be found a more outstanding example of vocal range and dazzling technique than in the *Trinkleid* in *Lucrezia Borgia*, which she sang for Victor-G&T in 1905. The lightness of touch, the amazing agility and the variety of colour, ending with a dropped interval of twelve tones makes this truly a show-piece, and sets one wondering how this compared with the renderings of Alboni and Trebelli when this opera depended upon singing such as this, and did not finally flicker out until the latter's retirement.

Schumann-Heink first recorded for Columbia in that company's small and select celebrity list in 1903, and for Victor-G&T from 1905 onward, retaining her matchless style and dramatic fire, with a considerable portion of her voice, well into old age.

ANASTASIA VIALTZEVA

ANASTASIA VIALTZEVA was one of the most famous of those Russian gipsy singers who occupied so high a place in Czarist Russia. Her records have the historical value of forming part of the first batch of red label titles, and are very much fancied by collectors. Vialtzeva had a smooth and luscious voice which she devoted to Russian folk music and gipsy songs. There were later recordings by her, but these missed much of the charm of the 1900 titles, a list of which will be found in the Appendix.

EDYTH WALKER

Although EDYTH WALKER became one of the most famous of the Viennese dramatic sopranos, it was as a contralto that she first recorded. At Covent Garden her first appearance was in 1900 as Amneris, Ortrud and Urbano, and did not appear again until Thomas Beecham brought her over as a fully developed dramatic soprano to open his season in 1910 with the London *premiere* of *Electra*, when immense sums must have been spent on pre-publicity, for, without waiting to hear what this opera really was, there was so great a rush for tickets for the first night that seats were re-sold at handsome premiums.

Records

There is something ironical in finding that the first records of so distinguished an Electra and no less distinguished an Isolde were of two over-popular English ballads, and which alone of the otherwise well-chosen titles appeared in the English catalogue. These have nothing in their favour, and not having heard any of the others in these Viennese recordings, I know nothing about them.

TENORS

GIUSEPPE ANSELMI

GIUSEPPE ANSELMI. One of the most polished and fastidious of Italian tenors with a ringing voice of traditional Italian purity. He recorded somewhat prolifically for Fonotipia, generally with meticulous care, but too often otherwise. Some of his recorded work suffered from over-emphasis and exaggeration, while at other times he seemed insufficiently familiar with the music—certainly in *Il mio tesoro*, and in *Ecco ridente* to some extent; and a tenor who falls down on either or both of these arias has much leeway to recover, but his best work was first-class, as shown in *Ah non credevi tu* in *Mignon* and *Quando le sere al placido* in *Luisa Miller*.

Anselmi sang in London in the first years of the century, winning the full admiration of the most critical. His Cavaradossi in *Tosca* was sung with excellent *cantelena*, but like all tenors since de Lucia he turned his back on the portrait and harangued the audience in full voice.

AMADEO BASSI

AMADEO BASSI came to London with a high European reputation to take part in the season of 1907 as relief tenor to Caruso. Without in any way compensating for Caruso's absence, he was fully acceptable, and in the autumn of the same year he returned to share the tenor leads with Vignas. So, with Litvinne, de Lucia, Sammarco and Luppi also present, the Fonotipia catalogue was well represented.

Records

Bassi's first records were for Pathe "hill and dale" in 1904, and his Fonotipias followed in 1906 and 1907. He had a true and full tenor which reproduced well, well produced if lacking in colour. But he had power and fulness which assured his reputation as a tenor of the nearly first class.

Both together. " Don't listen to the other chap. I can sing much louder than he can."

Barnaba .. Signor Sammarco.
Enzo .... Signor Bassi.

Punch, June 26, 1907
(with Sammarco)

ALESSANDRO BONCI

ALESSANDRO BONCI was, academically speaking, the perfect tenor, by which it is meant that his voice was a genuine and natural tenor and his style and technique classically correct. He was not comparable with Caruso, being altogether different; his style being more inclined towards the earlier school of de Lucia. He seemed to have discovered the art of singing without the necessity to breathe, and so was able to execute some miraculous feats of phrasing; and being so natural a singer he was completely free from tricks and mannerisms, and unafflicted by too much temperament.

His Covent Garden debut was as Rodolfo in *La Boheme* in 1900, and his success was never in doubt, and the curtain calls he received were said to have aroused Melba's wrath. He sang as principal tenor during Caruso's absence in 1903 and 1907, and in 1908 he partnered Tetrazzini in some magical performances of the *Barbiere* and *Pescatori di Perle*, always singing with an unforced and gracious tone in which the *legato* in its truest and most classical form was conspicuous, and with an exactitude of balance between notes and words which is an insoluble problem for most singers. And above all, he avoided exaggeration.

Records

The catalogue of Bonci's records made tempting reading, for everything that one could wish to hear from a classical tenor was there, and their tone was consistently fine. I think they are more forward than any records that were heard up to that date, in fact quite startlingly so, but that was a Fonotipia characteristic. The collector may find something of a similarity in his treatments, in which respect he chiefly differed from Caruso, but his unaffected style was quite disarming, and if somewhat lacking in imagination, was wholly faultless. The voice, although cold in quality, was full and flexible, and the easy confidence of his delivery at once strikes the listener. He used the *voix blanche* with masterly discretion, and his open-throated quality was one of his greatest points for admiration, and this is admirably shown in his *Che gelida manina*, which is sung absolutely straight and without deviations. The ease with which he surmounts the difficulties of the much-dreaded *Salve Dimora* makes one envious of those who heard it so sung in the opera. His *Spirito Gentil* is perhaps his finest rendering, and even prompts the thought that Caruso set himself to outrival it in his own record. Only in *La donna e mobile* does Bonci depart from his usually staid correctness, and he makes of it something of a show-piece of *bel canto*. Having heard him in the *Barbiere* I was naturally glad to get his duets with Corradetti, especially *Ah che d'amore* (entered as *Numero quindici*) of which in fact my memory of de Lucia is the more vivid.

There were several excellent concerted pieces, from which the collector may safely make his own selection, and even his modest part in the trio finale to *Faust* (with Russ and Luppi) gains from his singing of it.

His later Columbia records are less to be recommended.

ENRICO CARUSO

Of ENRICO CARUSO it may truly be said that none but himself could be parallel; and I will say frankly that what follows in this note is a eulogy and not a criticism, for I find nothing to criticise. The tendency to criticise a great artist is persuasive, but since I first heard Caruso in person in 1904 and nearly all his recorded work, I have learnt that Caruso was infallibly right, and that where I had thought otherwise I now know that it was I who was wrong. I have from time to time found myself in conflict with some who are unable to accept this, and I must respect their opinions, but it is my considered view that during the course of his twenty triumphant years, Caruso never ceased to study and to improve, until in the last years of his tragically short life (he died at forty-eight in 1921), he attained to a height of magnificence that has never been challenged. Even that famous darkening of the voice which caused so much perturbation was in no sense a deterioration, but rather an impressive richness which enabled him to adopt an even more opulent style; and his high Cs at the end of his life excel the more tentative and much-controlled Cs in the admired recordings of 1906.

As Caruso was supreme in every kind of singing I will mention in particular a trick of his which has served as a point of criticism, which is the audible release which has too often been taken as a sign of strain. There is no instance in all Caruso's recorded work where this is true. So immense were his resources that no such question arose.[1] And why pick on Caruso? This form of release was employed by practically all singers of the first class in the mid and late nineteenth-century style in varying degrees, where they judged it to be right and proper. Caruso generally confined its use to music of operatic character, and with a few exceptions eschewed it in the ballad form. I will not clutter up this page with examples, but in *The Lost Chord*, for all its declamatory fervour, it is conspicuously absent.

Caruso was not greatly interested in the *bel canto*, although he left two or three examples which amply prove that he was fully master of it. Exactly what *bel canto* means is something which every student of singing decides for himself. Du Maurier, in his immortal novel *Trilby*, writing of Paris in the eighteen-sixties—the days of Giuglini and the young Patti—puts the demise of "il bel canto" somewhere in the middle of the eighteenth century, which makes it still more difficult to define. It certainly did not mean singing which was sufficiently agreeable to the individual ear to warrant the term, nor does it now imply simply a proper use of *legato*, which after all is a *sine qua non* to any trained singer. Doubtless Du Maurier's characters heard it in their day, as a purely decorative use of fully trained vocal resources

---

[1] It is not always easy to understand what it is that critics have condemned as "strain". The writer supposes that it is a matter of definition of terms for surely the highest tenor notes in *fortissimo* require quite considerable strain.

employing chest, throat, mixed and head with a happy disregard for the printed note—possibly handed down from the male sopranos—in a rococco style of which de Lucia and Boronat (q.v.) were, for the gramophonist, the outstanding practitioners. Even in our own day there are Italian singers whom I have heard manage it very well, but they come and go with such bewildering speed that it is impossible to follow them up; but they seemed to receive little encouragement. There have been others who have unwisely attempted it and have received too much.

While on the subject of technical terms as sometimes applied to Caruso I will mention that of "the intrusive h", an expression which by its very imprecision may create confusion. I cannot understand how the term came into use in the loose way in which it is used, nor how any singer who used it succeeded in getting a public engagement. The meaning that it should carry is the aspirating of vowel sounds in *legato* (e.g. a turn) or in rapid *staccato*; and even a non-singer can prove to himself how much easier in a passage of either sort it is to sing "ha ha ha" than to sing "ah ah ah", and also how wrong it is. But where, as often happens, a connecting passage of, say, three ascending crotchets in "ah" may sometimes be given a trace of the aspirate the objection does not apply, since the singer is not using a paltry device to conceal his incompetence.

I am reminded of a famous court case in the nineteen-thirties in which the plaintiff collected witnesses to affirm that aspirating was a legitimate mode of singing. Well, I have just said the same thing, but with a vital difference; but I do not recollect that any distinction was made on that occasion.

Although Caruso was less at home with English ballads, the large group of Italian and Neapolitan songs which he recorded for those who were not operatically minded, make a special and most interesting group. He put so much of himself into them as to give them a personal value, and in my opinion it is a mistake to despise them. If there were one or two which we may think unworthy, we may feel sure that Caruso saw something in them which he hoped to embellish, even where some, as was obviously the case, were sung and recorded to please those friends who had obligingly written them for him. But by far the greater part of this group are worthy of our attention on their merits, and with Caruso's "fingerprints" on them they are made magnificent. Too many unfortunately suffer from the quite atrocious orchestral combinations—more resembling a hurdy-gurdy—and much inferior to many quite tolerable orchestras which accompanied the middle period opera selections. A piano would have been so much better.

*   *   *   *

G

I have said that Caruso continued to study and to improve, and although there would seem to have been little room for improvement even from the very beginning, his last records show him in a light of full maturity hardly possible to a youthful singer. If the *O Paradiso* was the highlight of his earlier days, so, I think, was the *Ombra mai fu* the peak of his recording career. This exhibits the perfect singer in every carefully-considered note and phrase, with a beautiful shake of which we might never have suspected him capable. Every type of singing is represented in the last year of his recording life, and there is not one which suggests a singer in decline—which of course Caruso never was. One dubious experiment, and that a very temporary one, and one more generally admired than condemned, I find in one or two operatic records of the late period being some rather savage attacks on big notes which I find disconcerting. This *coup de glotte* is generally the cause or effect of a damaged mechanism, and is used to conceal a *tremolo* which was something from which Caruso never suffered. In fact so close and firm was his *vibrato* that it sometimes seemed non-existent.[1]

[1] *Vibrato* is an effect deliberately applied to improve quality and carrying power, as also used by the violin group of instruments ; *tremolo* is a dire weakness due to faulty technique or to ill health, and is involuntary. The famous singer Emma Nevada summed up the difference for all time—"*Vibrato*" she said, "is life, and *tremolo* is death".

I suspect that some part at least of the lack of enthusiasm for the later records may be traced to ears that were becoming jaded by the *embarras du richesse* which tended to encourage overmuch selectivity in individual tastes.

*   *   *   *

But Caruso needs no defenders. He has passed into legend, and his very name is synonomous with the greatest of singing. He had an infallible instinct for what was right; he copied no one, and no one has been able to copy him. Although he succeeded to a succession of illustrious tenors, his conquest was immediate. He was at once hailed for what he was—the greatest tenor that ever sang.

As an actor Caruso was something of a law to himself. He could not be said to have been equal to Tamagno, de Lucia and Zenatello, any one of whom could have been a distinguished actor even if he had never sung a note. On the other hand, to say that he was a better actor than Bonci or Gigli would be to offer faint praise. He had something wholly his own in poise and neatness of movement which was so definitely "operatic" in character as might have served him better than the best of acting. He threw himself heart and soul into his roles, and that alone carried conviction. His singing carried him along, and whether on stage or platform he never failed to appear exactly right. In the innumerable photographs, especially those in stage costume, it is difficult to find even one in which he did not look stiff and awkward; but in the rare snapshots when he was unaware of the camera, he was his natural self, as when he sang.

*   *   *   *

It is accepted as a fact that it was Caruso's Milan record of 1902 of *E lucean le stelle* that secured for him his first Metropolitan engagement without further audition; but be this as it may, it need not be questioned that following the usual trend which was still running at that date, by which outstanding Covent Garden successes gravitated naturally to the Met., Caruso's course was clearly set. That he preferred New York to London is obvious, and he probably fitted in better, but had he, like Melba, remained as attached to the city which gave him world fame, the operatic centre of gravity might not have been so violently shifted.

Punch, June 8, 1904

Records

The first records, apart from some hill-and-dale Pathes, were made in the early weeks of 1902 for the light blue issue of the International Zonophone company of Milan. For many years they were not much thought of or sought after, and were wrongly regarded as having a precarious interest as showing Caruso's early immaturity. But as only a few weeks separated these from the first G&Ts, and followed Caruso's triumph in the *premiere* of Franchetti's *Germania*, it becomes obvious that there is no substance in this assumption. Musically, their only special interest lies in the realistic rendering of *La donna e mobile*, which is more alive than either of the later Victor-G&Ts, neither of which so well reflected the stage performance. The rather unexpected upsurge of demand for them has produced high values and a quite appreciable smattering of specimens.

Of the G&Ts some, through accident or otherwise have become major rarities, such as the 1902 version of *Dai campi dai prati* with its very slight false start, and a very fine *Celeste Aida* which was broken. In the 1903 issue there is the only recording by him of part of a duet in *Adriana Lecouvreur*, and in which the piano continues, standing in for the soprano part. In this, as just noted, Caruso sings in genuine *bel canto* style. The collecting cult has drawn a surprising number of these issues from their fifty-year-old hiding places, and their values vary very much, even within the same series, and depending wholly on scarcity.

There is an especially charming quality in the G&T records with which Fred Gaisberg jumped the gun, for they have a lightness and spontaneity all their own. The first in serial sequence, the *Questa o quella*, is seldom found in playable condition, which suggests that it was enjoyed to excess in the early days. The *Giunto sull' passo* is perhaps my favourite example of the earliest Caruso, with the *Manon Sogno* close behind. Of the 1903 series, remembering their slow speed, the first *Vesti la giubba* is the one which I most greatly like—perhaps because it is reminiscent of de Lucia's stage rendering. The least satisfactory, and perhaps for that reason one of the rarest, is the *Una furtiva* of 1902 which was ill-advisably compressed in a single record, a mistake soon to be corrected in New York, when in 1904 his twenty-five-year contract with G&T and the associated Victor company began.

These New York records seemed to suggest a step forward in Caruso's style, and certainly there was an aloof dignity about them which was most impressive. Some have detected a tightness, which improved reproduction has eliminated, and which was ascribed to a change in the voice—but more likely due to a different recording method. This is the more probable since on his return to Milan in 1904, Caruso's *Mattinata* evokes the earlier and more carefree style. The beauty of the *Huguenots* aria, recorded a few months before I heard him sing it at Covent Garden, with its finely played piano accompaniment, had that aloof perfection which the more opulent later recording missed, and in *Un solo istante* we hear a show-piece of the purest *bel canto* such as he seldom gave us. The *Brindisi* in *Cavalleria Rusticana* is another *tour de force*, and never repeated by him, and unapproachable until another Caruso is born, ending with a magnificently produced "mixed" note which has produced perplexity in some listeners to whom it was unfamiliar. It has now died with other *bel canto* forms.

A still further advance was apparent in 1906, with a *Spirito Gentil* comparable in execution to the *L'Elisir* item just noticed, the first *M'Appari* and the only *Che gelida manina*, sung lyrically and in an unbroken *legato*, these marking the assumption of the pink label and the raising of Caruso's records to £1 each (the company being then under contract to Melba not to price any solo records at a figure equal to hers). A month later came the magnificent best-seller *Solenne in quest' ora* with Scotti, and at the end of 1906 Caruso climbed to his peak (on which he stood for the rest of his life) with *O Paradiso*, which may be the greatest feat of singing recorded by him or any other tenor. The *Vesti la giubba* was perhaps less meritorious than the *Improvviso*, and our period worthily ends with the solitary duet with Melba.

Punch, May 31, 1905
(with Melba)

JOHN COATES

JOHN COATES was that intellectual type of singer who had all the attributes of a great operatic artist with one exception only, and that one was the voice. Except for this inequality Coates might have been the greatest singer of all time, for he had artistic and musical qualities in an uncommon degree, which enabled him to give one of the classic performances of Lohengrin and even of Tristan. This does not mean that the voice was an unpleasant one, as has so often happened with singers of Wagner, but it was too gentle, too refined, for big effects, and he did not make the mistake of attempting to force it. He sang also in *opera comique* on occasion, and although a man of big build he made a very pleasant stage figure. He did much opera in Germany, and passed through concert and oratorio with equal serenity, *The Dream of Gerontius* being one of his favourites. He was still singing with his peculiar charm shortly before his death at an advanced age.

EMILE COSSIRA

EMILE COSSIRA, a French tenor who made irregular appearances at Covent Garden between 1891 and 1900. He sang the French repertoire, and made his London debut in a hastily contrived season of chiefly French operas which was Harris' reply to a more interesting season offered elsewhere by Lago. He made only two black G&T records in Paris in 1903–4 and a single Zonophone in the next year.

BEN DAVIES

BEN DAVIES, who ranks next to Edward Lloyd as a festival tenor, may be regarded as the first celebrated singer to record for G&T. For fifty years his name was known to all, and when past the age of eighty he was one of the best of broadcasters, singing with a resonant and powerful voice with a breath control that proved the efficacy of his method.

"Caro mio Ben", as his friends called him, was a delightful man to know, full of good humour and at all times ready with a joke. When I remarked to him that he seemed to be singing better at seventy-five than he did when forty-five, he replied "Yes ? I think I have heard others say the same thing". I know of no biography of this interesting singer, but early in the 'eighties he was a leading tenor in the Carl Rosa company, and sometimes sang in the Grand Season at Covent Garden, where he was billed to appear in 1892 as Faust with Melba, Maurel and Plancon. He had lost all recollection of this, but the "special extra performance" was advertised for July 25th. He sang the lead in the original production of Cellier's popular *Dorothy*—the role later being taken by Coates—and in Sullivan's *Ivanhoe*. On leaving the dramatic stage, Ben, following the usual trend, took to concert and oratorio with inevitable success, for he was one of those who revelled in the vast spaces of the Crystal Palace, where his massive rendering of Rossini's *Cujus Animam*, on festival occasions which would include Agnes Nicholls, Ada Crossley, Watkin Mills and Santley, was something to remember.

Records

Ben Davies was a frequent recorder, his first records dating from 1900, consisting of five of his favourite encore pieces. This series exceptionally play at about 83 r.p.m. The catalogue for March 1906 erroneously states that the three records then offered, all 12-in., were made seven years previously, bringing the year back to 1899. Of course no 12-in. records appeared until 1903, and the confused reference would have been to these of 1900.

The recording of them was crude, but those of 1903 were excellent, if some of the 10-in. specimens were somewhat thinly recorded. His favourite ballad was *So fare thee well* from Cellier's *Doris*, which he continued to sing until the end of his life, and always with the same lilting humour. Following the 1903 issue, Ben Davies recorded again with conspicuous success in the "middle period" on the purple label—a somewhat ambiguous distinction which enabled H.M.V. to upgrade the prices of the best of their black label singers, and then in 1933, through my own urging he recorded electrically for Columbia, and it was these that prompted the little conversation I had with him which is mentioned above. Ben's voice on that occasion had nothing of the earlier baritonal quality, nor was there anything to suggest that he was an ageing, in fact, aged man. He died, universally beloved, in 1946, while the first version of this note was being written.

FERNANDO DE LUCIA

FERNANDO DE LUCIA was a close friend of Ben Davies, and we may believe that they were merry and good companions; and they would sometimes amuse their friends by singing Tosti's *La Serenata* as a duet—doubtless taking considerable liberties with it.

De Lucia was the last of that school of singing in which the Italians specialised in the early and middle nineteenth century—*bel canto in excelsis*, in fact, and although refined to the last degree his singing avoided the effeminacy of his type. He was engaged by Harris for his London debut in 1887, when, as we know, London was somewhat over-saturated with opera singers, and required much persuasion to recognise that a new era and an important new tenor had arrived. He returned in 1902 evidently much improved, for his singing genius was then unquestioned, and sang in all the twelve performances of *Cavalleria* with Calve in her first season. In the following year he made history by his marvellous Canio in the first London performances of *I Pagliacci*—a masterly study which has never been approached, even by Caruso himself, for de Lucia had a very personal touch to impart to all his work, and an unfailing artistic sense which forbade even the slightest hint of exaggeration or vulgarity. Opera-goers of 1905 had the good fortune to enjoy this Canio, together with the no less classic Tonio of Ancona, for these two artists had for twelve years made these roles their own. He was an extremely good actor, and his light-hearted Almaviva in the *Barbiere* entered into, or even led, the brisk humour of the *buffo* scenes, and how well I remember what I have never heard since, that lingering headnote with which he led up to the quartet *Buona sera, mio signore.* He had developed a control of his vocal mechanism which was unrivalled in his time, and could descend from a *fortissimo* of full power to a *diminuendo* in a long-drawn thread of sound, and no more sensitive or expressive singing has been heard in our time.

Records

The earliest records by de Lucia are pure gems. They were a 10-in. series made in Milan in 1903, and appeared in the English celebrity catalogue of that year. Many of them were unusually short, but all were remarkable both for the little touches in which he indulged and for the fresh and silvery quality of the voice. In *La donna e mobile* we get one verse only, sung in the oddly unconventional manner that we come to expect from him; and the *Recondite armonia* in Tosca has special historical interest since it was de Lucia who introduced the role to London. De Lucia as an artist was much to be commended in this work where he sang the aria quietly and reflectively while at work on his canvas. How right he was! In his first 12-in. record made in 1904, he gives a masterly and classic rendering of *Ecco ridente* in the *Barber* which will be an unattainable ideal to the hastily trained singers who come and go with such bewildering rapidity today. He saw possibilities in that rather commonplace aria *Dei miei bollenti spiriti* in *Traviata* which he was quick to exploit, but perhaps his real show-piece as an exposition of *bel canto* was *Addio, Mignon,* a wonderful instance of controlled and expressive singing. His duet with Boninsegna in *Tardi si fa* from *Faust* was the first recorded combination of two singers of equally high status, in which de Lucia begins in the softest of head production and rises to a *fortissimo* A from the chest of prodigious length. It is interesting to compare this version with that of Caruso and Farrar—for there is hardly a point of resemblance.

De Lucia also recorded for Fonotipia a large number of not very interesting Neapolitan songs, and then near the end of his life he made his now famous Phonotype issue of solo and concerted items which he had not previously recorded. These included his *Vesti la giubba* with its little twist that Leoncavallo knew nothing about, and his pathetically dramatic *No Pagliacci non son*; also a characteristic *Che gelida manina*, which improved (?) on Puccini and a great many others, all of which show how well the integrity of correct vocalisation survives the years, for at the age of sixty he was singing like a young man. De Lucia has suffered severely in the course of dubbing for LP from too slow speeds and consequently false pitch, but in some cases the work has been well done.

JEAN DE RESZKE

JEAN DE RESZKE's records are legendary but unknown, unless we are to credit cryptic stories of hidden hordes sealed up in some strong-room—which I do not. But it is certain that Jean did record for Fonotipia, and Bauer meticulously dates the event as 22nd April, 1905, the titles being *Scene du tombeau* in *Romeo* and the prayer in *Le Cid*. An Australian correspondent many years since claimed to have heard a test pressing of the *Romeo* scene many years earlier still, but for the rest, all is silence. He probably made test records for H.M.V. in or about 1908, for I have seen his portrait in a

brochure showing the H.M.V. celebrity
singers of that year. Evidently he
exercised his option in refusing to pass
any for sale, although in the case of
Fonotipia the first catalogue contained his
records, and also some by his wife Marie
de Reszke.

Punch, July 10, 1897

LEON ESCALAIS

LEON ESCALAIS was a French *tenore robusto* characteristic of his school. His
voice, to quote the Fonotipia catalogue, was "stupenda, estesa, vibrante e
robusta". His perseverance in study and his magnificent repertoire were
stressed, as well as a dramatic talent of the first order. At the Paris Opera
he was a star tenor, and his effortless singing and fine sense of rhythm are
well shown in the exciting male septet in *Les Huguenots*, which he finishes
with a "stupenda, estasa, vibrante and robusta" C sharp.

NICOLAI N. FIGNER

NICOLAI N. FIGNER is chiefly known to us as the husband of Medea Mey and
as one of the original Russian red label celebrity group of 1900. With his
wife he appeared at Covent Garden in 1887 under Lago's direction, and
received the honour of a command to a State Concert at Buckingham
Paris. His production was typically Russian, and unlike that of his contemporary Sobinoff, who, although Russian-trained, was more inclined to
the Italian school. Of the two I prefer Sobinoff, for Figner's voice, as
recorded, was pinched and puny.

EDOARDO GARBIN

EDOARDO GARBIN. To judge of Garbin's quality by his records may be
misleading unless we can hear a sufficient number of them, for he was
addicted to a white production not generally acceptable to English ears.
He could sing with equal ease and greater effectiveness without it, and
covered a wide range of roles from light to *robusto* in the style which he
applied to each. Although a star Fonotipia recorder in 1904–5, after
quitting G&T who had produced him on red label, it was not until 1910
that he reached Covent Garden, but without creating any noticeable stir.

Records

The G&T records above referred to were withdrawn within a matter of months, evidently due to the defection to Fonotipia. Like all the Milan red labels of that year, they require to be played at the low speed of 70 to 72, to obtain the correct pitch and *tempo*. The recording was no better than moderate, and for myself, I got no pleasure from listening to them, much the same being said for the Fonotipias with an occasional outstanding exception.

VILHELM HEROLD

VILHELM HEROLD, a Danish tenor of great distinction who sang in London in 1904 and 1907. It has been said of him that he recalled Jean de Reszke in his stage presence and in the classical purity of his voice and style. He was a very excellent Lohengrin, and it was in this role and as Walter in

A Hammer-us Trio.

Punch, June 1, 1904
(Alten, Rooy, Herold)

Die Meistersinger that I heard him in 1907 with Ackte as Elsa and Minnie Nast as Eva. He was not by preference a Wagnerian singer and had a great range of other roles, singing Faust and Romeo at Covent Garden. His records were black label, and very numerous. They were made in Copenhagen, including some Berliners, from 1903.

EDWARD LLOYD

EDWARD LLOYD will recall more effectively than any other singer the authentic atmosphere of the Victorian era. After Joseph Maas, Lloyd became the undisputed prime favourite of native tenors, and held immense prestige over a very long period. He was an oratorio and festival singer, and in him the now lost art of ballad singing was heard to perfection. His voice, if cold, was of singular sweetness, his style was massive and majestic, and his interpretations were classic. On big festival occasions at the Crystal Palace or the Albert Hall, Albani, Patey, Lloyd and Santley comprised a quartet which was a national institution. Lloyd retired in 1900 while still in possession of nearly the whole of his powers, but did not record until 1904.

It is to be hoped that when artistic evaluations have settled down, and attention can be spared from the world operatic celebrities, Edward Lloyd may be permitted to occupy the same place among gramophonists as he did in person in the years of his activity. Despite his black label and his relatively advanced age he had got something at his command which no other English-speaking tenor in my recollection possessed, and what this was can be heard but not explained.

Lloyd's farewell was at the Albert Hall on December 12th, 1900, and was a gala occasion. Lloyd himself sang the *Prize Song, Lend me your Aid*— to become his two most successful recordings—and *The Holy City* with its composer Stephen Adams at the piano. Ben Davies sang *Salve dimora*, and others who contributed were Evangeline Florence, Lane Wilson, Santley, Plunket Greene and Kennerley Rumford. Richter, Ganz and Elgar acted as conductors.

A few weeks before writing this revised note I drank a toast to Lloyd's memory using a crystal glass from a set which Lloyd had presented to his much-beloved impresario Pedro Tillett (of Ibbs and Tillett), whose widow was my hostess on that occasion. Mary Tillett gave me a letter from Lloyd to her husband which mentioned that he had completed his contract with G&T (i.e. as far as the 1905 series); and another from Landon Ronald dated February 4th, 1904, saying that Lloyd had on that day sung "quite beautifully" what was evidently the first batch, and thanking Tillett for having arranged the contract, in token of which G&T had sent him a complete gramophone outfit, to which Ronald added the injunction that he was free to change any records he might not have liked, mentioning his name. This interesting sidelight shows that Ronald stood high in the hierarchy of G&T, who always did things on the grand scale.

In Tillett's own handwriting I read that Lloyd had confessed to him that he was terribly nervous before the public and that his knees knocked together, although (added Tillett) he always looked calm and collected.

Records
     Lloyd's first records were of his favourite ballâds, which were of the
old-fashioned type always acceptable when sung as he sung them. He sang
Tom Bowling as no one else could, and gave a tenderness to *I'll sing thee
songs of Araby* which again cannot be conveyed in words. In 1905 he recorded
Bonnie Mary of Argyle so expressively that I used it to conclude my first
broadcast programme, when it was said to have made an excellent effect.
In the same year he recorded fine renderings of the recitative and opening part of the air *Lend me your Aid* in Gounod's *Queen of Sheba* (which,
to avoid offence to Victorian Anglicanism was re-named *Irene*—if this will
be believed!)—and the *Prize Song* in *Die Meistersinger*, his rendering of
which was considered equal to that of Jean de Reszke himself. He recorded
also the tenor parts in a more or less complete recording of *The Messiah*.

FRANCESCO MARCONI
FRANCESCO MARCONI takes us back to opera in the 'eighties, when he appeared
in London to replace Gayarre, whose health was becoming uncertain and his
appearances less regular. He opened with Ponchielli's *La Gioconda*, which
then was sweeping Europe with outbursts of enthusiasm as it never experienced in England, although at once recognised as a new work of great
interest and importance. In his first season Marconi sang also in *Aida*,
Faust, La Traviata, Marta, Puritani and *Mefistofele*. Then, either on account
of the generally confused situation in London opera or because Gayarre
decided to return, or for any one of the unlimited causes governing the
vagaries of a singer's life, Marconi after one more season was not heard there
again.

Records
     His records which were red G&T were fairly numerous, although one
only was listed in England—the air in *Eugene Onegin*. They were variable
in quality, some being roughly turned out, but his *Cielo e mar* in *La Gioconda*
is sung in grand style.

JOSEPH O'MARA
JOSEPH O'MARA was with hardly a doubt the finest English-speaking operatic
tenor of our period. He had a voice of true Italian quality which he delivered
with power and sweetness, and he was a first-rate actor. In the roles in which
I heard him—Tannhauser, Florestan, Canio, Don Jose and Hoffmann—he
was comparable with the best, and although his voice did not wholly survive
the heavy amount of work he put on it, it was always a pleasure to know that
O'Mara was the leading tenor. Unhappily, his recording was negligible;
a few primitive Berliners and a single G&T from the ballad opera *Shamus
O'Brien* by Stanford, completing his output.

GIUSEPPE OXILIA

GIUSEPPE OXILIA was known in England only for his connection with the most disastrous of Mapleson's final ventures in 1887. It is likely that Mapleson was compelled to recruit his talent from less costly sources than he would have wished, but it does not seem that Oxilia in any way disappointed him. He recorded in 1902 and 1903 on black G&T at Milan a pleasant selection of the most lyrical airs from Italian opera.

FRANCESCO TAMAGNO

FRANCESCO TAMAGNO was the mightiest of *tenori robusti*, the original and unapproachable creator of Verdi's Otello. Now that we can hear his voice under much improved conditions we may admire it as it deserves. Despite its immense volume there was a tenderness of *timbre* which indicated a natural feeling for his music which contributed to his proud title of *Il Re dei tenori*. He was a giant of a man, and as Samson must have realised the role. He had been famous in Italy and in South America before he came to England, although Frederick Gye had put Tamagno's name on one of his prospectuses several years before the event. That event, when it did come, was not due to Gye, but was no less than the transportation of the new production of Verdi's *Otello* from the Scala, Milan, with its original cast, including Tamagno and Maurel, to the Lyceum Theatre, London. This was in 1889, and the Covent Garden debut did not take place until 1895, when he again sang Otello with Albani as Desdemona. In this season Jean de Reszke absented himself, and thereafter Tamagno made no appearance until 1901, i.e., after Jean's retirement. In 1901 Tamagno appeared in the six performances of *Otello*, this time with Emma Eames, in de Lara's *Messaline*, *Les Huguenots* and as Radames in *Aida*.

He was a kindly and simple-minded man of peasant origin, and although earning fabulous fees he never forgot the penurious times, and it was related how he would quite openly make a parcel of the succulent remnants of a feast in his napkin, cheerfully explaining that they were for his *bambina*. Mme Arditi, the wife of the *maestro*, has left it on record [1] that ". . . Tamagno is an extremely pleasant man, and not a bit like the generality of tenors . . . but of cheerful and pleasant disposition".

[1] *My Reminiscences*, by Luigi Arditi.

A story for which I was indebted to Zelie de Lussan tells how she was present at a performance of *William Tell* at the Metropolitan when Tamagno was singing. In the duet with the Mathilde, sung by Libia Drog, the lady suffered a complete lapse of memory and was quite unable to proceed. Tamagno hummed the passage into her ear, but with no result; he repeated the cue *forte*, still without success, the orchestra meanwhile improvising something, until, seeing nothing but disaster ahead, Tamagno, now thoroughly exasperated, snatched the score from the prompter's hands, and holding it close to the eyes of the nearly fainting prima donna, bellowed the music with all his strength before the curtain was lowered.

Records

Until quite recent times it had been accepted that Tamagno's records were little more than historical souvenirs, with only a hint of the real Tamagno voice; and with primitive or ill-adjusted players there was some reason for this belief. As usual, it was the records and never the players that were held to be at fault, and it has been left to time and progress to prove otherwise. It has also been believed, owing to his comparatively early retirement, that Tamagno had lost his voice. Nothing could be further from truth. Tamagno retired owing to heart trouble and nothing else. The voice was unaffected, and although the strenuous work of opera was denied him, he certainly put all he possessed into the making of his records. The records were among the G&T company's finest, both technically and artistically, and it is simply proper reproduction that is needed to do them justice, and that has had to wait until quite recent times. For myself, I use top-grade amplification with thorn needle, coupled with a large speaker unit fitted to an out-sized non-commercial baffle of composite construction; and with this, used with intelligent adjustment, it is possible to hear the warm undistorted Tamagno voice at full strength and mellowness.

As high *tessituras* gave him no trouble, any suggestion that the recorded music was transposed to suit his allegedly failing powers may be dismissed peremptorily.

The *Otello* items have an especial interest as showing Verdi's own *tempi*, which by today's practices seem slow; and particularly magnificent is the declamatory splendour of the *Esultate*, especially, I think, on the 10-in. disc. As with Caruso, I prefer to accept everything Tamagno sang as being sung correctly and perfectly, and exactly as he intended to sing it. Of the two *Morte d'Otello* renderings, the 12-in. one is fuller and broader, besides being more complete, although the 10-in. has a peculiar charm of its own. Apart from this, I prefer the 10-in. set on the whole, and my complete set of these in original form I value as one of the high spots in my collection. The 10-in. *O muto asil* shows the completely effortless treatment of the high *tessitura*, the B flats with their cruel approaches ringing out sweetly, and in the following cabaletta *Corriam, corriam* the top Cs are sung with zest. The *Herodiade* air is really too dull for comment, but the *Samson* title, so disappointing under former conditions of reproduction, is now to be heard for what it is. Tamagno launched his top notes in a manner all his own, which precluded any question of shouting. In the *Andrea Chenier* he takes breath preparatory to the high notes, in which he differed from Caruso, and both methods have their points, neither being open to criticism: in the 10-in. version of this aria Tamagno ends at the middle. The *Inno*, or hymn, in *Le Prophete* is more like a conqueror laying down his terms than an appeal to heaven, and is sung with a sense of great urgency; and the pastorale *Sopra Berta* reveals a different mood of reflective lyricism remarkable in a *tenore robusto*, but in Tamagno a strain of tenderness is never far away, and that is one of the most endearing features of his singing. Both versions of *Ora e per sempre* are records of great splendour, as is *Di quella pira* with it two ringing high Cs, one of which is traditional but neither wholly conventional, but both highly effective, and we may assume Verdi's cordial concurrence in this as in other instances.

We should treasure our Tamagno records, for they are truly magnificent souvenirs of the great *tenore robusto* of his age.

FERNANDO VALERO

FERNANDO VALERO, whose red G&Ts provide some of the greater rarities, was a Spaniard, who sang throughout the Covent Garden season of 1890 and again in 1903, when his only records were made in London. His voice had a tendency to whiteness, and caused comparisons to be made with his great compatriot Gayarre who (in 1890) had lately retired. He sang chiefly as a relief tenor to de Reszke and Ravelli, and appeared in all the routine performances of *Carmen*.[1]

[1] It was in this season that Jean de Reszke decided to appear as Don Jose, and a special occasion was made for this, with de Lussan as Carmen and Lassalle as Escamillo; the Micaela was Pinkert, and in the following season Melba joined the brilliant *ensemble* in this role.

ERNEST VAN DYCK

ERNEST VAN DYCK was one of the finest of tenors, and ranged from Massenet to Wagner. He was outstandingly the finest Tristan I ever saw. Besides this splendid Tristan, Van Dyck was supreme as Tannhauser, Siegmund, Lohengrin and Walter, singing and acting with a vitality to astonish a later generation.

Unhappily, his Fonotipia recording was lamentable, and was never placed on sale, but a hill-and-dale Pathe of Siegmund's *Liebestlied* gives a fair approximation of his voice.

FRANCESCO VIGNAS

FRANCESCO VIGNAS was the tenor of the London *premiere* of *Cavalleria Rusticana* in Lago's season in 1891. He was duly spotted by Harris, and became a member of the Covent Garden establishment. He was certainly one of the truly fine tenors of this fruitful period, with that sense of style which is so instantly recognised when present. Although he frequently appeared as Tannhauser and Lohengrin in Italian versions, it was in the lyrical operas that he excelled, for in these he was comparable with Caruso himself, whom, in fact, he somewhat resembled in appearance.

Records
Although a singer of red label status, his only G&T records were under black label, and not issued in England. The only one that I heard was of poor quality. Like so many others, he was attracted to Fonotipia, where his records were better known. During the time he sang in England, our audiences had been regaled with such great tenors as de Reszke, Alvarez, de Lucia, Tamagno, Caruso, Zenatello and Anselmi; not to mention others whose names might have become household words in other conditions. It is not easy for collectors today to appreciate what a wealth of talent was nightly offered to English and American audiences in those days.

HERMANN WINKELMANN

HERMANN WINKELMANN's records will make a strong appeal to those interested in the history of Wagnerian opera. It was in 1882 that London heard for the first time the authentic uncut Wagnerian repertoire in the German language and sung by German artists. While _The Ring_ was being given at the old Her Majesty's Opera a company with Richter as musical director and fortified with Wagner's blessing opened at Drury Lane to produce, among other works, the London _premieres_ of _Tristan_ and _Die Meistersinger_ with very distinguished casts. Of the singers, Winkelmann was the leading tenor, singing also in all performances of _Lohengrin_ and _Tannhauser_. The artists, among whom were Sucher, Malten, Brandt and Eugen Gura, comprised probably the best exponents ever heard of the Wagnerian idiom, for they sang under Wagner's personal direction, and we know that he favoured lyrical methods in preference to the declamatory style which has supplanted them.
Winkelmann recorded on black G&T in Vienna.

GIOVANNI ZENATELLO

GIOVANNI ZENATELLO made a wholly successful London debut in the autumn of 1905, singing in the _Ballo_ with Boninsegna and Sammarco. His success was immediate, and thereafter for many years he ranked as one of the leading Italian tenors. He had a voice of warm and trumpet-like quality, and a vigorous method which suited particularly the more _robusto_ roles, but he sang the entire Italian repertoire in the styles best suited to each. Naturally he excelled as Radames and as Canio; as Cavaradossi, the Fausts of Gounod and of Boito, Rudolfo and Don Jose he was superb; but it was as Otello that he reached his highest stature. Zenatello sang this role many hundreds of times over the next twenty-five or so years, and with no falling off in his powers. His absolute debut in the role was at Covent Garden on 1st July, 1908, which was Covent Garden's peak season of that decade, with Melba, Scotti and McCormack in the cast. But it was Zenatello's night, and he was acclaimed as the true successor to Tamagno. Be this as it may, there has been no other since to compare with him, or any other who has attempted the role who could have hoped to continue in it with undiminished splendour for a like period of a quarter of a century.

Records

Zenatello made a few black label G&Ts in 1903, followed in 1904 by three reds evidently at the same session at which selections from Giordano's *Siberia* were made by Storchio (q.v. in Appendix). They were all withdrawn at the end of 1904 when Zenatello crossed over to Fonotipia, and in England are practically unknown. Two copies of the 1903 issue came briefly to light to be played at Scotland Yard (see "Strange Interlude") when it was found that like others of that year they were recorded at a slower speed than was generally used, and therefore unjustly condemned. The Fonos, however, are a most lively series and cover some of the best records made by the company, many being concerted pieces of great interest. Later, he and other Fonotipia artists recorded for Columbia, but with definitely less success, with the exception to two very fine duets by Zenatello and his wife Maria Gay from *Cavalleria* and *Aida*.

Signor ZENATELLO assists on three consecutive nights at the death of a different lady friend. From left to right, the corpses (suppressed in the picture) are those of *Carmen, Mimi,* and *Madama Butterfly*, respectively.

Punch, Oct. 17, 1906

H

BARITONES

HENRI ALBERS

HENRI ALBERS was a distinguished baritone who sang very frequently at Covent Garden in the 'nineties, being much admired in such roles as de Nevers, Mercutio, Wolfram, in *Manon*, and as Wotan in a French version of *Die Walkure*. He was also present on the occasion when Jean de Reszke essayed the role of Werther, with Eames and Arnoldson also in the cast.

The only records by Albers are a single black G&T made in Brussels in 1904, and five Odeons made in Brussels and Paris in 1906.

MARIO ANCONA

MARIO ANCONA, one of our favourite baritones both on records and on the stage, came to London in 1892, in one of Lago's less important seasons. Ancona, however, was one of the most important of Lago's recruits, a fact which the watchful Harris fully appreciated, for he carried the new baritone off to Covent Garden where he at once established his reputation with London audiences. It was said more than once by those who should know that Ancona lacked real musical sense and needed thorough coaching in all his roles. If that were indeed so, it only remains to say that he was a particularly apt pupil, for he gave no inkling of any such thing. He had a rich and steady voice, and the parts in which I heard him—Tonio, Valentine and Rossini's Figaro—he seemed in each the perfect representative. He was merry, grave and tragic, and his sonorous voice rolled easily over the orchestral background. In *Pagliacci* he made the role of Tonio his own, and with his inseparable partner de Lucia these two great artists carried the opera to its deserved triumphs in London and then to New York.

It must be a matter for lasting regret that G&T and Victor alike missed such golden opportunities of recording these two in partnership, as we may be sure Fonotipia would have done given the same chances. Not even in 1905, when both were in London, was any approach made; and as with Melba and Caruso, Melba and Scotti, and other combinations we all could think of, so were de Lucia and Ancona neglected.

Records

The fact that Ancona's first red label G&Ts were made (as the numbers suggest) in London in 1904 when he was singing in an autumn season suggests that the London headquarters were at least conscious of him, although for that short period only.

The London recordings were on offer for a few months only, to be withdrawn in favour of a Milan issue at near the same time, but whether before or after I cannot say—it doesn't matter much either way. The *Pagliacci* prologue was twice recorded under the same number, the second being followed by a cross following the numerals. It is rather disappointing—not as good as it should have been, being a little ponderous and inclined to lose resonance as it gets to halfway. Similarly, the *Credo* makes so bad a start that we may wonder why they didn't stop and start again, but once the first section is over the record comes to life, and a very excellent *Credo* is heard, the fine resonance of Ancona's voice being admirable. His *Mattinate* (Tosti) is a pleasing item, and was written specially for him, although, like most singers of this ballad, he uses *tempi* not contemplated by its composer: in fact Tosti is said to have declared that Melba was the only singer who sang it properly.

MATTIA BATTISTINI

By common consent MATTIA BATTISTINI was the most wonderful baritone of our Golden Age. His style has been well described as "oratorical", and it conformed rigidly to the strict tradition of mid-Victorian singing. Not only had he a voice of the richest *timbre*, but an understanding and skill in the uses of *bel canto*, in the true meaning of this lightly applied term, of the very highest order. Another cliche of criticism is "the grand manner", and this might have been coined especially for him, for Battistini executed feats of singing, both in technique and in range of expression, which would have lain beyond the powers of most renowned singers. He was most successful in Verdi, and especially in *Ernani*, an opera which gave him the fullest scope both for the fullness of his voice and for his magnificent skill in his use of it. He was magnificent also in appearance, which dominated the stage like the true aristocrat that he was. He first appeared in London in 1883, and returned as a fully matured artist in Harris' opening season, 1887, at Drury Lane. He did not re-appear at Covent Garden until 1905, and in the following year his Germont in the *Traviata* was of overwhelming splendour, actually overshadowing Melba and Caruso. Up to 1922 Battistini was still singing in opera, and gave a triumphant recital at the Queen's Hall in 1926, two years before his death.

Battistini provides us with an excellent example of the debt which a composer owes to those singers who by the sheer splendour of their singing could rescue from mediocrity much music which was inherently dull. Donizetti, for example, was not at his happiest when writing for the baritone voice, especially in solos, and the contrast between his baritone roles and those of Verdi is striking. Both composed *con amore* for their sopranos, and even their mezzos, but a cursory glance will show that while Donizetti showed much inspiration when composing for his tenors he generally treated his baritones as necessary but rather irksome appendages: Verdi on the other hand did some of his best work for his baritones, and one has to look to the opposite ends of the Verdian scale, from *Trovatore* to *Otello* and *Aida*, to find really worthy tenor roles.

Battistini seemed to choose much music of an intrinsically dull character, and then to transmute it to splendid life by his own gifts and talents. There are several examples of this. He would also exploit the unusually high range of his voice by singing tenor passages untransposed, for he could do a ringing B flat with the best, but I do not myself think that these experiments were wholly successful and certainly his *Ideale* is unexpectedly disappointing.

Both composers treated their unfortunate basses with open contempt, and it was to Gounod and Meyerbeer that these outcasts had to turn for salvation.

Records

The "Warsaw Batts", as I christened them in "Collectors' Corner", make a truly fascinating little set, and certainly they have fascinated collectors the world over. I remember them from my earliest days as an admirer of fine singing, and was fortunate enough to acquire some at second hand, in which were the *Deh non plorar* and the *Occhi di fata*, which I still consider the two I most greatly like. But I was also enraptured by the *Finch'an del vino*, despite its un-Mozartian style, and with applause and shouts for encore, to which Battistini can be heard directing his accompanist with "ancora". Without doubt he was dancing as he sang, and all present must have enjoyed a stimulating session. In Tosti's *Ancora* one may enjoy his suave phrasing and immaculate *legato*, and his noble Valentine is heard in *Dio possente*. *Largo al factotum* might have been better if on a 12-in. disc, for it is complete, but so well is it done that it is not a simple matter to place a finger on a fault. The only failure was in the *O tu bel astro*, which evidently had not been timed beforehand, and G&T were sometimes strikingly remiss about allowing bad records to go out. There are still two of the set that I have not achieved, one of which—the *Eugen Onegin*—is very rare and rather dull. The Spanish *La Mantilla* until lately has been unknown to us, but a fortunate collector has now secured a perfect original copy. The characteristic ditty is exquisitely sung, with its constantly recurring ornament executed with perfect neatness. The *Favorita* duet with Carotini is in this version introduced by a baritone solo most nobly sung.

The "Warsaw Batts", which were put out in 1903, were withdrawn two years later; then in 1907 came the superb orange label 12-in. set which made a great impact on gramophonists of the day including myself. The richly "forward" quality was something in advance of anything we had yet heard, and at fifteen shillings each they seemed even cheap, so splendid were they. Myself, I selected *Eri tu* and *A tanto Amor*, and as soon as I had restored

my shattered finances I added *O sommo Carlo*. Some of this issue were
musically rather dull, but the radiant beauty of Battistini's singing made
one forget that. He continued to record for twenty years, and as he never
lost his voice there was no falling off in his records, except for one, which
may have been the last he was ever to make—the *Non piu andrai*, in which
he seemed to feel no interest, and I would guess that his stamina was at last
failing. The question has been posed whether Battistini was a good singer
of Mozart, and certainly he would not vindicate himself by this record:
and in *La ci darem* he seemed strangely ill at ease, although of course there
was no nonsense about the *tempo* in those days.

Punch, July 11, 1906

DAVID BISPHAM

DAVID BISPHAM was a Philadelphian singer with Quaker tendencies who sang
the heavy baritone roles at Covent Garden throughout the 'nineties. He
appeared as Kurvenal, Wolfram, Alberic, Pizaro, Beckmesser and Telramund;
also as Wotan, in which, despite his lack of height, his forceful personality
brought well within his scope. On leaving grand opera he sang in London
in *opera comique*, in *La Basoche* and *The Vicar of Wakefield*, in which his
impressive acting compensated for some roughening of the voice.

Records

David Bispham's G&T records have always attracted the fancy of collectors on account of their rarity. They were made in London in 1902 and 1903, and although prepared for the red label catalogue were issued as black label at what must have been the last moment. Several copies evidently went out in the original form, and any of these that have turned up are naturally prized for their museum interest. Brahms' *Sappische Ode* is a fine piece of work, as is Schubert's *Hark, hark, the Lark*, which he sings with a lightness and tender feeling which is not always apparent in him. In fact he was temperamentally inclined to austerity and made little concession to charm. Perhaps the rarest is his *Quand'ero paggio*, which is sung twice on the short disc, but without verve or humour. Vocally, Bispham is best heard in the lugubrious Gounod setting of *O that we two were maying*, and the sad Philadelphian revels in the miseries of *The Sands of Dee*. He recorded very copiously for Columbia, showing a strong partiality for traditional British ballads to which he was unsuited, nor was his only operatic item *Dio possente* any more satisfactory, although the evident onset of age may have explained this. But in the American ballad *A Banjo Song* we hear the true Bispham well recorded.

FRANCESCO MARIA BONINI

FRANCESCO MARIA BONINI was one of Fonotipia's earliest recorders, his records being among the gold label single-sided original issue. Subsequently he recorded in many concerted scenes with Russ, Petri, Luppi and others. He had a powerful and resonant voice which recorded excellently, with a smooth *legato* or a fierce declamation. The two sides comprising the prayer in Leoncavallo's *Rolando di Berlin* and *Cortigiani vil razza* are most satisfying, and enough to show him as a singer of the top rank.

FERRUCIO CORRADETTI

FERRUCIO CORRADETTI was one of Fonotipia's most useful artists, his records covering three pages of Bauer's work, which leaves it to me to say simply that he must have recorded everything! Although a light baritone he did not allow that to prevent him from singing music from the heavy roles, and in *buffo* he was unsurpassed and of these there was no more exhilarating example than the comic trio *Di Pandolfetti medico* in *Crispino e la comare* which is listed in the Appendix under Magini-Colletti. The spontaneity of the *ensemble* with its absurd asides, with the patter well forward on the lips makes this record of very special interest.

Records

Corradetti made a number of Berliners, of which I possessed *Eri tu* (on a 7-in. disc!) with an impressive orchestra and outstandingly good, and I wish I could get it again. He made a number of G&Ts in 1904, some with secondary singers, and in 1905 he joined Fonotipia where he made himself quite at home, for Bauer catalogues sixty titles in the 39 series, and twenty-three in later ones.

ANTONIO COTOGNI

ANTONIO COTOGNI made his debut in 1852, so to say the least he was past his prime when he recorded on red G&T in a duet with the tenor Marconi in 1908. This was *I Mulattieri*, a comic patter into which both singers enter with tremendous gusto. This record is a world rarity. Two curious and unnamed recordings are ascribed to Cotogni, one being of *O casto fior*, which exists as a G&T unlabelled test pressing having a matrix number next to Santley's 12-in. records of 1903. When invited to give a name to this I saw no alternative, for it may convincingly be guessed that no other singer with so old and worn a voice would have been of sufficient prestige to have been asked to record. One could imagine Cotogni and Santley arriving arm in arm at the studio when Santley did his recording of *Non piu andrai* and *Thou'rt passing hence*, and when this was finished, what could be more natural than for Santley to say "Now you have a go, old boy; Willie Gaisberg will be only too pleased, won't you, William?" And that, I am convinced, is what happened. A precise repetition of this event seems equally certain to have taken place when Tamagno recorded in Milan in the same year; for the unpublished *Perche?* which was given the number 52685 was certainly not by Tamagno, but very much like the faded voice which recorded with Santley. Did Cotogni perhaps rather enjoyed his jaunts with his friends to recording studios?

FRANCESCO D'ANDRADE

FRANCESCO D'ANDRADE was a Portuguese baritone of immense vigour and vitality who was another of Lago's discoveries in due course to be annexed by the voracious Harris. In his first season, 1886, he made his London debut as Rigoletto, appearing also in *Faust, Les Huguenots, Ballo,* the *Trovatore, Ernani, Gioconda* and *Nozze di Figaro*. He continued his successful London career for a further four seasons, thus being the natural partner for Gayarre and Marconi.

Records

The only records so far traced were made for Lyraphone. One of these was re-issued by Parlophone shortly before the war, the title being the Champagne Air in *Don Giovanni*, sung at such an excessive speed as to leave us wondering whether that was how he usually treated it.

GIUSEPPE DE LUCA

GIUSEPPE DE LUCA was one of those red label G&T recorders of 1903 who soon afterwards moved to Fonotipia. The G&Ts are naturally rare collectors' specimens, and if played at the low speed that all these 1903 Milan recordings require, they are interesting if not thrilling to listen to, though the *Favorita* duet with Ceresoli is outstanding. De Luca attained to stardom in course of time, when he became really well-known he had great popularity, and he continued to sing into well past his seventieth year. He was as well-liked as a man as he was as an artist, and Dorothy Caruso writes of him as "this quiet and good man". He did not get a great deal of work in London, first being heard there in the autumn of 1907, and in Beecham's erratic season of 1910 he sang many leads. In 1915 he went to the Metropolitan, New York, and at once became a general favourite. He retired from active singing in 1934, but on a day in July 1935, De Luca was unexpectedly announced to sing at Covent Garden in *Il Barbiere*—an announcement that drew me from the country like a magnet, and in the years that followed I hardly met a musically inclined person who was not present on that night, when he was given an astonishing ovation. It was his only appearance, and his last in London. It was then that he presented me with the souvenir portrait, cordially inscribed, which formed the cover of the first edition of the G.A.R., but minus the inscription.

EUGENIO GIRALDONI

EUGENIO GIRALDONI was the son of another famous baritone of the same name, and is best remembered as the creator of Scarpia in *La Tosca*. In this role I thought he acted better than he sang, and it may be concluded that his voice was then in decline, being inclined to woolliness; nor did Giraldoni seem to give greater pleasure to New York audiences, for his stay at the Metropolitan was limited to the single season of 1904–5, which was three years before London heard him. In his youth he was much admired in Italy, and made his debut at Barcelona at the age of twenty. But lacking subtlety, Giraldoni was not a finished singer by our standard, although his inclusion here is imperative as a red label recorder of 1903.

Records

Giraldoni's first records were among the ill-fated red label issue of 1903, but when played at their proper speed the voice can be better heard, and Giraldoni was another of those who crossed over to Fonotipia, so the disappearance of his red label records causes no surprise.

Moreover, there is no special attraction in the singing of such specimens from this series as I have heard—the *Aida* and the *Herodiade* items—both of which are sung without charm or finish, although as museum specimens they have their attractions.

"SIGNOR FRANCISCO"

"SIGNOR FRANCISCO" (Emilio de Gogorza) appeared under this of his various *noms de guerre* in the G&T catalogues as black label Victor-G&Ts. Without doubt these few items which appeared in England were the finest operatic singing then to be found outside the red label series. His voice had a weight and sonority most impressive to hear, and the extreme skill of his delivery is shown in every one. The abbreviated *Largo al factotum* equals any, and he sings the *prestissimo* patter at the conclusion with its words clearly enunciated, which is more than can always be said, for too often are the words jettisoned in favour of La-la-la. As a side reflection on this particular, we have heard in very recent times at Covent Garden a Figaro who had the audacity to sing two dotted crochets in place of the six quavers—and get away with it, which gives some indication of the depths to which singing has sunk. Doubtless the excuse would be, why should a singer spend months or years in perfecting lip production when the audiences are equally content with this discreditable makeshift?

To return to Signor Francisco: his *Prologue*, or the part of it, was one of my first purchases, for having recently then heard Ancona in person, it did and always has reminded me of Ancona's rendering: and very long before I heard Edouard de Reszke's record of the Drinking Song in *Martha* I imagined the Francisco rendering as possibly resembling it.

These were 10-in. records, after which followed a 12-in. of the ever-popular *La Paloma*, which I immediately acquired, and of which I have never tired. There is a solemn dignity in this, combined with beautiful phrasing and tone which for me makes all other attempts sound cheap and rather common. This title was replaced, though with the same numbering, when de Gogorze's red label record was issued. There are easily detected differences between the two.

Signor Francisco's first records to be heard in England under his own name were in the duets with Emma Eames, whose husband he was.

HARRY PLUNKET GREENE

HARRY PLUNKET GREENE was one of the most skilful, quite the most lovable, and perhaps the most erratic of singers. Possessing originally a very fine low voice he attempted an operatic career at Covent Garden in 1890, appearing as the Commendatore in *Don Giovanni*, and in a minor role in *Die Meistersinger*. This was not his vocation, however, and he did not pursue it, devoting himself to the concert platform and giving particular attention to German *lieder*. Whether the comparatively early failure of his voice and his rather frequent difficulties with intonation were due to faulty production or to inherent weakness may be uncertain, but he was by no means put out by it, and proceeded with amazing success to teach and to demonstrate that although a good voice and good singing were helpful adjuncts, both were entirely subsidiary to clear enunciation and intelligent interpretation. His pupils may still be heard, proclaiming the same beliefs, and may generally be identified by their tendency to address their audiences in what they describe as "presenting a programme".

Records

The first record was a G&T made in 1903 or earlier, and very rare. This is of Schubert's *Abschied*, which, according to its numbering, was sung in German, although it might just as well have been in Arabic. In his later English and especially Irish songs however, his controlled enunciation was a joy to hear, for he had the gift or the skill not to let clear consonants interfere with the vocal line. He phrased in the grand manner and with a beautiful *legato* which was a model of fine singing.

RICHARD GREEN

RICHARD GREEN is one of the few early G&T black label singers to be carried into the new edition, for the reason of the historical importance of his membership of the famous cast in which *I Pagliacci* was first heard in London. With Melba, de Lucia and Ancona, Richard Green was the Silvio which he sang with evident success since he sang it unchanged throughout the seasons of 1893 and 1894. His records are among the 1900 issues, of which I have two verses of Maud Valerie White's *The Devout Lover.*

The name of Hermann Gura is catalogued by Bauer in "Historical Records": but this should not be confused with Eugen Gura who was one of the great Wagnerian singers of the 'eighties.

GIUSEPPE KASHMANN

GIUSEPPE KASHMANN, despite his name was an Italian, and made his debut at Turin in 1874. He was a baritone of high standing in Europe and America, although he never visited England.

His records were 12-in. red labels of 1904, and appeared in the English supplement of February 1905 and were deleted a year later.

JEAN LASSALLE

JEAN LASSALLE was one of the truly great baritones of the late Victorian epoch. His superb physique and exuberant vitality at once attracted attention and set off his fine voice to perfection. By his vigour and dominating presence he made an initial success of Massenet's *Le Roi de Lahore,* sung of course in Italian, at its London *premiere* in 1879, but not even he could repeat that feat for Rubinstein's dreary *Demon*. He was very close to the de Reszkes, and the three made a notable triumvirate. In the few Pathe records that he has left it is easy to detect the classic purity of style which he bequeathed to his no less distinguished successor at the Paris Opera, Maurice Renaud. Some unlikely looking single side Odeons sung by a young bass of the same surname are hopefully attributed by some collectors to Jean Lassalle, but the only authenticated records are taken from cylinders.

ANTONIO MAGINI-COLETTI

ANTONIO MAGINI-COLETTI, although unheard in England, was much admired in the two Americas and on the Continent in the 'nineties, and was a leading singer at La Scala. He modelled his style upon the great baritones Graziani and Cotogni, and made his debut in Rome in 1880.

Records

Magini-Colletti recorded for International Zonophone in 1902 on the light blue label used for the Zonos of Caruso, and these rank highly as collectors' rarities. In 1904–5 he recorded exclusively for Fonotipia, making some of the finest baritone records of the period. His voice was inclined to be heavy and dark, although his singing of Rossini's *La Danza* would seem to negative this, but by that time he had been singing for twenty-five years.

VICTOR MAUREL

VICTOR MAUREL—"the great Maurel"—"the best of all" as Zelie de Lussan described him. He made his debut at La Scala in 1870 as a pupil of Faure, and he continued with ever-increasing prestige until well after the turn of the century. I may be one of the few left who heard him at his two London recitals or his opera appearances in 1904 and 1905 when he was still a very great artist. As an actor he was first-rate, and did in fact desert the opera for French drama for a brief spell. He had great versatility and *finesse*, and could convey the fullest meaning with a minimum of action. As all know, his most notable achievement was his creation, under Verdi's eye, of the roles of Iago and Falstaff, although in London his interpretation of the latter

Doctor Maurel-Malatesta.
A Night Call—before the Curtain.   *Punch*, May 17, 1905

somewhat offended against Shakespearean susceptibilities, and was not seen more than twice in all the London productions of the time. But his dramatic renderings of *Quand'ero paggio* at his recitals, when he advanced to the edge of the platform and addressed the front rows *sotto voce* with completely different gestures for each of the numerous encores stirred his audiences to delirious joy. Each time he sang the *Credo* in Otello with the *finesse* I have mentioned, and once the *Largo al factotum* with full dramatic action. Of the various non-operatic items he sang I remember best *Pur dicesti*, and what a pity he didn't record it.

The absence of a memoir of this great man is a tragic gap in the musical library, for there must be a great story to tell. He was a talented painter and swordsman, an experienced and entertaining lecturer, and even made a hobby of surgery, although how this last accomplishment was acquired and practised remains unexplained.[1]

[1] This curious sidelight is taken from descriptive matter accompanying "Spy's" cartoon in *Vanity Fair* of October 20th, 1898.

Records

Maurel's first records were on red label G&T made in Paris in 1903. They were indifferently recorded, and were more than usually liable to the blast which was the bane of the early gramophones. Theirs was a short life, for which their technical deficiencies probably shared the blame with non-appreciation of their slow playing speeds, and with the singer's defection to Fonotipia. Some of them were degraded to the general catalogue with black labels. The Fonotipias, however, were altogether better, and if due allowance be made for their fast playing speeds may be said to be lifelike reproductions of Maurel at the end of his unusually distinguished career.

As collectors' specimens the G&Ts rank among the most coveted of all, and even on these, given reasonable copies, the fine chest resonance is well shown. It is a great loss and a great mystery why there was no record of the *Credo*, which was Maurel's *chef d'oeuvre*, as a souvenir of his great creation of Iago, but on Fonotipia he recorded the *Quand'era paggio* with great gusto and *elan*—three times on the same disc all slightly different, with studio applause, the first repetition being especially notable for its phrasing and rhythm.

GIUSEPPE PACINI

GIUSEPPE PACINI was one of the "gold label" Fonotipia singers—signifying the first issue by that company. It was a beautiful voice and used with restraint and good feeling. The *Il balen* in the *Trovatore*, with an introduced *bravura* flourish, is a fine example, and the *Description of London* in Mascagni's *Guglielmo Ratcliff*, music of a narrative type, is full of colour. The name role was created by Pacini at the Scala, and was a great personal success for him, though this record may be all that remains of the opera. He sang at St. Petersburg and spent much time in South America, though none, apparently, in England or the States.

ANTONIO PINI-CORSI

ANTONIO PINI-CORSI, the most accomplished *buffo* since the legendary Ciampi of Patti's day, was one of the most polished artists to appear in London opera. He seldom undertook a serious role, although making a few appearances as Tonio, but he had a serviceable voice and was a fine musician. As a *buffo* actor he was quite superlative, and he gave a distinction to the role of Bartolo in *The Barber* which was in high comedy. Here was none of the stage clown generally seen in this role, and we saw instead a crisp and precise little gentleman whose every action and movement were exactly to the point. In Paer's *Il Mastero di Capella*, the libretto of which I did not see, he gave directions to the orchestra, imitating the various instruments with a whimsical comicality that could hardly have been matched.

Records

Pini-Corsi's many black label records were never on sale in England, but on red label he took part in two or three concerted extracts from the *Barbiere* with de Lucia. Also, there was one red label G&T evidently made during the *Siberia* session with Zenatello and Storchio, and some black and silver Columbias of 1903—an issue which, it may be remarked, did not seem to have unduly disturbed the G&T company.

MAURICE RENAUD

MAURICE RENAUD almost calls for a page to himself, for none have ever shown a purer artistic sense or a deeper understanding of the operatic idiom. It was written of him in an obituary notice in a New York paper, "Distinction was the everyday mantle of Maurice Renaud", and this was well said. He was not merely a singing actor nor yet an acting singer, but was pre-eminently great in both these arts, and thus he was one of the greatest operatic artists of his time. He was the most profound and conscientious operatic scholar of our epoch, and none gave as detailed an attention as he did to the atmosphere and background of his work. He would infallibly catch the eye of the least initiated, for he was picturesque, forceful, insinuating, elegant and musicianly in a manner to delight all one's senses. He had a solemn and sombre manner, and so strong was the force that he emanated, and so compelling the thought that preceded his every action that he never for a moment lost the attention of his audiences. He gave particular attention to the costuming of his roles, and he took the stage with grace and grandeur, and moved with such artistry of finish that he never put a foot or a finger wrong.

Renaud, who was pupil and successor to Lassalle at the Paris Opera, made his London debut at the Diamond Jubilee gala performance in 1897, singing Wolfram in an act from *Tannhauser*, and de Nevers in the last act of *Les Huguenots*. He was one of the greatest of Don Giovannis, a role which he shared with Scotti, offering two perfect and contrasted interpretations. His last appearance in London was in Hammerstein's lavish but wasteful season of 1911–12 at the lavish and wasteful Opera House which the optimistic *entrepreneur* had erected in Kingsway. It was a fine theatre, although turned over to living pictures until in the late nineteen fifties it ended appropriately with a single and in many ways brilliant season of Italian opera which must have evoked many memories in those old enough to have seen it in its two opera phases, very shortly following which there was nothing to bear witness to its existence but a hole in the ground.

Records

Renaud recorded first for French G&T on black labels of 1901, these being converted to red label to conform to the "London Red" issue of 1902. They are inclined to austerity both in subject and treatment, though with the exception of a perfectly rendered *Promesse de mon avenir* in *La Favorita*, he being, as I believe, the only one to follow faithfully the rendering of his master who created the role.

The London records are all of great interest and if found in good condition will reproduce well. That so careful a singer should give the right emphasis and no more to the *Toreador Song* is to be expected, and the perfect rendering is the natural result. His *Star of Eve* is so full of sensitivity and subtlety as to open wide the question, which is not confined to this record, whether Renaud, profound musician that he was, obtained many fine effects by using the natural, or "just", scale in place of the "equal" (i.e. faked) scale in general use. With accompanying instruments presumed to be playing true only as

Punch, July 13, 1904
(Kirkby Lunn, Renaud,
   Calve, Gilibert)

Salomé Calvé. "Kindly pick up this dagger, as I want to put an end to myself and the Opera."

to their octaves, the result would be something off pitch, noticeable only to exceptional ears. It was said of the illustrious Joachim that he played "out of tune", until somebody discovered that by using the "just" scale against the "equal" scale of his colleague or colleagues he was accomplishing a very extraordinary feat. There was a similar tale of a new soprano who at rehearsal sang Elizabeth's Greeting throughout in this manner, creating at first consternation, followed by a round of applause at this audacious *tour de force.* I am unsure whether I unreservedly accept this story, believing, as a very humble violin player, that the "just" scale either comes naturally to a singer or a fiddler, or if not, that the teacher will see to it, the actual interval depending on the key in use at the time and the note on which the sharp or flat is to lean, both being extended something beyond those sounded by the piano. These self-contradictory ruminations leave me wondering what it is that Renaud did—if he did anything!

MARIO SAMMARCO

MARIO SAMMARCO was first known of in England from his portrait in the 1902 celebrity catalogue. His London debut was as Scarpia in *Tosca* in October 1904. While undoubtedly first-rate, Sammarco was just short of reaching the upper flights of baritones, for he lacked the picturesqueness of Scotti, the nobility of Renaud, the vigour of Lassalle, the vocal opulence of Battistini or the dominance of Maurel. This is not intended as dispraise, for he had attributes of his own, which perhaps those others had not got. He had a sardonic forcefulness and a look of ruthlessness, and in roles that lay well for his voice he sang gloriously. His Scarpia was an interesting study of cynical savagery, as was his Barnaba in *La Gioconda.*

Punch, Oct. 24, 1906

128 _The Golden Age Recorded_

Records

The first recordings were on red G&T at Milan, and formed part of the first celebrity catalogue. They were good examples, and the *Germania* title, which in the previous edition of this book I had written of with some lack of enthusiasm, is in fact a magnificent record when heard in unspoilt condition. Sammarco sang the *Prologue* to *Pagliacci* in a manner all his own, which the cut version here used hardly shows, although an impressive performance. The *Credo* also is naturally cut, but the short excerpt from *Zaza* is particularly good. There were some 12-in. records in 1904; and later recordings of about 1909 reflect the more subdued methods of that phase. It was on Fonotipia that Sammarco was heard at his best, though he never seemed able to rise beyond a certain level, some of his performances hardly escaping the dull and unimaginative, although in *La mia Bandiera* he comes very much to life, and in the trio *Che fate qui, signori ?* in *Faust* he sings the fragment of the discarding of the charm with truly beautiful tone and dramatic fire. His *La ci darem*, sung with Irene de Bohuss seems to have been the first recording, and shows, of course, the correct *tempo* of the six-eight section.

CHARLES SANTLEY

CHARLES SANTLEY stands alone as the greatest English baritone of the mid-Victorian period. His first London appearance, after singing with success in his native Lancashire, was in 1857. That he was a philosopher as well as a singer is evident from the many crisp and lively opinions which besprinkle his two volumes of memoirs. He seceded from the Royal Italian Opera in 1871, in pursuit of his dream of establishing opera in English, which, for an Italian-trained singer, seems something of a paradox. For so strict an advocate of artistic integrity in all things, this burning desire to use English texts seems oddly inconsistent. From that time onwards he became something of an operatic Ishmael, for he was as obstinate as he was conscientious, and preferred to sacrifice a great career for the sake of a demonstrably mistaken principle. He never forsook his ideals, and in his student days would decline a much needed fee rather than undertake a role to which he did not feel he could do justice.

When over seventy years old, Santley continued to appear on such festival occasions as the Good Friday concerts at the Crystal Palace and parts of the Handel festivals, which was more in response to public affection than to any remaining beauty of voice. It is, though, a precious memory to have seen the old man and to have heard exactly the voice with which he recorded.

Records

The records of Santley were made in London in 1903—the *Non piu andrai* having a special attraction for collectors for its great rarity, as well as special value for true lovers of Mozart as a pattern of Mozartian style before this became dragged into the arena of musical politics, and was made to conform with what we understand to be the present fashion. (I wish we could know how such "fashions" originate, and why.) This was the first record of the 052 series, i.e., the first 12-in. disc to be sung in Italian by a male voice. With this, Santley recorded Sullivan's rather depressing song *Thou'rt passing hence, my Brother*, which is equally rare and nearly as interesting, for although it does not solve any controversies, it exactly reproduces the effect made by Santley's rendering of it on the public platform at that time of his life. The 10-in. trio are of less interest, although showing how well he expressed the sly opportunism of the *Vicar of Bray* and the bibulous sentiments of *Simon the Cellarer*.

KARL SCHEIDEMANTEL

KARL SCHEIDEMANTEL was one of the most famous Wagnerian baritones of the 'seventies and 'eighties, and was a leading singer in the first all-German performances of the master's works to be given at Covent Garden. This was in 1884, under the direction of Richter. In those days Wagner, outside Germany, was still struggling for existence, and the declamatory singing style, so disagreeable to him, was becoming the vogue, and which limited the proper appreciation of the "new music". Scheidemantel was an exception to this trend, and was much admired for his lyrical singing.

Scheidemantel's records are rarely seen, but their historical importance is attested by the enquiries from collectors over a wide area. The short list of his titles, recorded in Dresden where he worked and died, will be found in the Appendix.

ANTONIO SCOTTI

ANTONIO SCOTTI was everybody's favourite, both in London and in New York, as well he might have been, for not only was he a fine operatic artist, but he was unusually well favoured by nature, having a tall and elegant figure, handsome presence and an easy and charming manner. In him, as with Battistini, there was nothing of the intelligent student picked by nature from lowly beginnings, for he also was of high stock and of unforced natural dignity. In recalling Scotti to memory one can almost detect the aroma of his super-quality English cloth and Havana cigar, which latter, curiously enough, always reminded me of the quality of his voice, which was of an uncommon *timbre*—somewhat woody—the cigar box, perhaps? But so varied were its tones and so perfectly applied its colouring, that Scotti will always be remembered as one of the great stage baritones. Thus, as the consul in *Madama Butterfly* his kindness and tact at the significant moment of

I

the reading of the letter was something that could not be taught, and in *La Boheme* it was easy to understand how the unhappy Mimi confided in so sympathetic and gallant a Marcello. His fun and high spirits at the mock duel in the fourth act was a vivid trifle, and he brought the second act to its triumphant end by picking up Parkina as though she were weightless and carrying her at arm's length from the stage.

Scotti retired in 1933 after a career of forty-four years.

Records

The "London Scottis" have always had a special attraction for collectors not only being rare, but perhaps as being so representative of their period. *O Nuit d'amour* in de Lara's *Messaline* is, as I believe, the only record of this passage, and is sung by Scotti with a sensuous charm all his own. I have had them all except the *Quand'ero paggio*, sung twice and in my judgement the best balanced rendering known. Doubtless owing to its rather extreme brevity, the accompanist, who was Landon Ronald, thought fit to fill up with piano-playing on his own account, and with music in no way suitable to the occasion. This improvisation is based upon Wormser's *L'Infant Prodigue*, the mime-play in which Ronald had been playing the piano part in London, and much popularised by him.

Punch, May 31, 1905

"Nous voici encore! O mon p'tit chou!"
Alcindoro-Dufriche, Marcello-Scotti, Musetta-Parkina, Schaunard-Gilibert.

In 1903 Scotti made three black and silver Columbia records of the series already referred to, and which included, besides Scotti, Edouard de Reszke, Schumann-Heink, Suzanne Adams, Sembrich and Gilibert.

RICCARDO STRACCIARI

RICCARDO STRACCIARI was for long well known to gramophonists for his later Columbia records. Some will remember his appearances at Covent Garden in the autumn of 1905 with the San Carlo Opera Company of Naples, singing with Boninsegna, Zenatello and Didur. He was a striking and dramatic stage figure, and his entrance as the captive Amonasro left no doubt about his quality. His first records were for Fonotipia in 1903–4.

ANTON VAN ROOY

ANTON VAN ROOY was a singer of such mighty artistic stature as may well place him above any of the leading baritones in the Wagnerian roles. For many years he was the finest Wotan in the world, and his Kurvenal was, if possible, an even greater achievement, for it was conceived upon a plane of such lofty nobility as touched upon pure genius. There was an alertness and intelligence in Van Rooy's Kurvenal when keeping watch beside the unconscious Tristan with an unwavering and rocklike immobility which lifted him out the rut of the routine Kurvenals who have succeeded him:

Van Rooy. A regular nailer at a Sole-o, when   *Punch*, June 1, 1904
he makes another striking hit.

the kindly humanity of *Nicht doch*: *in Kareol* was an outstanding touch, and the eloquent expression imparted by such a trio as Ternina, Van Dyck and Van Rooy gave a unique significance to the rather static drama.

Van Rooy's voice was of astonishing power and weight, with an organlike quality of great dignity and solemnity most appropriate to his superb Wotan, and with a roundness and softness which, as an old opera-goer of my youth said, "made you want to stroke it!" In whatever selection that one might be tempted to make of the *greatest* voices of this marvellous epoch, the name of Van Rooy would infallibly be included; and without question the same can be said of his powers as an actor. He continued to appear at Covent Garden from 1898 till 1914, and except for the season of 1912, when his voice was evidently in need of a rest, he sang as only Van Rooy could sing.

Records

As may be supposed, a voice such as Van Rooy's was hardly the kind to suit the early recording machine. None the less, his London red labels of 1902, although unmanageable on the primitive machines of their day, made valuable souvenirs in the ears of those who remembered him. They need to be played at a low speed, and inattention to this has produced some bad listening.

Later "pre-dog" 12-in. records of 1908 must be accounted as failures, excepting for that of Wotan's greeting to Walhalla which was preserved for some years in the company's Historical Catalogue. Some later Columbias were better than any that had previously been made, and although not especially powerful, caught the quality of Van Rooy's voice with fair smoothness.

BASSES

VITTORIO ARIMONDI

VITTORIO ARIMONDI was a *basso* who found little scope in his first London season in 1894 in face of the competition of Edouard de Reszke, Plancon, and Castlemary, all singing in French and Italian opera. In the following year he appeared in *Otello* with Albani and Tamagno, but his first big chance was as Basilio in *Il Barbiere* at Patti's re-entry in that year. It was ten years after that I heard him in that role, and with Pini-Corsi in this or in *Fra Diavolo* this pair of rich comedians could be relied upon to stop the show, so perfectly complementary were they to each other.

Arimondi had a true bass, full and round and of immense power, and his Mephistopheles, although not particularly satanic, was sung with easy fluency.

Records

The only records by this fine artist to be sold in England were the ineffective Nicoles, but there were some black G&Ts made at Vienna in 1904. (It has already been remarked that the Vienna branch showed no interest in red labels, and in fact did not use them until Selma Kurz recorded in 1906); there were also some Columbias of 1907.

FEDOR CHALIAPIN

FEDOR CHALIAPIN will be remembered as a great interpreter of Russian opera. He had a vivid personality and was a good actor so long as the entire stage belonged to him, for lacking all sense of proportion he missed true greatness. Thus in Boito's *Mefistofele* he was well suited, and gave a vital and even frightening performance, but in Gounod's *Faust* or as Leporello in *Don Giovanni*, or as Basilio in *Il Barbiere* he was out of his natural element. The voice was rough and unpleasing but there was no denying that he was a finished singer. On the concert platform he would give a virtuoso display of the whole art of voice production, and seemed able to sing in any *tessitura* with equal ease.

Records

Chaliapin was first tentatively brought to our notice in a very restricted sphere by his portrait as a young man at the end of the G&T celebrity catalogue of 1902. Such records are of extreme scarcity, and indeed it would be difficult to imagine it otherwise with singers of such fame and so well known to us to choose from. One of these discs reached me many years ago from Russia—the *Veau d'or*, sung in Russian, but lacking in character; but a record Karganoff's *Elegie* better showed him as the true bass that he was at that time. Generally his singing suffered from too much guttural expression and a tendency to slur on dropping notes. To many, Chaliapin was the greatest singer of all time; to others—he wasn't.

JEAN FRANCOIS DELMAS

JEAN FRANCOIS DELMAS, the great bass of the Paris Opera, recorded on black Zonophone in Paris in 1902, and immediately thereafter on black G&T. He transferred to Fonotipia in 1903 or 1904, and continued with them for the next year, and was then relegated to Odeon; from all of which it may be remarked either that the singers did not then pay much regard to their recording value or that some were more astute than others.

For forty years Delmas was one of the great opera stars, and, according to an obituary notice, he created over a hundred roles.

EDOUARD DE RESZKE

EDOUARD DE RESZKE's great career has been excellently told in Clara Leiser's *Jean de Reszke*. His London debut was in 1880, and in the next twenty years he sang as leading bass in seventeen seasons. Edouard was one of the most well liked of artists, and his great good nature endeared him to everybody with whom he came into contact. Three records only stand to his credit, made in 1903 in the Columbia black and silver label series, but some with red labels. By that time Edouard had been some time retired, with his voice, like his brother Jean's, sadly worn by excessive singing of Wagner. It is difficult for us today to arrive at any conclusion about the merits of the brothers' Wagnerian performances, since it was an article of faith that neither could do wrong. Whether it was by their own wish that they took the step or whether they were dragooned into it by the fanatical Wagnernites of the day, whipped up by the critic Bernard Shaw, in whose view they were acting almost criminally in not laying their great talent at the feet of the Master, the fact remains that they paid dearly for it.

Records

The record of *Infelice* in *Ernani* is fairly good and is generally much admired. The voice has little resonance, but the fine phrasing is always apparent. The *Serenade de Don Juan* (Tschaikowsky) is announced by Edouard himself in English with a foreign accent. It is too laboured to be wholly pleasant, and he seems none too sure of his breath: but the *Drinking Song* in *Marta* is excellent, sung with ease and distinction and without exaggeration.

ADAMO DIDUR

ADAMO DIDUR was a Polish bass and a pupil of Battistini. He had some European and South American reputation before he came to London in 1905 with the San Carlo Opera Company, when he made a clear impression with a fine voice and a distinctive personality. In that year he sang in Boito's *Mefistofele* with Zenatello as Faust, and later sang frequently in London and New York where he had a career of great brilliance.

Didur recorded for G&T on black label in 1904, shortly to leave for Fonotipia who did him better justice.

HAMILTON EARLE

HAMILTON EARLE was a prominent English bass of the 'nineties and after, and was much admired on the concert platform, appearing frequently at Covent Garden in *utilite* roles. He had a voice of great depth and musical quality which he used with unfailing taste.

Records

Hamilton Earle's black G&T records were made in London in 1903 and were of fine quality, Jupiter's slumber song in *Philemon et Baucis* and *Vision fugitive* in *Herodiade* being models of fine *cantilena*.

PIERRE GAILHARD

PIERRE GAILHARD was one of the great names at Covent Garden from 1879 till 1883, and was principal bass at the Paris Opera, of which he became director on his retirement. Like Maurel he was a pupil of Faure. During his London engagements he sang both the bass roles in *Les Huguenots*, in *Faust*, *Der Freischutz*, *Don Giovanni*, *Semiramide*, *Le Prophete*, *Mignon*, *Seraglio*, *L'Etoile du Nord*, *Mefistofele* and *La Gazza Ladra*. Gailhard's records were Fonotipia, very rare, but may be heard as transferred to LP, fortunately agreeable to hear.

GIOVANNI GRAVINA

GIOVANNI GRAVINA. I am assured by those who should know that records by Gravina reveal a bass of quite exceptional quality. He made three records only—for red G&T, the Invocation in *Robert le Diable* and the air of Alvise in *La Gioconda* and another, the first of which appeared in the first English red label catalogue in 1902. I trust that my informants heard Gravina's singing from original records, as I should be sorry to judge him from the over-pitched LP which is all that I have heard.

MARCEL JOURNET

MARCEL JOURNET's undeserved fate in the early days of his great career was to serve as a sort of understudy to Plancon. He came to Covent Garden in 1897, and later succeeded Plancon as principal bass. Like all good basses (and most tenors too) Journet appeared impressively bearded, to the great advantage of the spectacle, and saving us from the awful sameness of unprepossessing shaven faces. This fashion added greatly to Journet's vivid and vital personality, and it may have been his successor Marcoux—a bass of dry voice and austere personality—who set the fashion of shaven basses.[1]

[1] Of all the wilful and perverse affronts to operatic tradition which have been afflicted on us, surely none have surpassed the presumption of presenting a bare-faced Flying Dutchman, which not only was in defiance of Wagner's explicit instruction, but would seem to have been beyond the Dutchman's contriving.

ORESTE LUPPI

ORESTE LUPPI was another well-bearded *basso* in the old tradition, and who was known to us for some time before we saw him. For he was Fonotipia's star bass, and his records which date from the company's beginnings were of fine quality and splendid execution. It would be some exaggeration to say that he was the equal in quality of Arimondi or Journet, without mentioning Plancon, for his voice had a quality of dryness which, judged by our standards, was something below the best. This is not to say that Luppi was not one of the true operatic basses, for his very presence on the stage carried the certainty of a fine performance. There was more than a hint of Arimondi in the ease and flexibility of his delivery, and he sang with a clarity and sonority only to be heard in the true bass. Luppi appeared at Covent Garden in 1907, with the Fonotipia representative already mentioned (see under Bassi).

WATKIN MILLS

WATKIN MILLS was the last, perhaps, of the true Handelian basses, by which I mean those basses who devoted their careers to perfecting their execution of the Handelian idiom, and not merely capable singers who would undertake *The Elijah* or *Messiah* when invited to do so. Watkin Mills' massive and perfectly trained voice was one of the delights of the late Victorian musical festivals. In no musical form is the loss of tradition more startlingly apparent today than the singing of oratorio, for no longer is it studied by singers or musical directors as a separate art form. In Victorian times the first object in view was an understanding of the correct manner of delivering the sacred text, which implied a deep feeling for the symmetrical architecture of the work as a whole, a crystal clarity of utterance, both of words and music, and perfect definition in divisions. No departures from accepted *tempi* were tolerated.

Watkin Mills fulfilled these requirements to perfection, as well as possessing a terrific physical strength to support the tense flexibility of delivery and the spontaneous joy of utterance that so greatly distinguished the master singer. No oratorio singer of his time, not even Santley, sang with a greater weight of authority, and those of us who remember him could comfortably feel certain that if any conductor had been in need of correction, Mills would have administered it in no uncertain manner. The records were Odeon, of about 1907–8 and despite their terrible orchestral accompaniments, are of the greatest possible value to those who may wish to study traditional oratorio singing.

FRANCESCO NAVARRINI

FRANCESCO NAVARRINI, strictly speaking, falls just outside our scope, his records being of the Fonotipia 62 series and therefore presumably of post-1907. However, Bennett has stated that 1907 was the date, and I do not doubt that he was right—it would be somewhere right on the borderline. The Fono illustrated catalogue dated January 1907 does not mention any records of the 62 series, and neither does my appendix, but oddly enough, Navarrini's name is found in the consolidated list of Fonotipia artists on the cover, rather strongly suggesting that the records were taken perhaps some considerable time before their issue. Now that advanced collectors are giving ever greater attention to records which hitherto had escaped the limelight it is natural that Navarrini should be favoured, and it is more than likely that these collectors know a great deal more about him than I do.

In 1907 he was fifty-two, which speaks volumes for the glorious quality of his voice even at such an age, and which makes one incline to the belief in an earlier recording date, though even so it is the voice of a singer in his prime. One could hardly over-estimate the beauty of Navarrini's voice and style, the controlled phrasing and the unfailing artistry, but the importance of judging him from an original record needs stressing, as a LP which I also heard was much over-pitched—the same applying to Gravina, which I heard only through this dubious medium. The disservice which has been done where "engineers" have taken the place of artists is serious, and one hopes that errors in this direction will be detected and liquidated.

Navarrini sang the role of Ludovico at the *premiere* of *Otello*, and it is a curious circumstance that a "Signor Navarrini" sang the same role in Zenatello's all-time debut season as Otello at Covent Garden in 1908—but quite evidently not the same.

I have used the spelling "Navarrini" in preference to the obviously misprinted label in which one "R" is omitted. The Fono catalogue, prospectus, and the "*Otello*" vocal score may safely be accepted.

POL PLANCON

POL PLANCON, by common consent, ranks as the greatest bass of our period. It would not be possible to compare him with Edouard de Reszke in point of musicianship, but for the pitch of perfection to which he had brought his wonderful organ he was surely unique among basses. The tone quality was wonderful in itself, but no other than a virtuoso of the voice could have brought it under such control or have given to it so varied a range of tone colour. His singing was a model for all types, for it was classically correct—in slow passages he demonstrated the true meaning of *legato*, in dramatic scenes he pointed every phrase, and he could execute *coloratura* with wonderful skill, having a shake of the genuine kind. There was a flexibility and resiliency about his production by which he was immediately recognised,

138

and at all times he showed a deep artistic feeling for his music. Plancon seemed to add something vital to everything he sang, and it is inevitable that history will acclaim him as the most distinguished among basses. Needless to add, he was traditionally bearded.

Records

It was natural that Plancon should have been included in the group of G&T's original red label artists, and on the first appearance of their records, the idea of being able to hear the great Plancon on the gramophone was something too exciting to be missed. So famous was his Mephistopheles that his *Faust* excerpts attracted immediate attention, and in both the *Veau d'or* and the *Serenade* he has never been equalled. Following a second issue in 1903, he recorded exclusively for Victor, the greater part of his repertoire being issued in Europe as Victor-G&T. Of the original series the air in *Le Caid* is an excellent example of his many-sided gifts, and the air of Vulcan in *Philemon et Baucis*, although most unnecessarily cut, is another with a strong appeal. The 12-in. Victor-G&Ts were a magnificent group, from the solemn grandeur of Gounod's *Le Vallon* to the cheerful Husbandman's Song in Haydn's *Creation* it would be impossible to pick any under tip-top form. A final choice, however, might fall on Flegier's *Le Cor*, recorded in 1905 in which all Plancon's art is shown at its best and most mature—colour, phrasing, *sostenuto*, and over all that sense of sheer style only to be heard in artists of the highest class.

All admirers of this great singer—and who is not?—will have their own recorded favourites, the *Faust* excerpts are naturally model renderings, and the weight and serenity of the *Magic Flute* airs beyond praise or criticism. In songs of lighter texture, such as *Le Soupir*, *Embarquez vous*, or *Au pays bleu* Plancon employed his huge resources with a delicacy and charm which proved his versatility, and his rendering of Gounod's *Nazareth* was massive and mellifluous.

A sketch by Phil May showing the whole cast of Faust
apparently singing the Soldiers Chorus: left to right:
Brazzi, Plancon, de Vigne, Ancona, Eames, Saleza (*Punch*
May 22, 1897)

A Covent Garden group from *Punch* of July 27, 1904.
Foreground, left to right: Kirkby Lunn, Calve, Caruso,
Gilibert, Van Rooy, Melba, Alten, Scotti. *Background,*
(*left to right*) Alice Nielsen, Parkina, Suzanne Adams,
Journet, Herold, Destinn, Van Duyke.

INSTRUMENTAL AND SPOKEN RECORDS

THE RECORDINGS of instruments during the G&T period was not so successful as to warrant a detailed examination, but a very brief survey may be acceptable.

The violinist Kubelik was then at the height of his great popularity, and G&T recorded him on red label for the 1902 catalogue. Of the two titles, St. Lubin's arrangement of the sextet in *Lucia di Lammermoor* for unaccompanied violin was, even by today's standard an astounding *tour de force*. Although it was hardly possible to appreciate it on machines of the old type, it now stands out as a seemingly incredible piece of fiddling, the melody weaving in and out of massive double-stopping, variations, harmonics, and sometimes a *pizzicato* accompaniment to his own double-stopping with trilling added.

More solid fare is provided by Josef Joachim, the *doyen* of violinists of his time. These also were on red label, but made in 1903, at the same time as the records of Santley. I had the privilege as a schoolboy of hearing Joachim when he came at the invitation of his old friend Paul David, our head music-master, son to Ferdinand—and all friends of Brahms, to bring his quartet to the school concert hall, and although too juvenile to appreciate it fully, I recall it very clearly.

Joachim's handling of Brahms' Hungarian Dance in G minor is monumental, played in his own arrangement, with the sonority of his glorious Stradivari pealing like an organ; and his records, alone of early violin recordings, did reproduce a genuine violin quality, and comment by him is clearly audible at the finish.

Other well-known players who made records for G&T included Sarasate, Drdla, Marie Hall, Kreisler and Von Vecsey when a "child prodigy". How right was Gaisberg in his book that with electrical recording the true violin quality (as recorded in the Heifetz period) was lost for ever.

*   *   *   *

Some of the spoken records of the turn of the century period have much interest. Those of Sarah Bernhardt are surely great prizes. These were made on French G&T, and although not powerful, and to our ears somewhat monotonous, they are true records of the greatest tragedienne of our time. On Fonotipia we have the voice of Sardou, the French playwright of the lurid dramas in which the divine Sarah thrilled her audiences both in Paris and in London. The only red label speaking records were made in 1902 by "Carmen Sylva", the *nom-de-guerre* of the Queen of Roumania who was known as a poetess, and these were of considerable beauty, for her voice is well reproduced and her diction quite beautiful.

Of the English actors of pre-eminence, the greatest in the recording field was without question Beerbohm Tree, or Sir Herbert as he became. Tree carried on the Irving tradition of spectacle and large-scale drama, with a versatility which Irving did not wholly possess. Irving's extraordinary personality and even more extraordinary voice sufficed to establish him as the greatest of English actors, but Tree managed to isolate his innumerable characters from himself and from each other, and created a gallery of contrasting portraits without parallel since the days of Charles Matthews. The day of the actor manager was indisputably the day of great acting, for this race of stage giants held the doctrine that an actor's business was to act, with an appearance appropriate to the character, and to make himself both seen and heard. Tree's skill in disguise was truly astounding, and in case it may be objected that disguise was not the same thing as acting, the range of his records was such that the contrasts between them might defy detection from the voice alone, which must of necessity omit the touches of genius which he gave to his portrayals. Thus, in his G&T records of 1906 few listeners today would readily recognise the voice that spoke in the character of Falstaff as being the same as that of Svengali—one of Tree's greatest successes—or the two similar voices used in such differing manner as in Mark Anthony's lament and the calm reflectiveness of "To be or not to be". The period of ridiculing Tree by those who never saw him nor could hope to imitate him, may, it is to be hoped, be on the wane, and there are signs that he is again becoming an entity in public consciousness.

The voice of Ellen Terry was recorded too late to show its beauty; but there was a 10-in. G&T of 1902-3 by Lady Bancroft speaking two short poems in a richly arch manner, its number being G.C. 1238. It was an opportunity missed that Sir Squire was not induced to record also, especially a scene with his wife. I recall seeing them in a box some time after their retirement, watching their illustrious contemporary Mrs. Kendal. Although I had never previously seen him, the luxuriant white hair, the black moustache and rimmed monocle with its wide black ribbon could not have belonged to any other.

Sir Charles Wyndham, the first actor to be knighted in the new century, might be called the successor to Sir Squire Bancroft, although formerly contemporary with him. This suave and polished high-comedian recorded for Berliner in 1898 an extract from Tom Robertson's *David Garrick*, which was his greatest acting success, and frequently revived in periods of doldrum. The handling of the name-part required a very special style, without which it would flop badly, but the sheer grace and charm of Wyndham's polished manner carried its mechanical artifices through without question.

Lewis Waller, who graduated under Tree, rivalled Forbes Robertson as the greatest of elocutionists, and in Tree's stupendous production of *The Three Musketeers* it was Waller as Buckingham who was most admired. Tree's d'Artagnan has been dismissed as negligible by later commentators—who probably never saw it—a view from which I most emphatically dissent. Superb also as Brutus in Tree's *Julius Caesar* of 1899 (it was Shakespeare's also, which might have been overlooked) Waller certainly outshone Tree's Mark Anthony. On entering into management himself, Waller had two reliable stand-bys in *Henry V* and *Monsieur Beaucaire*. His elocution in Shakespeare attracted all his admirers, whether Shakespeareans or not; and in the French period piece his ovation never failed him.

There was no more genuinely amusing comedian than G. P. Huntley, who played a high-life type very much in his own manner which could appeal only to English audiences. His only record (G&T) was a duologue on a golf course in *Three Little Maids*: "Stymied, was he? I thought he looked a bit funny at lunch".

There was a duologue between Fred Terry and Julia Neilson from their perennial success *The Scarlet Pimpernel*—not a play I particularly cared for. For me there were none in their repertoire to equal *Sweet Nell of Old Drury*, a romantic drama of Nell Gwyn and Charles. I saw it first just sixty years ago, and returned the following week. While on leave from the Flanders front in 1915 I took my fiancee; and in about 1930 we took our son. Fred and Julia were a little older, but not much. Long after Fred's death, and Julia was in retirement we eventually met, and I told her all about it, and how she was my first love, always with her picture postcard in my pocket-book—adding for the sake of honesty and truth that I had made the same avowal to Ellaline Terriss.

Julia was not a great actress, but a very good one, and perhaps the best remembered of her time. She had the advantage of large features, and she used them. She used the whole of the stage, with just that amount of exaggeration in speech and gesture which enabled the audience to hear what she was saying and to see what she was doing. I just can't imagine what modern producers would make of Julia Neilson—or she of them! She had a beautiful mezzo singing voice, which she used in the plays, and the specially composed "Nell Gwyn's Song" by Raymond Roze remains one of my most nostalgic memories. She recorded her singing voice for Berliner, and one of these has survived—*The Cuckoo Song*.

Fred Terry, who was Julia's husband, and father of Dennis and Phyllis Neilson-Terry, besides being the youngest brother of Ellen, was a magnificent Shakespearean actor. He, also, had the large features of so many stage celebrities, was quite absurdly handsome, and had a fine speaking voice and very clear enunciation. I met him after that occasion in 1930, and was much impressed by his very kindly and dignified bearing. I have a long letter from him in which he said that although they had always had to work very hard, they loved every moment of it. On going into management they confined themselves to period drama, and good—that is, paying—examples were not easy to find. In consequence they spent much time "on the road", where the quality of the play mattered less, but were sure of their welcome on their returns to the West End; and if a production went wrong, as Fred said, there was always *Sweet Nell* and *The Scarlet Pimpernel* to restore the money chest.

Fred and Julia were a unique combination on the English stage, and nothing like them has been seen since.

For a full and wholly fascinating account of their lives in the theatre, Julia's book of reminiscence *This for Remembrance* cannot be too highly recommended—if copies can be found.

MUSICAL COMEDY

MUSICAL COMEDY at the turn of the century succeeded the great vogue of Burlesque which flourished at the old Gaiety. It had nothing in common with a present-day "Musical". It was not until about 1914 that the Gramophone company turned to the idea of recording the stage performers in the countless delightful songs in which musical comedy was so rich in the pre-jazz—in fact pre-ragtime—age, and surprisingly little was recorded at all. The wondrous Edna May made a Berliner from *The Belle of New York*, and Connie Ediss of the old Gaiety also left a few relics. Otherwise there was little enough. Evie Greene recorded a good rendering from her creation *A Country Girl*— she was a good singer—and Louie Freear, a feminine low comedian, with no voice at all, made a few not very articulate examples of her style. Marie Tempest, then a brilliant musical comedy lead, recorded (subject to correction) one song only from her creation of *The Geisha*, and the exquisite but now contemned *Merrie England* was then represented only by *The Yeomen of England* sung by the original Essex, Henry Lytton, though neither he nor Isabel Jay were yet identified with musical comedy, although in due course they drifted into it. The popular Maurice Farkoa moved from Berliner to G&T, and that, I think, is all there is to chronicle about the recording of one of the most lovable memories of the Edwardian London theatre, and which, except for some good examples by Fraser-Simpson, did not survive the first war.

But I am not forgetting Ellaline Terriss of affectionate memory, who recorded in 1903 and 1906 some charming echoes of her charming self, in pleasantly sentimental songs which she sang without sentimentality.

K

MUSIC HALL

THE defunct English institution the Music Hall was in its heyday when recording began, and G&T may be thanked for their far greater objectivity in their attitude to it than in the case of muscial comedy. The Music Hall stars were real stars—not just anybody—and were a race apart, with a technique all their own. London was their hunting ground, spreading to all parts. From the Music Halls were recruited the principals for the Christmas pantomimes—dames, demon kings, princes, babes and the like, and of all these the greatest partnership was Dan Leno and Herbert Campbell at Drury Lane. Even today most people have heard of Marie Lloyd—saucy and as clever as they came—Vesta Tilley, one of the aristocracy of the Halls; Mark Sheridan, irresistibly funny if less aristocratic; Gus Elen, the tough old coster; Arthur Roberts on board H.M.S. *Irresponsible*; Lil Hawthorne, serio-comic or "serio" for short, although neither one nor the other, but much beloved; Eugene Stratton, the king of coon singers and creator of *Dolly Daydream, Lily of Laguna* and *The Coon Drum Major*; G. H. Chirguin, the "white-eyed Kaffir", in reality a good old cockney type with his one-stringed fiddle and *The Blind Boy*. Victoria Monks, another "serio", and that true old trouper Vesta Victoria whose ma pinched her young man. Oh dear! there is enough material here to fill a book.

Is it necessary to apologise for this rather personal survey of a very precious youthful memory? It is part of a picture, and it reflects a very special and characteristic phase of what was certainly the most wonderful epoch of our era—that period of peace, prosperity, spaciousness, brilliance, "happy-go-lucky" and "devil-may-care", but oh, how short—the Edwardian decade

APPENDIX

NOTE ON APPENDIX

THERE can be no very obvious formula for a method of selecting records for inclusion in this Appendix, nor is it easy to define what is its exact purpose; but I expect an Appendix will be considered necessary, and I rather agree. It is a "collector's" Appendix and not a discographer's, which means that it is intended to be characteristic rather than complete.

I am showing some temerity in suggesting correct playing speeds where I have felt able to do so, and since speed (i.e. r.p.m.) governs pitch, the importance of this is obvious, especially since we can find no direct authority beyond the erratic and therefore unreliable directions issued by the G&T company in some of their catalogues. (What a lot of painful research and speculation would have been saved if the companies had printed the dates and correct speeds on their labels.) I assume all these records to have been sung in their original keys, having found no occasion for thinking otherwise, and I am full of scepticism when I hear of music having been transposed to suit certain singers. To me, it is merely a matter of a record being played too slowly—as simple as that. Not being afflicted with perfect pitch, I am dependant on my piano for fixing r.p.m. to match keys, and while there exists the possibility of error, it would not, I think, be of such an extent as to falsify the key.

One cannot guess what method was used in the early days for determining r.p.m. The first disc machines were without calibrated regulators, and we would occasionally check up our machine's performance with the aid of a watch! Fonotipia were silent on the subject, but as a general rule, G&T tended to slow speeds and Fono to high, and it is not even certain that a consistent speed was maintained even throughout a session. I stand wide open to correction by those with better ears than mine on matters of pitch, and I very vividly remember a well-known conductor who was listening to some "London Reds" I was proudly demonstrating at Broadcasting House who asked "why are we playing this record in the key of E-flat major instead of C?"—the reason being that the B.B.C.'s player was fixed at 78 r.p.m.

147

But these are matters on which collectors generally prefer to trust to their own ears, and perhaps also to what they have become accustomed to, but when a bass comes over like a baritone or a tenor like a soprano, the presumption—even probability—is that there is something wrong.

*   *   *   *   *

Without soliciting sympathy for my views I have latterly been assailed by doubts about the propriety of disinterring unpublished recordings, as these were generally faulty in some degree, and to dig them up and distribute them seems unfair to all concerned—with one shining exception, in which Melba sang a false note and can distinctly be heard to say "Now I shall have to sing it all over again"!

For these reasons, then, I have omitted unpublished records from the Appendix.

SOPRANOS

SUZANNE ADAMS

RED LABEL, G&T. LONDON, 1902

			R.P.M.
3291	Jewel Song, *Faust*	Gounod	78
3292	Coquette	Stern	75
3293	Valse aria, *Romeo et Juliette*	Gounod	74
3294	Home, Sweet Home	Bishop	75
3295	Printemps nouveau	Vidal	75

There was a second recording of Home, Sweet Home under the same numbers, but on black label. Both the rendering and the accompanying are different.

EMMA ALBANI

RED LABEL, G&T. LONDON, 1904

			R.P.M.
3505	Home, Sweet Home	Bishop	76
3540	Robin Adair		
53325	Ombra mai fu	Handel	
03014	Angels ever bright and fair	Handel	

TERESA ARKEL

BLACK LABEL, G&T. MILAN, 1903

53312	Spunta l'aurora pallida, *Mefistofele*	Boito
53315	Preghiera, *Norma*	Bellini
053004	Tacea la notte, *Trovatore*	Verdi

1904–5

53385	Strofe d'Alice, *Robert le Diable*	Meyerbeer
53405	Porgi Amor, *Nozze di Figaro*	Mozart
53406	Toglietemi la vita ancor	Scarlatti
053039	Cieli azzuri, *Aida*	Verdi
053059	Canto di Veneri, *Tannhauser*	Wagner
053060	Aria del Sonno, *L'Africaine*	Meyerbeer
053061	Casta Diva, *Norma*	Bellini
053062	Quant'e bello, *Lucrezia Borgia*	Donizetti

FONOTIPIA, MILAN, 1904–5

39360	D'amor sull' ali, *Trovatore*	Verdi
39361	Siccome un di, *Pescatori di Perle*	Bizet
39386	L'altra notte, *Mefistofele*	Boito
39447	Ebben! Ne andro lontana, *Wally*	Catalani

SIGRID ARNOLDSON
RED LABEL, G&T. BERLIN, 1906

			R.P.M.
33609	Seguidilla, *Carmen*	Bizet	76
33610	Habanera, *Carmen*	Bizet	
33611	Serenade	Gounod	
33612	Connais tu le pays, *Mignon*	Thomas	
33613	Jewel Song, *Faust*	Gounod	
43777	Echo Song	Eckert	
53465	Bolero, *Vespri Siciliani*	Verdi	
53466	Voi – chc sapete, *Nozze di Figaro*	Mozart	
53467	Ah fors' e lui, *Traviata*	Verdi	
83597	Fjorton Ar, (Swedish Song)	Dannstrom	

MARIA BARRIENTOS
FONOTIPIA, MILAN, 1903

			R.P.M.
39010	Son vergine vezzosa, *Puritani*	Bellini	80
39011	Ah non giunge, *Sonnambula*	Bellini	
39012	Voci di Primavera	J. Strauss	
39013	Bell Song, *Lakme*	Delibes	
39026	Deh vieni non tardar, *Nozze di Figaro*	Mozart	
	1904		
39457	Come per me sereno, *Sonnambula*	Bellini	
39458	Sovra il sen, *Sonnambula*	Bellini	
39459	Una voce poco fa, *Barbiere de Siviglia*	Rossini	
39460	Io sono docile, *Barbiere di Siviglia*	Rossini	
39461	Io son Titania, *Mignon*	Thomas	
39462	Solveig's Song, *Peer Gynt*	Grieg	
39463	No se que siento, *Chateau-Margaux*	Caballero	
39464	(a) Las hijas del Zebedeo	Chapi	
	(b) Artistas en miniatura	Hernandez	
39465	Air of Armida, *Rinaldo*	Handel	
39480	El cabo primero	Caballero	
39503	Ombra leggera, *Dinorah*	Meyerbeer	
39504	Qui sola soletta, *Dinorah*	Meyerbeer	
39538	Or son las, *Fra Diavolo*	Auber	
39539	Gia per la danza, *Fra Diavolo*	Auber	
39542	Caro Nome, *Rigoletto*	Verdi	
39543	Tutte le feste, *Rigoletto*	Verdi	
69002	Ombra leggera, *Dinorah*	Meyerbeer	
	1905		
39825	Sulla tomba, *Lucia di Lammermoor* (with Zenatello)	Donizetti	

GEMMA BELLINCIONI
RED LABEL, G&T. MILAN, 1903

053014	O grandi occhi lucenti, *Fedora*	Giordano
053017	L'altra notte, *Mefistofele*	Boito
053018	Voi lo sapete, *Cavalleria Rusticana*	Mascagni
053019	Ah fors' e lui, *Traviata*	Verdi

The *Mefistofele* and *Cavalleria items only were issued in England, in February, 1905, and were withdrawn in March, 1906.*

CELESTINA BONINSEGNA
RED LABEL, G&T. MILAN, 1904

R.P.M.

53372	In quello trine morbide, *Manon Lescaut*	Puccini	76
53373	Suicidio, *Gioconda*	Ponchielli	
53374	Letter Song, *Le Maschere*	Mascagni	
53375	D'Amor Sull' Ali, *Trovatore*	Verdi	
53376	Voi lo sapete, *Cavalleria Rusticana*	Mascagni	
53392	Ninna Nanna	Leoncavallo	
54056	Miserere, *Trovatore* (with Vals)	Verdi	
053049	O Patria mia, *Aida*	Verdi	
053050	Casta Diva, *Norma*	Bellini	
054043	Tardi si fa, *Faust* (with de Lucia)	Gounod	
054044	Il ciel, *Aida* (with Vals)	Verdi	

1905

53415	Morro ma prima in grazia, *Ballo in maschera*	Verdi
53416	La vergine degli Angeli, *Forza del Destino*	Verdi
53417	Ernani involami, *Ernani*	Verdi
53418	Quai celesti concenti, *L'Africaine*	Meyerbeer
53419	Bolero, *Vespri Siciliani*	Verdi

1906

053063	Tacea la notte, *Trovatore*	Verdi
053065	Ma dall' arrido stelo, *Ballo in maschera*	Verdi
053067	Madre pietosa, *Forza del Destino*	Verdi
053068	Gia l'odio m'abbandona, *L'Africaine*	Meyerbeer
054062	Sal quel di che t'ho veduta, *Ernani* (with Cigada)	Verdi
54264	Mira d'acerbe lagrima, *Trovatore* (with Cigada)	Verdi
54266	Vivra contende il giubilo, *Trovatore* (with Cigada)	Verdi

1907

53481	Al bello a me ritorna, *Norma*	Bellini
53492	Te solo	Sabaino
053088	Pace mio Dio, *Forza del Destino*	Verdi
053089	Madre pietosa, *Forza del Destino*	Verdi
053101	Notturno	Cantoni
054097	Deh non volerli vittime, *Norma* (with Collazza and de Segurola)	Bellini
054098	Non sa tu, *Sallo in maschera* (with Ischierdo)	Verdi
054109	O dolce voluta, *Ruy Blas* (with Collazza)	Marchetti

OLIMPIA BORONAT
RED LABEL, G&T. ST. PETERSBURG, 1904

R.P.M.

23420	The Nightingale	Alabieff	76
53346	Sempre libera, *Traviata*	Verdi	
53347	Senza l'Amore	Tosti	
53348	Caro Nome, *Rigoletto*	Verdi	
53349	Valse, *Mireille*	Gounod	
53350	Air, *Zabava*	Ivanow	
53351	Qui la voce (andante), *Puritani*	Bellini	
53352	Desiderio	Zardo	
53353	Cavatina, *Pescatori di Perle*	Bizet	
53354	Rose Aria, *Marta*	Flotow	

EUGENIA BURZIO

FONOTIPIA. MILAN, 1904

			R.P.M.
39513	Ma dall'arrido stelo, *Ballo in maschera*	Verdi	80
39514	Mezzanotte, *Ballo in maschera*	Verdi	
	1907		
39934	Tacea la notte, *Trovatore*	Verdi	

Also duets with Zenatello and Magini-Coletti.

EMMA CALVE

RED LABEL, G&T. LONDON, 1902

			R.P.M.
3281	Habanera, *Carmen*	Bizet	76
3282	Magali (Provencal Song)		
3283	Enchantement	Massenet	
3284	Serenade, *Zanetto*	Massenet	
3285	Seguidilla, *Carmen*	Bizet	
3286	Voi lo sapete, *Cavalleria Rusticana*	Mascagni	

There are two recordings of 3285 under the same numbers and evidently made at the same time. One of these probably was not intended for issue.

EMMA CARELLI

RED LABEL, G&T. MILAN, 1904

53341	Vissi d'arte, *Tosca*	Puccini
053028	Voi lo sapete, *Cavalleria Rusticana*	Mascagni
053029	Addio, *Boheme*	Puccini
053032	Addio piccolo desco, *Manon*	Massenet
053033	La piovra, *Iris*	Mascagni
053034	La mamma morta, *Andrea Chenier*	Giordano
053035	Dopo	Tosti
053036	Marechiare	Tosti
054026	Scena della bagno, *Lorenza* (with Sammarco)	Mascheroni
054028	Gia midicon venal, *Tosca* (with Sammarco)	Puccini
054034	Morte di Fedora, *Fedora* (with Ventura)	Giordano

FONOTIPIA. MILAN, 1906

39647	Nel suo amor, *Siberia*	Giordano
39648	Non odi la il martir, *Siberia*	Giordano
39649	Vissi d'arte, *Tosca*	Puccini
39650	Ancor son io, *Manon*	Massenet
39730	Suicidio, *Gioconda*	Ponchielli
39731	Dopo	Tosti
39734	Io sono l'umile, *Adriana Lecouvreur*	Cilea
39735	Poveri fiori, *Adriana Lecouvreur*	Cilea

ZELIE DE LUSSAN

RED LABEL, VICTOR. 1903

2187	Lili	Guetary
2188	Connais tu le pays ? *Mignon*	Thomas
2198	Habanera, *Carmen*	Bizet
2199	Rosy Morn	Ronald
2301	La Paloma	Yradier

BEKA GRAND, 1906

8312	**Tribut de Zamora**	Gounod
8313	**Habanera,** *Carmen*	Bizet
8314	**Styrienne,** *Mignon*	Thomas
8315	**I know a lovely garden**	D'Hardelot

None of de Lussan's records were issued in England.

EMMA DESTINN

BLACK LABEL, COLUMBIA. BERLIN, 1904

R.P.M.

40483	**Habanera,** *Carmen*	Bizet	76
40587	**Kennst du das Land?** *Mignon*	Thomas	
40588	**In Kahn**	Grieg	

The following Fonotipias, although sung in German, were labelled as from Milan. They were soon afterwards issued from Berlin as Odeon. The unnumbered titles, although here entered as Fonotipia, may have belonged to the extensive Odeon recordings which it is not thought necessary to include here.

There were also many recordings by the Gramophone Company and other manufacturers of later dates, including an interesting and historically significant Aida-Amneris duet with Kirkby Lunn of about 1910–11.

FONOTIPIA. 1904

R.P.M.

39417	**Ritorna vincitor,** *Aida* (sung in German), Pt. 1	Verdi	85
39418	**Ritorna vincitor,** *Aida* (sung in German), Pt. 2	Verdi	85
39420	**Kennst du das land ?** *Mignon*	Thomas	85
39422	**Styrienne,** *Mignon*	Thomas	85
–	**From "Das Hohe Lied"**	Mendelssohn	
–	**Air,** *The Bartered Bride*	Smetana	
–	**Aufenthalt**	Schubert	
–	**Die liebe Farbe**	Schubert	

EMMA EAMES

RED LABEL, VICTOR-G&T. U.S.A., 1904–1905

R.P.M.

043058	**Still wie die Nacht**	Bohm	76–78
03041	(*a*) **L'Incredule** (Hahn)	Beach	
	(*b*) **The year's at the spring**	Beach	
03042	**Ave Maria**	Gounod	
03043	**Good-bye**	Tosti	
03044	(*a*) **Star-spangled Banner**		
	(*b*) **Dixie**		
03045	**Who is Sylvia?**	Schubert	
033013	**Jewel Song,** *Faust*	Gounod	
033014	**Elegie**	Massenet	
033015	**Valse Aria,** *Romeo et Juliette*	Gounod	
053058	**Vissi d'arte,** *Tosca*	Puccini	

1906

033018	Elegie (with 'cello obl. by Hollmann)	Massenet
033019	Chanson d'Amour (with 'cello obl. by Hollmann)	Hollmann
033020	Micaela's Air, *Carmen*	Bizet
033022	Valse Aria, *Romeo et Juliette*	Gounod
033023	Jewel Song, *Faust*	Gounod
033024	Le Roi de Thule, *Faust*	Gounod
03067	Ave Maria (with 'cello obl. by Hollmann)	Gounod
053091	Ave Maria, *Otello*	Verdi
053092	Voi lo sapete, *Cavalleria Rusticana*	Mascagni
054071	La ci darem, *Don Giovanni* (with de Gogorza)	Mozart
054072	La dove prende, *Flauto Magico* (with de Gogorza)	Mozart
034000	Le Crucifix (with de Gogorza)	Faure

1907 GREEN LABEL

034015	Trio finale, *Faust* (with Dalmores and Plancon)	Gounod

ALICE ESTY

BLACK LABEL, G&T. LONDON, 1904

			R.P.M.
3568	I dreamt that I dwelt, *Bohemian Girl*	Balfe	76
3569	Waltz Song, *Romeo and Juliette*	Gounod	
3570	Scenes that are brightest, *Maritana*	Wallace	
3571	The Night was calm, *Trovatore*	Verdi	

1905

3585	Elizabeth's Greeting, *Tannhauser*	Wagner
03038	Breeze of the Night, *Trovatore*	Verdi
03039	Elsa's Dream, *Lohengrin*	Wagner
03040	Sweet Spirit hear my prayer, *Lurline*	Wallace

CESIRA FERRANI

BLACK LABEL, G&T. MILAN, 1903

53281	Mi chiamano Mimi, *Boheme*	Puccini
53282	Addio, *Boheme*	Puccini
53283	In quelle trina morbide, *Manon Lescaut*	Puccini
53284	Addio piccolo desco, *Manon*	Massenet
53285	L'altra notte, *Mefistofele*	Boito
53286	Se tu m'ami	Pergolesi
53287	Serenata inutile	Brahms
54035	Tardi si fa, *Faust* (with Apostolu)	Gounod

EVANGELINE FLORENCE

BLACK LABEL, G&T. LONDON, 1902

			R.P.M.
3421	April Morn	Batten	74
3438	The Swallows	Cowan	
3442	Grande Valse	Verzano	
3443	Charming Bird, *Pearl of Brazil*	David	

MARIA GALVANY

BLACK LABEL, G&T. MILAN, 1903

53293	Caro Nome, *Rigoletto*	Verdi
53295	Rondo, *Sonnambula*	Bellini
53296	Variations	Proch
53297	Una voce, *Il Barbiere*	Rossini

RED LABEL, G&T. MILAN, 1907

53482	Gli angui dell' inferno, *Flauto Magico*	Mozart
53483	Valse, *Mireille*	Gounod
53484	Una voce, *Il Barbiere*	Rossini
53485	Qui la voce, *Puritani*	Bellini
54315	Veglia o donna, *Rigoletto* (with Ruffo)	Verdi
54316	Si vendetta, *Rigoletto* (with Ruffo)	Verdi
054000	Piangi fanciulla, *Rigoletto* (with Ruffo)	Verdi
054001	Dite alla giovine, *Traviata* (with Ruffo)	Verdi
054110	Chieda all'ura, *L'Elisir d'amore*	Donizetti
054111	Tornami dir che m'amo, *Don Pasquale* (with Giorgini)	Donizetti
054112	Son geloso dello zeffiro, *Sonnambula* (with Giorgini)	Bellini

Also several pre-dog records of 1908 including duets with Marconi and de Lucia.

MARY GARDEN

BLACK LABEL, G&T. PARIS, 1904

33447	Melisande's Song, *Pelleas et Melisande*	Debussy
33449	Ariette 1	Debussy
33450	Ariette 2	Debussy
33451	Ariette 3	Debussy

The above were accompanied by the composer.

SALOMEA KRUSZELNICKA

RED LABEL, G&T. WARSAW, 1903

			R.P.M.
23355	L'alta notte, *Mefistofele*	Boito	73
23356	Zobaczycie		
23359	Amore amor	Tirindelli	
23360	Melodia	Quaranta	
23361	Solveig's Song, *Peer Gynt*	Grieg	
23362	Vizzi d'arte, *Tosca*	Puccini	

Also two Polish songs of same series.

FONOTIPIA. 1906 (as Krusceniski)

			R.P.M.
39908	Di Dice	Quaranta	80
39909	Capelli d'oro	Oddone	
39919	Ebben ? Ne andro lontana, *Wally*	Catalani	
39920	Lasciali dir tu m'ami	Quaranta	
39921	L'altra notte, *Mefistofele*	Boito	
39922	Io sono l'umile, a ancell, *Andriana Lecouvreur*	Cilea	

SELMA KURZ

RED LABEL, G&T. VIENNA, 1906–7

			R.P.M.
53494	Ah non giunge, *Sonnambula*	Bellini	76
43885	Der Vogel im Valde	Taubert	
33592	Vilanelle	Dell'Acqua	
43737	Styrienne, *Mignon*	Thomas	
43738	Saper vorreste, *Ballo in maschera*	Verdi	
43739	Queen of Night aria, *Magic Flute*	Mozart	
53431	Caro Nome, *Rigoletto*	Verdi	
43887	Legends, *Lakme*	Delibes	
43897	Mad Scene, *Lucia di Lammermoor*	Donizetti	
43898	Ave Maria	Tosti	
53486	Il Pensieroso	Handel	
53491	Parla, Valse	Arditi	
54396	Air de Mysoli, *Perle de Brasil*	David	

LILLI LEHMANN

BLUE LABEL, ODEON. BERLIN, 1905

50071	Long, long ago	Traditional
50078	Air, Egmont	Beethoven
50094	Auf dem Wasser zu singen	Schubert
50096	Ave Maria	Gounod
50097	Robin Adair	
50098	Air of Anna, *Don Giovanni*, Pt. 1	Mozart
50099	Air of Anna, *Don Giovanni*, Pt. 2	Mozart
50100	Im kahn	Grieg
80003	Air, *Traviata*	Verdi
80004	Erlkonig	Schubert

1907

50353	Ah fors' e lui, *Traviata*, Pt. 1	Verdi
50354	Ah fors' e lui, *Traviata*, Pt. 2	Verdi
50356	Abscheulicher, *Fidelio*	Beethoven
50372	Intermezzo	Schumann
50373	Mondnacht	Schumann
50374	Alfredo, Alfredo, *Traviata*	Verdi
50389	Heiden roslein	Schubert
50390	Air, *Egmont*	Beethoven
50391	Frohe Botschaft	
50392	Air, *Joshua*	Handel
50393	Du bist der Lenz, *Walkure*	Wagner
50394	Queen's Aria, *Les Huguenots*	Meyerbeer
50395	Heilge Quelle, *Figaro*	Mozart
50396	Aria, *Don Giovanni*, Pt. 1	Mozart
50398	Or sai chi l'onore, *Don Giovanni*	Mozart
50399	Aria, *Don Giovanni*, Pt. 2	Mozart
50432	Du bist die Ruh	Schubert
50433	Die Loreley	arr. Bungert
80005	Marten aller Arten, *Seraglio*	Mozart
80006	Air, *Fidelio*, Pt. 1	Beethoven
80007	Air, *Fidelio*, Pt. 2	Beethoven
80008	Ach ich liebte, *Seraglio*	Mozart

80009	Air, *Robert le Diable*	Meyerbeer	
52698	Casts Diva, *Norma*	Bellini	

50355	Crucifix (with Helbig)	Faure	
50357	Duet, *Figaro* (with Helbig)	Mozart	
50358	Duet, *Norma* (with Helbig)	Bellini	
50397	Duet, *Cosi fan tutti* (with Helbig)	Mozart	

FELIA LITVINNE
RED LABEL, G&T. PARIS, 1903

			R.P.M.
23196	Le Nuit	Rubenstein	73
33158	Pleurez mes Yeux, *Le Cid*	Massenet	
33160	Mon coeur s'ouvre, *Samson et Dalila*	Saint-Saens	
33163	Brunnhilde's Cry, *Walkure*	Wagner	
33182	J'ai pardonne (Ich grolle nicht)	Schumann	
033000	Stances, *Sappho*	Gounod	
033001	Priere, *Faust*	Gounod	

See in Artists' Section.
FONOTIPIA. PARIS, 1903-4

			R.P.M.
39052	Voi lo sapete, *Cavalleria Rusticana*	Mascagni	80
	1904		
38182	Reve d'Elsa, *Lohengrin*	Wagner	
39217	Grace, pitie, *Aida*	Verdi	
39218	Air du Sommeil, *L'Africaine*	Meyerbeer	

BLANCHE MARCHESI
BLACK LABEL, G&T. BERLIN, 1906

			R.P.M.
33593	L'Ete	Chaminade	77
43754	Im Mai	Goldschmidt	
43755	Eiapopeia		
43756	Bist du bei mir	Bach	
53439	Se Saran Rose	Arditi	
53440	Vissi d'arte, *Tosca*	Puccini	
53441	Voi lo sapete, *Cavalleria Rusticana*	Mascagni	

NELLIE MELBA
LILAC LABEL, G&T. LONDON

MATRIX		MARCH 1904 (with piano)		R.P.M.
1	03015	Mattinata	Tosti	70
2	03016	Nymphes et Sylvains	Bemberg	71
6	03017	Ah fors' e lui, *Traviata*, Pt. 1	Verdi	71
9	03019	Se Saran Rose	Arditi	71
12	03020	Mad Scene, *Lucia de Lammermoor*	Donizetti	74
15	03021	Sweet Bird (cadenza)	Handel	74
16	03022	Good-bye (two verses)	Tosti	72
		(with orchestra)		
20	03023	Mad Scene, *Hamlet*, Pt. 1	Thomas	75
21	03024	Mad Scene, *Hamlet*, Pt. 2	Thomas	75
22	03025	Caro Nome, *Rigoletto*	Verdi	75
23	03026	Ah fors' e lui, *Traviata*, Pt. 2	Verdi	75
		(with piano)		

25	03027	Three Green Bonnets	D'Hardelot	75
26	03028	Porgi Amor	Mozart	75
27	03029	Si mes vers avaient des ailes	Hahn	75

OCTOBER 1904

	3575	Chant Venitien	Bemberg	75
	3576	Les Anges pleurent	Bemberg	75
	03033	Ave Maria (violin obl. by Kubelik)	Gounod	75
	03034	La Serenata	Tosti	75
	03035	Valse Aria, *Romeo et Juliette*	Gounod	75
	03036	Chant Hindu	Bemberg	75
	03037	Addio, *Boheme*	Puccini	75

SEPTEMBER 1905

	3619	Away on the Hill	Landon Ronald'	75
	03046	Sur le Lac	Bemberg	75
	03047	Lo here the Gentle Lark	Bishop	75
	03048	Jewel Song, *Faust*	Gounod	75
	03049	Home, Sweet Home	Bishop	75
	03050	Good-bye (three verses)	Tosti	75

JULY 1906

	03069	Ave Maria ('cello obl. by Squire)	Gounod	78
	03070	Pastorale	Bizet	78
	03071	Mi chiamano Mimi, *Boheme*	Puccini	78
	03072	Aubade, *Le Roi d'Ys*	Lalo	78

ANNA VON MILDENBURG

BLACK LABEL, G&T. VIENNA, 1903

43630	Recitative to scena Ozean, du ungeneuer,	
	Oberon	Weber

MEDEA MEY-FIGNER

RED LABEL, G&T. ST. PETERSBURG, 1900–1

			R.P.M.
23122	Remembrance	Tosti	74
23123	The Night	Rubinstein	
23124	Tears, *Werther*	Massenet	
23125	Habanera, *Carmen*	Bizet	
23131	Chanson boheme, *Carmen*	Bizet	
23132	Night, Love and Moon	Davidoff	
23133	Fior che Langue		
23134	Vissi d'arte, *Tosca*	Puccini	
23135	Air de Lisa, *Pique Dame*	Tschaikovsky	
23146	Lullaby, *Harold*	Nopravnik	
23147	Vissi d'arte, *Tosca*	Puccini	

Duets with Figner

24057	Crucifix	Faure
24058	You tempt me so	Glinka
24059	The Sea Gull's Cry	Grodski
24060	Lontano, lontano, *Mefistofele*	Boito
24061	French duet	Doubrovsky

ALICE NIELSON
RED SEAL, VICTOR. 1907–8

64068	Addio del passato, *Traviata*	Verdi
64091	Ne fuis pas, *Romeo et Juliette* (with Constantino)	Gounod
74062	Mi chiamano, *Boheme*	Puccini
*74063	E'il sol dell'anima, *Rigoletto* (with Constantino)	Verdi
*74064	Una voce, *Barbiere*	Rossini
74075	Pariga o cara, *Traviata* (with Constantino)	Verdi
74066	Dammi ancor, *Faust* (with Constantino)	Gounod
74087	Quel guardo il cavalier, *Don Pasquale*	Donizetti
74107	Il Bacio	Arditti
74108	Ange adorable, *Romeo et Juliette* (with Constantino)	Gounod
74117	Convien partir, *Figlio del Reggimento*	Donizetti
74121	Last Rose of Summer	Flotow

These two recordings were issued as Red Label G&T as 054164 and 053137 respectively.

REGINA PACINI
FONOTIPIA. MILAN, 1904

			R.P.M.
39212	Gli Angui dell' inferno, *Flauto Magico*	Mozart	80
39232	Air and Variations	Proch	
39333	Sempre libera, *Traviata*	Verdi	
39234	Paquita	Zardo	
39235	Caro Nome, *Rigoletto*	Verdi	
39236	Valse, *Mirella*	Gounod	
39237	Ah fors' e lui, *Traviata*	Verdi	
39238	Qui la voce, *Puritani*	Bellini	
74011	Bel raggio, *Semiramide*	Rossini	
74012	Io son Titania, *Mignon*	Thomas	
	1906		
39769	Mi chiamano Mimi, *Boheme*	Puccini	
39770	Povera Mamma	Tosti	
39771	Ah vieni al tempio, *Puritani*	Bellini	
39772	Ideale	Tosti	
39773	Vissi d'arte, *Tosca*	Puccini	
39774	Gentil Augel, *Perle de Brasil*	David	
39775	Ave Maria	Gounod	
39776	Second Nocturne	Chopin	
39777	Non paventar, *Flauto Magico*	Mozart	
39778	Leggenda Valacca	Braga	
39781	Mi Patria	Alvarez	
39782	Vidatita		
39783	Una voce, *Il Barbiere*	Rossini	
39784	Io son docile, *Il Barbiere*	Rossini	
39785	Aprile	Tosti	

ESTHER PALLISER
BLACK LABEL, G&T. LONDON, 1902

			R.P.M.
3288	Spring	Tosti	72
3289	The sweetest flower that blows	Hawley	
3290	La Folletta	Marchesi	
4179	Bolero (with W. Palliser)	Saint-Saens	

ANGELICA PANDOLFINI
RED LABEL, G&T. MILAN, 1904

53333	Chanson de Florian	Godard
53340	Sortita di Adriana, *Adriana Lecouvreur*	Cilea
053037	Deh vieni, *Nozze di Figaro*	Mozart
053038	All'ombra di quel faggio	Taubert
053044	L'altra notte, *Mefistofele*	Boito

ELIZABETH PARKINA
BLACK LABEL, G&T. LONDON, 1904

			R.P.M.
3511	Comin' thro' the rye		74
3515	Vilanelle	Dell' Acqua	
	1905		
3581	When you speak to me	D'Hardelot	76
3583	The little grey linnet	Willeby	
3584	'Tis the day	Leoncavallo	
3586	Should he upbraid?	Bishop	
3587	Killarney	Balfe	
3588	I know a lovely garden	D'Hardelot	
33532	Ouvre tes yeux bleus	Massenet	
	1906-7		
3651	Spring	Tosti	77
3659	La Serenata	Tosti	
03088	La Fee aux Chansons	Bemberg	

ADELINA PATTI
PINK LABEL, G&T. LONDON
Recorded December 1905, issued February, 1906

			R.P.M.
03051	Voi che sapete, *Figaro*	Mozart	76
03052	Pur dicesti	Lotti	
03053	Home, Sweet Home	Bishop	
03054	Old Folks at Home	Foster	
03055	Batti, batti, *Don Giovanni*	Mozart	81
	In key of F major.		
03056	Jewel Song, *Faust*	Gounod	
03057	Kathleen Mavourneen	Crouch	
03058	La Serenata	Tosti	
03059	Robin Adair		
03060	Si vous n'avez rien a me dire	Rothschild	
03061	Comin' thro' the rye		
03062	The Last Rose of Summer	Moore	
03063	On Parting	Patti	
03064	'Twas within a mile of Edinburgh Town	Hook	
	Recorded 1906, issued February 1907		
03078	Kathleen Mavourneen	Crouch	
03079	La Serenata	Tosti	
03080	'Twas within a mile of Edinburgh Town	Hook	
03081	Home, Sweet Home	Bishop	
03082	Casta Diva, *Norma*	Bellini	
03083	Connais-tu le pays? *Mignon*	Thomas	
03084	Ah non credea, *Sonnambula*	Bellini	
03085	La Calesera	Yradier	

The last title was prepared but was not issued.

Appendix

ELISA PETRI

FONOTIPIA. MILAN, 1903

R.P.M.

39023	L'ombra di Carmen	Tirindelli	80
39074	Salve d'amor, *Tannhauser*	Wagner	
	1904		
39156	Aria di chiesa	Stradella	
39157	Sola nei miei prim'anni, *Lohengrin*	Wagner	
39158	Amore, amor	Tirindelli	
39449	Ideale	Tosti	
39483	Voi lo sapete, *Cavalleria Rusticana*	Mascagni	
39484	Perduta ho, *Damnation de Faust*	Berlioz	
39062	Si donna infame, *Gioconda* (with Luppi)	Ponchielli	
	1906		
39823	Sogno	Tosti	
39824	Occhi turchini	Denza	
39838	Nonna sorride	Tosti	
39839	Dio siete buono	Bossi	
39849	Io sono l'umile ancella, *Adriana Lecouvreur*	Cilea	
39850	O mia lia immortale, *Sappho*	Gounod	
39910	Canzone del pastore, *Tannhauser*, Pt. 1	Wagner	
39911	Canzone del pastore, *Tannhauser*, Pt. 2	Wagner	

With Corradetti

39515	Fa correggio, *Educande di Sorrento*	Usiglio
39516	Un bacio rendimi, *Educande di Sorrente*	Usiglio
39517	Quanti fischi, *Pipele*	De Ferrari
39518	So ben lo scemo, *Pagliacci*	Leoncavallo
39840	Io vi dico che partiate, *Linda di Chamounix*	Donizetti
39841	A dir il vero, *Linda di Chamounix*	Donizetti
39842	Chi siete? *Linda di Chamounix*	Donizetti
39843	Un buono servo, *Linda di Chamounix*	Donizetti
39880	Cantar, *Maestro di capella*	Paer
39881	Perche crudele, *Maestro di capella*	Paer
39890	Io son ricco, *L'Elisir d'amore*	Donizetti

39847	Per di qua, *Faust* (with Bonini)	Gounod
39848	Stammi ad udire, *Faust* (with Bonini)	Gounod

See also under *Magini-Coletti.*

AMELIA PINTO

RED LABEL, G&T. MILAN, 1902

R.P.M.

53232	Vissi d'arte, *Tosca*	Puccini	72
53233	Voi lo sapete, *Cavalleria Rusticana*	Mascagni	
53238	Aria, *Ero e Leandra*	Bottesini	
53239	Tu son sei buono, *Germania*	Franchetti	
53240	Suicidio, *La Gioconda*	Ponchielli	

Two recordings of 53232 under same catalogue number.

L

ROSINA STORCHIO

RED LABEL, G&T. MILAN, 1904

53331	Non sol un pensier, *Siberia*	Giordano
53332	Non odi le il martir, *Siberia*	Giordano
54248	Quest'orgoglio non a noi, *Siberia* (with de Luca)	Giordano
054027	E qui con te il mio destin (with Zenatello)	Giordano

FONOTIPIA. MILAN, 1904

39400	Quel guardo il cavalier, *Don Pasquale*	Donizetti
39401	So anch'io la virtu, *Don Pasquale*	Donizetti
39402	O luce di quest' anima, *Linda di Chamounix*	Donizetti
39597	Si domani, *Fra Diavolo*	Auber

GIANNINA RUSS

BLACK LABEL, G&T. MILAN, 1903

053008	Voi che sapete, *Nozze di Figaro*	Mozart
	1904	
53342	In quelle trine morbide, *Manon Lescaut*	Puccini
053025	Mi chiamano Mimi, *Boheme*	Puccini

Also in a number of concerted pieces with lesser singers.

FONOTIPIA. MILAN, 1903

39031	La Vergine degli Angeli, *Forza del Destino*	Verdi
39046	Ave Maria	Gounod
39047	Voi che sapete, *Nozze di Figaro*	Mozart
39049	Leggenda Valacca	Braga
39055	E l'amante, *Forza del Destino* (with Luppi)	Verdi
39056	Il Libro santo	Pinsuti
39064	Venite fidente, *Forza del Destino* (with Luppi)	Verdi
	1904	
39299	All'erta, all'erta, *Faust* (with Bonci and Luppi)	Gounod
39308	Mi chiamano Mimi, *Boheme*	Puccini
39354	Ritorna vincitor, *Aida*	Verdi
39355	I sacri nomi, *Aida*	Verdi
39357	Figlio del sol, *L'Africaine*	Meyerbeer
39380	Prendi quest'imagine, *Traviata* (with Ventura and Corradetti)	Verdi
39481	In quelle trine morbide, *Manon Lescaut*	Puccini
39388	Piu presso al Ciel, *Amica* (with Corradetti)	Mascagni
39535	Cosi mantieni il patto, *Gioconda* (with Blanchart)	Ponchielli
74001	Angeli Dei, *Gioconda* (with Parsi-Pettinella)	Ponchielli
69003	Trio, *Ballo in maschera* (with Longobardi and G. Pacini)	Verdi
69004	Non m'inganno, *Trovatore* (with Longobardi and G. Pacini)	Verdi
	1906–7	
39789	Sento un forza indomita, *Il Guarany* (with Martinez Patti)	Gomez
39869	Madamigella Valery? *Traviata* (with Bonini)	Verdi
39870	Pura siccome un Angelo, *Traviata* (with Bonini)	Verdi
39871	E grave il sacrificio, *Traviata* (with Bonini)	Verdi
39872	Dite alla giovine, *Traviata* (with Bonini)	Verdi
39873	Imponete, *Traviata* (with Bonini)	Verdi

39892	Casta Diva, *Norma*	Bellini
74017	Sextet, *Lucia di Lammermoor* (with Martinez-Patti, Bonini, Luppi, etc.)	Donizetti
	See also under Magini-Coletti.	

FRANCES SAVILLE

BLACK LABEL, G&T. WIEN, 1902-3

43300	Heiden-Roslein (7-inch)	Schubert	
43224	Gavotte, *Manon*	Massenet	
43240	Doll's Song, *Tales of Hoffmann*	Offenbach	
43241	Elsa's Song to the Breezes, *Lohengrin*	Wagner	
43277	Air of the Rose, *Marta*	Flotow	
33333	Maman, dites-moi	Traditional	82 R.P.M.

MARCELLA SEMBRICH

COLUMBIA, 1903

1364	Ernani involami, *Ernani*	Verdi
1365	Voices of Spring	J. Strauss
1366	Ah fors' e lui, *Traviata*	Verdi

RED LABEL, VICTOR-G&T. U.S.A., 1904-5

			R.P.M.
53394	Ah non giunge, *Sonnambula*	Bellini	77-78
43656	Standchen	R. Strauss	
43657	Der Nussbaum	Schumann	
23455	The Maiden's Wish	Chopin	
053054	Ah fors' e lui, *Traviata*	Verdi	
053055	Voci di Primavera	J. Strauss	
053056	Jewel Song, *Faust*	Gounod	
053057	Batti, batti, *Don Giovanni*	Mozart	
	1906		
053075	Parla Valse	Arditi	
053076	Mad Scene, *Lucia di Lamme rmoor*	Donizetti	
053077	Ernani involami, *Ernani*	Verdi	
053078	Caro Nome, *Rigoletto*	Verdi	
053096	Ah fors' e lui, *Traviata*	Verdi	
053097	Voci di Primavera	J. Strauss	
053099	Deh vieni, *Nozze di Figaro*	Mozart	
053100	Ah non giunge, *Sonnambula*	Bellini	
054074	Norina ed Malatesta, *Don Pasquale* (with Scotti)	Donizetti	
	1907		
034019	Doute de la lumiere, *Hamlet* (with de Gogorza)	Thomas	

LUISA SOBRINO

BLACK LABEL, G&T. LONDON, 1903

			R.P.M.
3465	Le Baiser	Goring Thomas	74
043002	Dich teure Halle, *Tannhauser*	Wagner	
053000	Ernani involami, *Ernani*	Verdi	

SUSAN STRONG
BLACK LABEL, G&T. LONDON, 1907

			R.P.M.
43958	Todessehnsucht	Bach	76
043078	Die junge Nonne	Schubert	

BLACK LABEL, PRE-DOG. LONDON, 1908

3725	Birthday Song	Korbay
3738	The Brain Spinning Swains	Beethoven
03099	Mary Gray of Allandale	arr. Lane Wilson
03116	Air of Salome, *Herodiade*	Massenet
03128	Stehe still	Wagner

LUISA TETRAZZINI
ZONOPHONE RECORDS. U.S.A. (?) 1904
(See Artists' Section)

10000	Rondo, *Lucia di Lammermoor*	Donizetti
10001	Caro Nome, *Rigoletto*	Verdi
10002	Una Voce, Barbiere, *Il Barbiere*	Rossini
10003	Valse Aria, *Romeo et Juliette*	Gounod
10004	Ah non giunge, *Sonnambula*	Bellini

CONTRALTOS

GUERRINA FABBRI
RED LABEL, G&T. MILAN, 1903

			R.P.M.
053006	Cavatina di Arsace, *Semiramide*	Rossini	74
053007	Rondo, *Italiana in Algeri*	Rossini	
053009	Cavatina, *Romeo e Giulietta*	Vaccai	
053015	Una voce, *Barbiere di Siviglia*	Rossini	

1904

53318	Cavatina, *Romeo e Giulietta*	Vaccai
53321	Ah se tu dormi, *Romeo e Giulietta*	Vaccai
53322	Brindisi, *Lucrezia Borgia*	Donizetti
053041	Figlio mio, *Prophete*	Meyerbeer

053007 and 053009 only were issued in England, in February, 1905, and were withdrawn before March, 1906.

MARIA GAY
BLACK LABEL, G&T. PARIS, 1904

33384	La Brise	Saint-Saens
33385	Chanson Boema, *Carmen*	Bizet
33412	La Feria	Fuentes

1905

33557	Divinites du Styx, *Alceste*	Gluck

FAVORITE. PARIS, 1907

1-46008	Spanish Song	
1-46009	Spanish Song	
1-6026	Habanera, *Carmen*	Bizet
1-6027	Air des Cartes, *Carmen*	Bizet

PINK PRE-DOG, GRAMOPHONE COMPANY. 1908

53516	Seguidilla, *Carmen*	Bizet
033039	Habanera, *Carmen*	Bizet
033040	Printemps qui commence, *Samson et Dalila*	Saint-Saens
033041	Mon coeur s'ouvre, *Samson et Dalila*	Saint-Saens
053140	Che faro, *Orfeo*	Gluck
Also		
2-053011	Giorni poveri, *Trovatore*	Verdi
2-063000	Chanson Boema, *Carmen*	Bizet

ALICE GOMEZ
BLACK LABEL, G&T. LONDON, 1902

			R.P.M.
3404	Melisande in the Wood	Goetz	77
3406	Irish Love Song		
3407	Beloved it is Morn	Aylward	
3408	Folk Song	Clutsam	

KIRKBY LUNN
BLACK LABEL, G&T. LONDON, 1902

3276	When the stars were young	Rubens
3277	One spring morning	Nevin
3280	The pretty creature	Storace

COLUMBIA. LONDON, 1905–6

3278	Willow Song	Cowen
3279	For a dream's sake	Cowen

ROSA OLITZKA
BLACK LABEL, G&T. LONDON, 1901

			R.P.M.
3430	Awake	Pelissier	Slow
3431	If thou wert blind		
3452	Let me dream again	Sullivan	
3453	Say yes, Mignon	D'Hardelot	

PARIS, 1902

33151	Habanera, *Carmen*	Bizet
33171	Romance de Siebel, *Faust*	Gounod
33181	Gavotte, *Mignon*	Thomas
53291	Voi lo sapete, *Cavalleria Rusticana*	Mascagni
331—	Air of the Page, *Huguenots*	Meyerbeer

BERLIN, 1906

43741	Gesange der Amneris, *Aida*	Verdi
43742	Sieh mein hertz, *Samson et Dalila*	Saint-Saens

ARMIDA PARSI-PETTINELLA
FONOTIPIA. MILAN, 1903

			R.P.M.
39068	Amore e maggio	Faini	80
39072	Ah se tu dormi, *Giulietta e Romeo*	Vaccai	
	1904		
39115	Stride la vampa, *Trovatore*	Verdi	
39394	Non conosci il bel suol? *Mignon*	Thomas	
39395	Voce di donna, *Gioconda*	Ponchielli	

1905

39623	Seguidilla, *Carmen*	Bizet
39624	Serenata	Gounod
39645	Vaga donna, *Huguenots*	Meyerbeer
39646	No, no, giammi da giovine paggio, *Huguenots*	Meyerbeer

1906

39792	Fernando, Fernando, *Favorita*	Donizetti
39793	Che fino al ciel, *Favorita* (with chorus)	Donizetti
39817	Al suon del tamburo, *Forza del Destino* (with chorus)	Verdi
39818	Rataplan, *Forza del Destino* (with chorus)	Verdi
39827	O mio Fernando, *Favorita*	Donizetti
39828	Ah veder l'amata stanza, *Mignon*	Thomas

1907

| 39912 | Figlio mio, *Prophete* | Meyerbeer |

See also Zenatello and Sammarco.

ERNESTINE SCHUMANN-HEINK

COLUMBIA. U.S.A., 1903

1378	Aria, *Prophete*	Meyerbeer
1379	Trinklied, *Lucrezia Borgia*	Donizetti
1380	Air, *Samson et Dalila*	Saint-Saens
1381	Bolero	Arditi
1382	Tod und das Madchen	Schubert

RED LABEL, VICTOR-G&T. U.S.A., 1906

043066	Sieh mein Hertz, *Samson et Dalila*	Saint-Saens
043067	Ach mein Sohn, *Prophete*	Meyerbeer
043068	Trinklied, *Lucrezia Borgia*	Donizetti

ELENA TEODORINI

BLACK LABEL, G&T. MILAN, 1903

53299	Rondo, *Lucrezia Borgia*	Donizetti
53300	M'odi, ah m'odi, *Lucrezia Borgia*	Donizetti
53301	Preghiera, *Gioconda*	Ponchielli
53302	Parla Valse	Arditi
53298	Habanera, *Carmen*	Bizet

N. D. VIALTZEVA

LARGE RED LABEL, G&T. ST. PETERSBURG, 1901

R.P.M.

23110	Tender embraces forgotten		76
23111	The daily Question		
23112	Why?	Meyer-Hellmund	
23114	Trifle not with Love	Davidoff	
23128	Should I love—I shall love whom I choose		
23130	Longing for thee		
23118	Russian Song		

As stated in the catalogue of 1903, the titles of these Russian songs have been translated literally into English.

TENORS

AMADEO BASSI
FONOTIPIA. MILAN, 1906

39643	Orride steppe, *Siberia*	Giordano
39644	T'incontrai per via, *Siberia*	Giordano
39651	Stanotte ho fatto un sogno, *Tess*	D'Erlanger
39652	Il sogno e la coscienza, *Tess*	D'Erlanger

1907

*39726	Canzone guerresca	Giordano
39727	Amor ti vieta, *Fedora*	Giordano

ALESSANDRO BONCI
FONOTIPIA. MILAN, 1903

			R.P.M.
39079	Addio Mignon, *Mignon*	Thomas	81
39080	Giunto sul passo, *Mefistofele*	Boito	

There were two published recordings of the Canzone
guerresca *on this catalogue number.*

39081	La Donna e mobile, *Rigoletto*	Verdi
39082	Recondita Armonia, *Tosca*	Puccini
39083	Una furtiva lagrima, *L'Elisir d'Amore*	Donizetti
39084	A te O cara, *Puritani*	Bellini

1904

			R.P.M.
39111	Una Vergine, *Favorita*	Donizetti	above
39127	Spiagge amate, *Elena e Paride*	Gluck	80
39128	Caro mio ben	Giordani	
39129	O cara imagine, *Flauto Magico*	Mozart	
39239	Questa o quella, *Rigoletto*	Verdi	
39240	Il Fior, *Carmen*	Bizet	
39241	O del mio dolce Ardor, *Elena e Paride*	Gluck	
39242	La Violetta	Mozart	
39248	I'll sing thee Songs of Araby	Clay	
39292	Tre giorni son che Nina	Ciampi	
39338	Spirito gentil, *Favorita*	Donizetti	
39339	O Paradiso, *L'Africaine*	Meyerbeer	
39331	E fia vero, *Favorita* (with Luppi)	Donizetti	
39336	Voi dovreste, *Barbiere di Siviglia* (with Corradetti)	Rossini	
39337	Numero quindici, *Barbiere di Siviglia* (with Corradetti)	Rossini	
39340	Del Tempio al limitar, *Pescatori di Perle* (with Magini-Coletti)	Bizet	
39341	Tornami a dir, *Don Pasquale* (with Pinkert)	Donizetti	
74000	Che gelida manina, *Boheme*	Puccini	
74006	Salve Dimora, *Faust*	Gounod	
69007	Ah non credevi tu, *Mignon*	Thomas	
69008	Dalla sua Pace, *Don Giovanni*	Mozart	
69017	Cielo e Mar, *Gioconda*	Ponchielli	
69018	Se tu m'ami	Pergolesi	
69019	Bella figlia, *Rigoletto* (with Pinkert, Lucacewska and Magini-Coletti)	Verdi	

1905
39673	Di Pescator ignobile, *Lucrezia Borgia*	Donizetti
39674	M'appari tutt' Amor, *Marta*	Flotow
39685	Cerchano lontana terra, *Don Pasquale*	Donizetti
39686	Mi par d'udir, *Pescatori de Perle*	Bizet
39687	Se il mio nome, *Barbiere di Siviglia*	Rossini
39691	Ah fede negar potessi, *Luisa Miller*	Verdi
39692	Quando le sere al placido, *Luisa Miller*	Verdi
39693	Tomba degli avi miei, *Lucia di Lammermoor*	Donizetti
39694	Fra poco, *Lucia di Lammermoor*	Donizetti
39695	Celeste Aida, *Aida*	Verdi
39696	Amor ti vieta, *Fedora*	Giordano
39697	Tu che a Dio, *Lucia di Lammermoor*	Donizetti
39698	Ah non mi ridestar, *Werther*	Massenet

ENRICO CARUSO
LIGHT BLUE LABEL, INTERNATIONAL ZONOPHONE. MILAN, 1902

			R.P.M.
1550	Un Bacio ancora	Trimarchi	78
1551	Luna fedel	Denza	
1552	Una furtiva lagrima, *L'Elisir d'Amore*	Donizetti	
1553	E lucean le stelle, *Tosca*	Puccini	
1554	No non chiuder, *Germania*	Franchetti	
1555	La donna e mobile, *Rigoletto*	Verdi	
1556	Siciliana, *Cavalleria Rusticana*	Mascagni	

RED LABEL, G&T. MILAN
Recorded March 1902

			R.P.M.
52344	Questa o quella, *Rigoletto*	Verdi	73
52345	Il Sogno, *Manon*	Massenet	
52346	Una furtiva lagrima, *L'Elisir d'Amore*	Donizetti	
52347	Giunto sul passo, *Mefistofele*	Boito	
52348	Dai campi, dai prati, *Mefistofele* (matrix 1789)	Boito	
52349	E lucean le stelle, *Tosca*	Puccini	
52368	Serenata, *Iris*	Mascagni	
52369	Celeste Aida, *Aida*	Verdi	
52370	No non chiuder, *Germania*	Franchetti	
52378	Studenti udite, *Germania*	Franchetti	

Recorded November, 1902, issued in 1903

			R.P.M.
52417	Cielo e Mar, *Gioconda*	Ponchielli	71
52418	Siciliana, *Cavalleria Rusticana*	Mascagni	
52419	No piu nobile, *Adriana Lecouvreur*	Cilea	
52439	Amor ti vieta, *Fedora*	Giordano	
53440	Vesti la giubba, *Pagliacci*	Leoncavallo	
52441	Non t'amo piu	Denza	
52442	Luna fedel	Denza	
52443	La mia Canzone	Tosti	
52448	Dai campi, dai prati, *Mefistofele* (matrix 2871)	Boito	
52369	Celeste Aida, *Aida* (matrix 2873)	Verdi	

Recorded October, 1903
052066 **Mi par d'udir,** *Pescatori di Perle*   **Bizet**
The Aida *and* Mefistofele *items were re-recorded and
issued under the old catalogue numbers. The matrix
numbers will serve to distinguish them, though the renderings
differ in certain respects.*

VICTOR-G&T. NEW YORK, 1904   R.P.M.

52062	**La Donna e mobile,** *Rigoletto*	**Verdi**	78–80
52063	**E lucevan le Stelle,** *Tosca*	**Puccini**	
52064	**Siciliana,** *Cavalleria Rusticana*	**Mascagni**	
52065	**Una furtiva Lagrima,** *L'Elisir d'Amore*	**Donizetti**	
52066	**Vesti la giubba,** *Pagliacci*	**Leoncavallo**	
52191	**Recondita Armonia,** *Tosca*	**Puccini**	
2-52479	**Il Sogno,** *Manon*	**Massenet**	
2-52480	**Questa o quella,** *Rigoletto*	**Verdi**	
052073	**Una furtiva Lagrima,** *L'Elisir d'Amore* (2nd verse)	**Donizetti**	
052074	**Celeste Aida,** *Aida*	**Verdi**	

NEW YORK, FEBRUARY, 1904

52193	**Brindisi,** *Cavalleria Rusticana*	**Mascagni**	78
052086	**Serenata,** *Don Pasquale*	**Donizetti**	
052087	**Romanza del Fiore,** *Carmen*	**Bizet**	
052088	**Bianca al par,** *Huguenots*	**Meyerbeer**	
052089	**Cielo e Mar,** *Gioconda*	**Ponchielli**	

MILAN, APRIL, 1904

52034	**Mattinata**	**Leoncavallo**	74

NEW YORK, FEBRUARY, 1906

2-52489	**Di quella Pira,** *Rigoletto*	**Verdi**	81
052120	**Spirito gentil,** *Favorita*	**Donizetti**	76
052121	**M'appari,** *Marta*	**Flotow**	
052122	**Che gelida Manina,** *Boheme*	**Puccini**	80
032030	**Salut Demeure,** *Faust*	**Gounod**	82

NEW YORK, MARCH, 1906

054070	**Solenne in quest' Ora,** *Forza del Destino* (with Scotti)	**Verdi**	82

December, 1906

052153	**Triste ritorno**	**Barthelemy**	82
052154	**Ideale**	**Tosti**	78
052157	**O Paradiso,** *L'Africaine*	**Meyerbeer**	78

1907

054117	**Bella figlia,** *Rigoletto* (with Abbott, Homer and Scotti)	**Verdi**	80
052158	**Improvviso,** *Andrea Chenier*	**Giordano**	80
052159	**Vesti la giubba,** *Pagliacci*	**Leoncavallo**	80
054127	**Ah Mimi,** *Boheme* (with Scotti)	**Puccini**	82
054134	**Del tempio al limitar,** *Pescatori di Perle* (with Ancona)	**Bizet**	80
054129	**O soave fanciulla,** *Boheme* (with Melba)	**Puccini**	77

BEN DAVIES

BLACK LABEL, G&T. LONDON, 1900-1

			R.P.M.
2-2500	Serenade	Schubert	82
2-2501	Songs of Araby	Clay	82
2-2502	My pretty Jane	Bishop	82
2 2503	When other lips, *Bohemian Girl*	Balfe	82
52329	Salve dimora, *Faust*	Gounod	

1903

2-2778	To Mary	M. V. White	76
2-2779	An Evensong	Blumenthal	
2-2780	Yes, let me like a soldier fall, *Maritana*	Wallace	
2-2781	So fare thee well, *Doris*	Cellier	
2-2782	A Sailor's Grave	Sullivan	
02000	Tom Bowling	Dibdin	
02003	Songs of Araby	Clay	
02004	Salve Dimora, *Faust*	Gounod	

FERNANDO DE LUCIA

RED LABEL, G&T. MILAN, 1903

			R.P.M.
52410	Ideale	Tosti	72
52411	La Donna e mobile, *Rigoletto*	Verdi	
52412	Marechiare	Tosti	
52413	Napulitanata	Costa	
52414	Recondita Armonia, *Tosca*	Puccini	
52415	Funesta che lucivi		
52416	Sogno, *Manon*	Massenet	
52427	Se il mio Nome, *Barbiere di Siviglia*	Rossini	
52435	Ah non mi ridestar, *Werther*	Massenet	
52436	Amor ti vieta, *Fedora*	Giordano	
52437	Il Fior, *Carmen*	Bizet	
52438	Tu sei morta nella mia vita	Costa	
52650	Cigno gentil, *Lohengrin*	Wagner	
52651	A suon di Baci	Baldelli	
52652	Siciliana, *Cavalleria Rusticana*	Mascagni	

1904

52077	Mia Madre, *Fedora*	Giordano	75
52078	Vedi io piango, *Fedora*	Giordano	
52079	Occhi di Fata	Denza	
52080	Un di felice, *Traviata*	Verdi	
52081	Una Vergine, *Favorita*	Donizetti	
52082	Serenata	Tosti	
52083	L'Anima ho stanca, *Adriana Lecouvreur*	Cilea	
52084	Lontananza	Cilea	
052078	Ecco ridente, *Barbiere di Siviglia*	Rossini	
054043	Tardi si fa, addio, *Faust* (with Boninsegna)	Gounod	

1906

2-52472	Di non t'incantan, *Lohengrin*	Wagner	76
2-52473	S'ei torna alfin, *Lohengrin*	Wagner	
2-52474	Della mia vita, *Pescatori de Perle*	Bizet	

2-52475	La tua bel alma, *Mignon*	Thomas
2-52518	Ah non credevi tu, *Mignon*	Thomas
2-52519	Salve Dimora, *Faust*	Gounod
2-52520	Mi par d'udir, *Pescatori di Perle*	Bizet
54293	Numero quindici, *Il Barbiere* (with A. Pini-Corsi)	Rossini
052111	Addio Mignon, *Mignon*	Thomas
052129	Dei miei bollenti spiriti, *Traviata*	Verdi
054080	All'idea, *Il Barbiere* (with A. Pini-Corsi)	Rossini
054081	Pariga O cara, *Traviata* (with Huguet)	Verdi
054082	Non hai compreso, *Pescatori di Perle*	Bizet
054083	Ah qual colpo inaspetatto, *Il Barbiere* (with Huguet and A. Pini-Corsi)	Rossini
054084	E'il Sol dell' anima, *Rigoletto*	Verdi

LEON ESCALAIS

FONOTIPIA. PARIS, 1904–5

39326	Dio! mi potevi scagliar, *Otello*	Verdi
39362	Dio m'inspira, *Juive*	Halevy
39371	Arretez mes freres, *Samson et Dalila*	Saint-Saens
39379	Dieu m'eclaire, *Juive*	Halevy
39392	Stances	Flegier
39293	Ah parair, *Mage*	Massenet
39414	Sicilienne, *Robert le Diable*	Meyerbeer
39426	O Paradis, *L'Africaine*	Meyerbeer
39427	Asile hereditaire, *Guillaume Tell*	Rossini
39428	Rachel, quand du Seigneur, *Juive*	Halevy
39429	Roi du Ciel, *Prophete*	Meyerbeer
39431	Hosanna	Granier
39532	Celeste Aida, *Aida*	Verdi
39533	La mia Letizia, *Lombardi*	Verdi
39546	Pastorale Languedocienne	Rupes
39562	Je veux encore entendre, *Jerusalem*	Verdi
39563	Priere de Roderiguez, *Cid*	Massenet
39564	O toi mon seul espoir, *Trovatore*	Verdi
39565	Tout m'abandonne, *Otello*	Verdi
39566	Source delicieuse, *Polyeucte*	Gounod
39573	Rachele allor che Iddio, *Juive*	Halevy
39577	Supplice infame, *Trovatore*	Verdi
39578	Dieu tu pouvais m'infliger, *Otello*	Verdi
39579	Scene pour tenor, *Pierre l'Ermite*	Granier

39196	Troncar suoi di, *Guillaume Tell* (with Magini-Coletti and Luppi)	Rossini
39342	La gloria inflamma, *Guillaume Tell* (with Magini-Coletti and Luppi)	Rossini
39370	Sextet, *Les Huguenots* (with Magini-Coletti, Corradetti, Luppi, etc.)	Meyerbeer
39525	Avec ces fleurs, *Sigurd* (with Talexis)	Reyer
39526	Oublios les maux, *Sigurd* (with Talexis)	Reyer

N. N. FIGNER
RED LABEL, G&T. ST. PETERSBURG, 1901

22547	Morning, *and* The Lovers	
22548	In a Garden	Balabanoff
22554	A moment of peril	Tschaikowsky
22555	Song	Doubrovski
22556	Laugh, Pajazo, *Pagliacci*	Leoncavallo
22596	Sicilienne, *Cavalleriu Rusticana*	Mascagni
22597	Air, *Otello*	Verdi
	1903	
2-22508	You are my Morning	Wrangel
032000	Air, *Les Huguenots*	Meyerbeer
	See also under Mey-Figner (soprano).	

EDOARDO GARBIN
RED LABEL, G&T. MILAN, 1903

			R.P.M.
52428	Un di felice, *Traviata*	Verdi	71
52429	Donna non vidi mai, *Manon Lescaut*	Puccini	
52430	Guardate pazzo son, *Manon Lescaut*	Puccini	
52431	Aspetti signorina, *Boheme*	Puccini	
52432	Mimi e una civita, *Boheme*	Puccini	
52433	Brindisi, *Cavalleria Rusticana*	Mascagni	
52434	Una Vergine, *Favorita*	Donizetti	
052010	Donna non vidi mai, *Manon Lescaut*		

FONOTIPIA. MILAN, 1903

39029	Una Vergine, *Favorita*	Donizetti
39036	No piu nobile, *Adriana Lecouvreur*	Cilea
39038	Sogno, *Manon*	Massenet
39039	Siciliana, *Cavalleria Rusticana*	Mascagni
39043	E lucean le stelle, *Tosca*	Puccini
39065	Sento che t'amo	Fatuo
39075	E un riso gentil, *Zaza*	Leoncavallo
	1904	
39116	Donna non vidi mai, *Manon Lescaut*	Puccini
39117	E dunque vero, *Adriana Lecouvreur* (with Stehl)	Cilea
39223	Ah Mimi, *Boheme*	Puccini
	1905	
69011	Brindisi, *Cavalleria Rusticana*	Mascagni
69014	Quartet, *Boheme* (with Stehl, Camporelli and Sammarco)	Puccini
69015	Solenne in quest'ora, *Forza del Destino*	Verdi
69016	Nume custode e vindice, *Aida*	Verdi

EDWARD LLOYD
BLACK LABEL, G&T. LONDON, 1904

3-2024	I'll sing thee songs of Araby	Clay
3-2025	Tom Bowling	Dibden
3-2026	The Holy City	Adams
3-2027	Death of Nelson	Braham
3-2028	Alice, where art thou?	Ascher
3-2029	Yes, let me like a soldier fall, *Maritana*	Wallace

3–2081	When all the world is fair	Cowen
3–2082	The Sea hath its Pearls	Cowen
3–2083	When other lips, *Bohemian Girl*	Balfe
3–2085	If with all your hearts, *Elijah*	Mendelssohn
3–2086	Lend me your aid, *Queen of Sheba*	Gounod
3–2087	The Maid of the Mill	Adams

1905

3–2294	Bonnie Mary of Argyle	
3–2299	The Minstrel Boy	Moore
02062	Lend me your aid, *Queen of Sheba*	Gounod
02063	Prize Song, *Meistersinger*	Wagner

Edward Lloyd's recording was completed in 1907 and 1908.

Speeds to conform with keys as given on labels.

FRANCESCO MARCONI

RED LABEL, G&T. MILAN, 1903–4

			R.P.M.
52016	Dai campi, dai prati, *Mefistofele*	Boito	74
52017	Stanze, *Nerone*	Rubinstein	
52788	Questa o quella, *Rigoletto*	Verdi	
052054	Romanza del Duello, *Eugen Onegin*	Tschaikowsky	
052055	O Paradiso, *L'Africaine*	Meyerbeer	
052056	Cielo e Mar, *Gioconda*	Ponchielli	
052057	Ingemisco, *Requiem Mass*	Verdi	
052058	Bella cantiam l'amore	Mascagni	
052065	Non guardarmi cosi	Paloni	

In 1908 the famous record

54373	I Mulattieri (with Cotogni)	Massini	80

FRANCESCO TAMAGNO

RED LABEL, G&T. MILAN, 1903

			R.P.M.
53673	Esultate, *Otello*	Verdi	79
52674	Morte, *Otello*	Verdi	
52675	Ora e per sempre, *Otello*	Verdi	
52676	Improvviso, *Andrea Chenier*	Giordano	
52677	Inno, *Il Profeta*	Meyerbeer	
52678	Di quella pira, *Trovatore*	Verdi	
52679	Sopra Berta, *Il Profeta*	Meyerveer	
52681	Figli miei v'arrestate, *Sansone e Dalila*	Saint-Saens	
52682	O muto asil, *Guglielmo Tell*	Rossini	
52683	Corriam, *Guglielmo Tell*	Rossini	
52684	Quand nos jours, *Herodiade*	Massenet	

1904

052068	Morte, *Otello*	Verdi	73

1905

052100	Improvviso, *Andrea Chenier*	Giordano	73
052101	Esultate, *Otello*	Verdi	
052102	Ora e per sempre, *Otello*	Verdi	
052103	O muto asil, *Guglielmo Tell*	Rossini	

Deserta sulla terra *in* Trovatore *was also recorded in*
1903, *but was not issued until* 1910, *numbered* 7–52277
with, of course, a Dog label. It opens *with the words*
"Dedicato alla memoria di mio padre" *spoken by*
Tamagno.
Of the 12-in. *series, the matrix numbers of* 052068 *and*
052100 *are consecutive, i.e.* 269 *and* 270 ; *while those of
the remainder run,* 10, 12 *and* 17.
   *The above dates are those of issue: all were recorded
in* 1903, *over three sessions, and it would be unrewarding
to search for vocal differences.*

FERNANDO VALERO
RED LABEL, G&T.   LONDON, 1903

			R.P.M.
52716	**Dormi pure**	Scuderi	73
52717	**Siciliana,** *Cavalleria Rusticana*	Mascagni	
52718	**Brindisi,** *Cavalleria Rusticana*	Mascagni	
52719	**Al Amor y la vida**		

FRANCESCO VIGNAS
BLACK LABEL, G&T.   MILAN, 1903

			R.P.M.
52735	**Studenti udite,** *Germania*	Franchetti	74
052002	**Racconto,** *Lohengrin*	Wagner	
052004	**O Paradiso,** *L'Africaine*	Meyerbeer	
052007	**Celeste Aida,** *Aida*	Verdi	
05200–	**Canzone della Primavera,** *Walkure*	Wagner	
052005	**Addio,** *Lohengrin*	Wagner	

FONOTIPIA.   MILAN, 1904

39122	**Mi Nina**	Guetary	80
39123	**La Partida**	Mandeno	
39131	**Ecco la gia Giovinezza,** *Lorenza*	Mascheroni	
39134	**O Paradiso,** *L'Africaine*	Meyerbeer	
39135	**Se ti dicessi,** *Stornello*	Amadai	
39136	**Celeste Aida,** *Aida*	Verdi	
39137	**Donna Clara**	Gastaldon	

1905

39794	**Maria**	Guetary
39805	**Sopra Berta,** *Prophete*	Meyerbeer
39806	**Cigno fedel,** *Lohengrin*	Wagner
39813	**Un Plieto**	Gazambide
39814	**A Granada**	Alvarez
39853	**Di non t' incantan,** *Lohengrin*	Wagner
39854	**Di Pescatore ignobile,** *Lucrezia Borgia*	Donizetti
74019	**Da voi lontan,** *Lohengrin*	Wagner
74020	**Dall 'alba tinto,** *Meistersinger*	Wagner

1906

62082	**Ora e per sempre,** *Otello*	Verdi
62083	**Ma se m'e forza,** *Ballo in maschera*	Verdi

HERMANN WINKELMANN
BLACK LABEL, G&T. VIENNA, 1905-6

3-42299	Air, *Dalibor*	Smetana
3-42370	Song to Venus, *Tannhauser*	Wagner
3-42417	Serenade, *Trovatore*	Verdi
3-42465	Prize Song, *Meistersinger*	Wagner
042110	Hochstes Vertrauen, *Lohengrin*	Wagner

FAVORITE. 1905-6

	Dream Song, *Meistersinger*	Wagner
	Liebesgluck	Sucher

GIOVANNI ZENATELLO
BLACK LABEL, G&T. MILAN, 1903

			R.P.M.
52703	Salve Dimora, *Faust*	Gounod	70
52711	Aria, *Dannazione di Faust*	Berlioz	
52712	Un di felice, *Traviata*	Verdi	
52702	Improvviso, *Andrea Chenier*	Giordano	

RED LABEL, G&T. MILAN, 1904

52764	Orride Steppe, *Siberia*	Giordano
52775	T' incontrai per via, *Siberia*	Giordano
054027	E qui te il mio destin, *Siberia* (with Storchio)	Giordano

FONOTIPIA. 1904

39243	Vesti la giubba, *Pagliacci*	Leoncavallo	75-82
39244	Improvviso, *Andrea Chenier*	Giordano	
39259	La Rivedro nell' estasi, *Ballo in maschera*	Verdi	
39260	Di tu se fedele, *Ballo in maschera*	Verd.	
39507	Celeste Aida, *Aida*	Verdi	
39529	Dai campi dai prati, *Mefistofele*	Boito	

39509	Fin da stanotte, *Mefistofele* (with Didur)	Boito
39527	Gia sacerdoti s' adunansi, *Aida* (with Frascani)	Verdi
39528	Misero appien mi festa, *Aida* (with Frascani)	Verdi

1905

39663	Dei miei bollenti spiriti, *Traviata*	Verdi
39664	Questa Donna conoscete, *Traviata*	Verdi

39665	Non sai tu, *Ballo in maschera* (with Burzio)	Verdi
39666	O qual soave brivido, *Ballo in maschera* (with Burzio)	Verdi

1906

39767	Che c'e egli, *Figlia di Jorio* (with Giraldoni)	Franchetti
39768	Rinverdisca per noi, *Figlia di Jorio*	Franchetti
39819	Ai nostri Monti, *Trovatore* (with Parsi-Pettinella)	Verdi
39825	Sulla Tomba, *Lucia di Lammermoor* (with Barrientos)	Donizetti

1907

39973	Niun mi tema, *Otello*	Verdi
39993	Donna non vidi mai, *Manon Lescaut*	Puccini
39994	Guardate pazzo son, *Manon Lescaut*	Puccini
39995	Un tal gioco, *Pagliacci*	Leoncavallo
39996	Vieni	Denza

BARITONES

MARIO ANCONA
            RED LABEL, G&T. LONDON, 1904

			R.P.M.
52072	Mattinata	Tosti	76
52073	Il Sogno, *Otello*	Verdi	
52074	Lucia (Ballata)		
3-32180	Chanson de l'Adieu	Tosti	
052075	Prologo, Pagliacci	Leoncavallo	
052076	Don Juan's Serenade	Tschaikowsky	

            RED LABEL, G&T. MILAN, 1904

52128	Mattinata	Tosti	77
52129	Il Sogno, *Otello*	Verdi	
52130	Serenata, *Don Giovanni*	Mozart	
3-32305	Chanson de l'Adieu	Tosti	
3-32306	Serenade de Don Juan	Tschaikowsky	
052075	Prologo, *Pagliacci*	Leoncavallo	
052080	Credo, *Otello*	Verdi	

There were two recordings of the **Prologo** *under this
number, and probably of the* **Credo** *also.*

MATTIA BATTISTINI
            RED LABEL, G&T. WARSAW, 1903

			R.P.M.
52663	Finch' an del vino, *Don Giovanni*	Mozart	74-75
52664	O tu bel Astro, *Tannhauser*	Wagner	
52665	Aria, *Eugen Onegin*	Tschaikowsky	
52666	Serenata, *Don Giovanni*	Mozart	
52667	La Mantilla	Alvarez	
52668	Occhi di Fata	Denza	
52669	Ancora	Tosti	
52670	Deh non plorah, *Demon*	Rubinstein	
52671	Largo al factotum, *Barbiere di Siviglia*	Rossini	
52672	Aria Valentino, *Faust*	Gounod	
54034	Ah l'altro ardor, *Favorita* (with Carotini)	Donizetti	

            ORANGE LABEL, G&T. MILAN, 1907

052141	O dei verd'anni, *Ernani*	Verdi	78
052142	Alla vita che t'arride, *Ballo in maschera*	Verdi	
052143	Il mio Lionel, *Marta*	Flotow	
052144	A tanto Amor, *Favorita*	Donizetti	
052145	O Lisbona, *Don Sebastiano*	Donizetti	
052146	Eri tu, *Ballo in maschera*	Verdi	
052147	Su queste Rose, *Damnation de Faust*	Berlioz	
052148	Perche tremar, *Zampa*	Herold	
054103	Da quel di, *Ernani* (with Corsi)	Verdi	
054104	La ci darem, *Don Giovanni* (with Corsi)	Mozart	
054105	La vedremo o veglio audace, *Ernani* (with Corsi)	Verdi	
054106	Vieni meco sol di rosee, *Ernani* (with Corsi)	Verdi	
054107	O sommo Carlo, *Ernani* (with Corsi, Colazza and		
	Sillich)	Verdi	

DAVID BISPHAM
BLACK LABEL, G&T. LONDON, 1902

R.P.M.

2-2682	Sapphische Ode	Brahms	72
2-2683	Drink to me only		72
2-2684	Hark, hark, the Lark	Schibert	72
2-2686	Quand'ero paggio, *Falstaff*	Verdi	72
2-2687	The pretty Creature	Storace	73
2-2688	Creation's Hymn	Beethoven	71
2-2689	My love Nell		70
	1903-4		
2-2941	The lass with the delicate air	Arne	76
2-2942	Maid of Athens	Gounod	77
2-2977	Who is Sylvia?	Schubert	77
2-2979	To none will I my·love discover	Wolf	77
02045	The Sands of Dee		78
02046	O that we two were maying	Gounod	78
040050	Als du im kuhnen Sange, *Tannhauser*	Wagner	78

FRANCESCO MARIA BONINI
FONOTIPIA. MILAN, 1903-4

39045	Pari siamo, *Rigoletto*	Verdi
39057	O monumento, *Gioconda*	Ponchielli
39071	Cortigiani, vil razza, *Rigoletto*	Verdi
39124	Preghiera, *Rolando di Berlino*	Leoncavallo
39125	Affo si ghiuto ammore	Carelli
	1905	
39671	Il Balen, *Trovatore*	Verdi
39672	Pieta rispetto amore, *Macbeth*	Verdi
	1906	
39740	Son sessant 'anni, *Andrea Chenier*	Giordano
39741	Un di m' era gioia, *Andrea Chenier*	Giordano
39742	Dio possente, *Faust*	Gounod
39743	O Lisbona, *Don Sebastiano*	Donizetti
39759	O dei verd' anni, *Ernani*	Verdi
39760	Quest'e dunque, *Due Foscari*	Verdi
39831	O vecchio cor, *Due Foscari*	Verdi

FRANCESCO D'ANDRADE
LYRAPHONE RECORDS. 1906-7
(*With acknowledgements to Robert Bauer*)

SERIAL NUMBERS D'A

1	Caro mio ben	Giordani
2	Pur dicesti	Lotti
3	Aprite un po', *Nozze di Figaro*	Mozart
4	Largo al factotum, *Barbiere di Siviglia*	Rossini
5	Resta immobile, *Guillaume Tell*	Rossini
6	Si vuol ballare, *Nozze di Figaro*	Mozart
7	Viens Leonora, *Favorita*	Donizetti
8	Toreador, *Carmen*	Bizet
11	Serenade, *Don Giovanni*	Mozart
12	Finch' an del vino, *Don Giovanni*	Mozart

M

GIUSEPPE DE LUCA
RED LABEL, G&T. MILAN, 1903

			R.P.M.
52420	Monologo di Michonnet, *Adriana Lecouvreur*	Cilea	70
52421	Caro mio ben	Giordani	
52422	O casto Fior, *Roi de Lahore*	Massenet	
52423	Vien Leonora, *Favorita*	Donizetti	
52424	Eri tu, *Ballo in maschera*	Verdi	
52425	Come il romite Fior, *Hamlet*	Thomas	
52426	Serenata, *Don Giovanni*	Mozart	
52444	Bella siccome un Angelo, *Don Pasquale*	Donizetti	
54021	Ah l'altro Ardor, *Favorita* (with Ceresoli)	Donizetti	

1904

52773	La conobbi quand'era fanciulla, *Siberia*	Giordano	
54048	Quest 'orgoglio, *Siberia* (with Storchio)	Giordano	
054039	Mattinata (with G. Pini-Corsi and others) *Siberia*	Giordano	

FONOTIPIA. MILAN, 1904

39165	Canzone della Pulce, *Damnation de Faust*	Berlioz	82
39168	Che fai tu qui, *Damnation de Faust*	Berlioz	

*De Luca recorded thirty-three further titles in the
Fonotipia 39 series.*

"SIGNOR FRANCISCO" (Emilio de Gogorza)
BLACK LABEL, VICTOR-G&T. U.S.A., 1903

			R.P.M.
52787	Largo al factotum, *Barbiere di Siviglia*	Rossini	78
52715	Prologo, *Pagliacci*	Leoncavallo	78
52720	Toreador's Song, *Carmen*	Bizet	78

1904

3–2098	La Paloma	Yradier	
3–2099	Brindisi, *Marta*	Flotow	

1905

062004	La Paloma	Yradier	74

*The above were the only European issues by this
prolific recorder under several names apart from the
large number of titles under his own.*

EUGENIO GIRALDONI
RED LABEL, G&T. MILAN, 1903

			R.P.M.
52401	Notturno, *Cristoforo Colombo*	Franchetti	72
52402	Deh non plorar, *Demon*	Rubinstein	
52403	O tu bel astro, *Tannhauser*	Wagner	
52404	Aria Morte, *Don Carlos*	Verdi	
52405	Visione fuggitiva, *Herodiade*	Massenet	
52406	Quest' assisa, *Aida*	Verdi	

FONOTIPIA, 1904

39443	Non pianger, no, *Demon*	Rubinstein	80
39444	O casto fior, *Roi de Lahore*	Massenet	
39445	Era le notte, *Otello*	Verdi	
39446	Credo, *Otello*	Verdi	
39536	Brindisi, *Hamlet*	Thomas	

1907

39918	S'ebben d'Imen, *Eugen Onegin*	Tschaikowsky	

PLUNKET GREENE
BLACK LABEL, G&T. LONDON, 1904

2–42776	Abschied	Schubert
3–2016	Off to Philadelphia	Haynes
3–2017	Two Songs	
3–2018	Father O'Flynn	arr. Stanford
3–2059	Eva Toole *and* Trotting to the Fair	
3–2060	The Donovans	
3–2089	The Farmer's Song	

1905–6

3–2334	The Gentle Maiden
3–2356	Little Mary Cassidy
4–2017	Molly Branigan
4–2355	Little Red Fox

RICHARD GREEN
BLACK LABEL, G&T. LONDON, 1901

2409	To my first Love	
2410	A Song of Thanksgiving	Allitsen
2411	The Devout Lover	Maud Valerie White

GIUSEPPE KASHMANN
RED LABEL, G&T. MILAN, 1905

052031	Carlos che solo, *Don Carlos*	Verdi
052032	O dei verd' anni, *Ernani*	Verdi
052036	Brindisi, *Hamlet*	Thomas
052037	Serenata, *Medici*	Leoncavallo
052038	Credo, *Otello*	Verdi

ANTONIO MAGINI-COLETTI
INTERNATIONAL ZONOPHONE, LIGHT BLUE LABEL. MILAN, 1902

1509	Pari siamo, *Rigoletto*	Verdi
1535	Deh vien alla finestra, *Don Giovanni*	Mozart
1536	All'erta Marinar, *L'Africaine*	Meyerbeer
1537	Sei vendicata assai, *L'Africaine*	Meyerbeer
1538	Barcarolla, *Gioconda*	Ponchielli
1897	Canzone della pulce, *Damnation de Faust*	Berlioz
1898	Su queste Rose, *Damnation de Faust*	Berlioz
1899	Serenata, *Damnation de Faust*	Berlioz

FONOTIPIA. MILAN, 1904–5

39335	Sei vendicata assai, *L'Africaine*	Meyerbeer
29351	La Danza	Rossini
39369	Vieni la mia vendetta, *Lucrezia Borgia*	Donizetti
39374	Con voi ber, *Carmen*	Bizet
39375	Non t'amo piu	Denza
39377	Lakme quel ciglio, *Lakme*	Delibes
39387	Senza fetto, *Guarany*	Gomez
39389	Musica proibita	Gastaldon
39410	Il sol per me, *Cristofero Colombo*	Franchetti

39411	M'odi, l'estrema e quella, *Cristofero Colombo*	Franchetti
39434	Pari siamo, *Rigoletto*	Verdi
39441	Cortigiani vil razza, *Rigoletto*	Verdi
39442	Miei Signori, *Rigoletto*	Verdi
39439	Qual voce, *Trovatore* (with Burzio)	Verdi
39440	Conte! ne cessi, *Trovatore* (with Burzio)	
39196	Troncar suoi di, *Guillaume Tell* (with Escalais and Luppi)	Rossini
39340	Del tempio al limitar, *Pescatore di Perle* (with Bonci)	Bizet
39342	La gloria infiammi, *Guillaume Tell* (with Escelais and Luppi)	Rossini
39370	Sextet, *Huguenots* (with Escalais, Corradetti, Luppi, etc.)	Meyerbeer
39373	Suoni la tromba, *Puritani* (with Luppi)	Bellini
39381	C'e Rudolfo? *Boheme* (with Petri)	Puccini
39396	Di Pandolfetti medico, *Crispinio e la Comare* (with Corradetti and Luppi)	Ricci
39397	Puoi tornare, *Crispino e la Comare* (with Corradetti and Luppi)	Ricci
39398	Figlia! mio padre, *Rigoletto* (with Russ)	Verdi
39399	Veglia o donna, *Rigoletto* (with Russ)	Verdi
39403	Quella pieta, *Linda di Chamounix* (with Luppi)	Donizetti
39404	La mia figlia, *Linda di Chamounix* (with Luppi)	Donizetti
39415	Signor! Va non ho niente, *Rigoletto* (with Luppi)	Verdi
39430	Quand'ero Paggio, *Falstaff* (with Petri)	Verdi
39432	Bimba non ti crucciar, *Adriana Lecouvreur* (with Petri)	Cilea
39435	Reverenza! Buon giorno, *Falstaff* (with Petri)	Verdi
39436	Ma c'e un'altra ambasciate, *Falstaff* (with Petri)	Verdi

VICTOR MAUREL
RED LABEL, G&T. PARIS, 1903

			R.P.M.
2-32809	Air, *Iphigenie*	Gluck	72
2-32810	Marquise	Massenet	
2-32811	L'Heure exquise	Hahn	
2-32812	Rondel de l'Adieu	De Lara	
2-32813	Fedia	Erlanger	
2-32814	Le Reve de Cassio, *Otello*	Verdi	
2-32815	Chanson de Printemps	Gounod	

FONOTIPIA. PARIS, 1903-4

			above
39032	Marechiare	Tosti	80
39041	Serenata, *Don Giovanni*	Mozart	
39042	Era la notte, *Otello*	Verdi	

1904

39245	Mandolinata	Paladilhe
39246	Rondel de l'Adieu	De Lara
39247	Ninon	Tosti

1907

62016	Quand'ero paggio, *Falstaff*	Verdi	82
62017	Marquise (Au temps du grand Roi)	Massenet	82

GIUSEPPE PACINI
FONOTIPIA. MILAN, 1903-4

			R.P.M.
39002	Prologo, *Pagliacci*	Leoncavallo	80
39003	Il Balen del suo sorriso, *Trovatore*	Verdi	
39004	Eri tu, *Ballo in maschera*	Verdi	
39005	O casto fior, *Roi de Lahore*	Massenet	
39007	Barcarola, *Gioconda*	Ponchielli	
39008	Un di m'era di gioia, *Andrea Chenier*	Giordano	
39009	E sempre vecchio andazzo, *Guglielmo Ratcliffe*	Mascagni	
39024	Credo, *Otello*	Verdi	

1905

69003	Terzetto, *Ballo in maschera* (with Russ and Longobardi)	Verdi
69004	Non m'inganno, *Trovatore* (with Russ and Longobardi)	Verdi

MAURICE RENAUD
LARGE BLACK LABEL, G&T. PARIS, 1901
(Converted to Large Red Label in 1902)

			R.P.M.
32076	Andante, *Favorite*	Donizetti	74
32077	Voici des Roses, *Damnation de Faust*	Berlioz	
32078	Jadis quand tu luttas, *Tannhauser*	Wagner	
32079	Priere, *Guillaume Tell*	Rossini	
32080	Rondel de l'Adieu	De Lara	
32081	Air, *Roi de Lahore*	Massenet	
32082	Le Soir	Gounod	
32083	Pour tant d'Amour, *Favorite*	Donizetti	
32084	Comme une pale Fleur, *Hamlet*	Thomas	

1902
RED LABEL, G&T. LONDON, 1902

			R.P.M.
2-2702	Romance de l'Etoile, *Tannhauser*	Wagner	75
2-2703	Le Chemin de Ciel	Holmes	
2-2704	Noel Paien	Massenet	
2-2705	Air du Toreador, *Carmen*	Bizet	
2-2713	Serenade, *Damnation de Faust*	Berlioz	

The above titles, with a few others added, were repeated in Paris recordings—Red Label in 1906, and Black Label in 1908-1909.

MARIO SAMMARCO
RED LABEL, G&T. MILAN, 1902

			R.P.M.
52371	Racconto, *Germania*	Franchetti	72
52372	Pari siamo, *Rigoletto*	Verdi	
52373	Zaza piccola zingara, *Zaza*	Leoncavallo	
52374	Prologo, *Pagliacci*	Leoncavallo	
52375	Credo, *Otello*	Verdi	

1903-1904

52011	Canzone della Pulce, *Damnation de Faust*	Berlioz	75
52782	Gia l'ignea colonna, *Mose*	Perosi	
052020	Racconto di Gerace, *Lorenza*	Mascheroni	
052025	Ballata d'Adamastor, *L'Africaine*	Meyerbeer	
052026	Monologo, *Andrea Chenier*	Giordano	
052027	Racconto, *Germania*	Franchetti	
052033	O dei verd'anni miei, *Ernani*	Verdi	
052034	Credo, *Otello*	Verdi	
052039	Sogno, *Otello*	Verdi	
052040	Arioso di Cascart, *Zaza*	Leoncavallo	
052041	Prologo, *Pagliacci*	Leoncavallo	
052063	Canzone delle Rose, *Damnation de Faust*	Berlioz	
054026	Scena di Susanna, *Lorenzo* (with Carelli)	Mascheroni	
054028	Gia mi dicon venal, *Tosca* (with Carelli)	Puccini	

FONOTIPIA. MILAN, 1903-4

39000	Canzone d'Amore, *Serenata rococo*	Meyer-Hellmund
39001	Serenata, *Don Giovanni*	Mozart
39006	A tanto Amor, *Favorita*	Donizetti
39025	Gia l'ignea colonna, *Mose*	Perosi
39077	O dei verd'anni miei, *Ernani*	Verdi
39078	Di Provenza, *Traviata*	Verdi

Sammarco recorded twenty-two further titles in the
Fonotipia 39 and 69 series.

CHARLES SANTLEY
RED LABEL, G&T. LONDON, 1903

R.P.M.

2-2862	Simon the Cellarer	Hatton	74
2-2863	The Vicar of Bray	Watson	
2-2864	To Anthea	Hatton	
02015	Thou 'rt passing hence	Sullivan	
052000	Non piu andrai, *Nozze di Figaro*	Mozart	

KARL SCHEIDEMANTEL
BLACK LABEL, G&T. DRESDEN, 1902

42843	Ich liebe dich	Grieg
42844	O Kehr zuruck, *Tannhauser*	Wagner
42869	Heinrich der Vogler	Loewe

1907-8

3-42821	Sohn knie' nieder, *William Tell*	Rossini
3-42822	Als du im Kuhnen, *Tannhauser*	Wagner
3-42936	Ich sell ein Gluck, *Figaro*	Mozart
3-42937	Champagnerlied, *Don Giovanni*	Mozart

ANTONIO SCOTTI
RED LABEL, G&T. LONDON, 1902

R.P.M.

2-2706	O Nuit d'Amour, *Messaline*	De Lara	75
2-2707	Serenata and Finch' an del vino, *Don Giovanni*	Mozart	
2-2708	Serenata	Rotoli	
2-2709	Dio possente, *Faust*	Gounod	
2-2710	Invano	Tosti	

2–2711	Toreador's Song, *Carmen*	Bizet	
2–2712	Quand'ero paggio, *Falstaff*	Verdi	

COLUMBIA. U.S.A., 1903

1205	Toreador's Song, *Carmen*	Bizet	
1206	Prologo, *Pagliacci*	Leoncavallo	
1207	Serenata and Finch'an del vino, *Don Giovanni*	Mozart	

RED LABEL, VICTOR-G&T. 1903–5

52059	Anch'io pugnai, *Aida*	Verdi	78
52061	Bella siccome un angelo, *Don Pasquale*	Donizetti	
52067	Dio possente, *Faust*	Gounod	
2–52433	Mandolinata	Paladilhe	
2–52434	O casto fior, *Roi de Lahore*	Massenet	
2–52435	Alla vita, *Ballo in maschera*	Verdi	
2–52481	Prologo, *Pagliacci*	Leoncavallo	
2–52482	Vi ravviso, *Sonnambula*	Bellini	
2–52483	Brindisi, *Otello*	Verdi	
052091	Eri tu, *Ballo in maschera*	Verdi	
052092	Credo, *Otello*	Verdi	
052107	Prologo, *Pagliacci*	Leoncavallo	
052108	Per me giunto, *Don Carlos*	Verdi	
052109	Come Paride, *L'Elisir d'amore*	Donizetti	
052112	Dio possente, *Faust*	Gounod	
052113	Serenata, *Don Giovanni* (**Mozart**) and		
	Quand'ero paggio	Verdi	
052115	Deh non parlar, *Rigoletto* (**Verdi**) and		
	Finch'an del vino, *Don Giovanni*	Mozart	

RICCARDO STRACCIARI

FONOTIPIA. MILAN, 1903

39058	Cruda funesta, *Lucia di Lammermoor*	Donizetti
39066	Prologo, *Pagliacci*	Leoncavallo

1904

39159	Ferito prigionier, *Germania*	Franchetti
39160	Quest'assisa, *Aida*	Verdi
39166	Dio possente, *Faust*	Gounod
39167	Ed or che tu coll'estro, *Tannhauser*	Wagner

1905

39625	Di Provenza, *Traviata*	Verdi
39626	O vecchio cor, *Due Foscari*	Verdi

ANTON VAN ROOY

RED LABEL, G&T. LONDON, 1902

			R.P.M.
2–2685	Wotan's Abschied, *Walkure*	Wagner	72
2–2700	Das Muhlrad		77
2–2701	Closing Scene, *Rheingold*	Wagner	77
2–2714	Opening Scene, *Rheingold*	Wagner	74
2–2715	Sangerkrieg, *Tannhauser*	Wagner	74
2–2716	Schusterlied, *Meistersinger*	Wagner	72

BASSES

FEDOR CHALIAPIN
RED LABEL, G&T. MOSCOW, 1901

			R.P.M.
22820	How the King went to War	Koenenmann	72
22821	O thou red Sun		
22822	Elegie	Karganoff	
22823	Le Veau d'or, *Faust*	Gounod	
22824	Prince Igor	Borodin	

JEAN FRANCOIS DELMAS
BLACK LABEL, G&T. PARIS, 1902–3

3–32622	Air, *Patrie*	Paladilhe
3–32623	Priere de la Symphonie legendaire	
3–32624	Scene de l'Eglise, *Faust*	Gounod
3–32625	Adieu de Wotan, *Walkure*	Wagner
3–32626	Air, *Jolie Fille de Perth*	Bizet
3–32627	Conte bleu, *La Tousseint*	
3–32629	Air, *Don Giovanni*	Mozart

FONOTIPIA. PARIS, 1903–4

39027	Benediction dea Poignards, *Huguenots*	Meyerbeer
39028	Ronde du Veau d'or, *Faust*	Gounod
39085	Air du pauvre Martyr, *Patrie*	Paladihle
39051	Serenade, *Faust*	Gounod
39053	Le Soir	Gounod
39106	Adieu de Wotan	Wagner
39107	Le Chemin du Ciel	Holmes
39130	Voici des Roses, *Damnation de Faust*	Berlioz
39210	Pater Noster	Neldermeyer
39—	Les deux Grenadiers	Schumann

EDOUARD DE RESZKE
COLUMBIA. 1903

			R.P.M.
1221	Infelice, *Ernani*	Verdi	70
1222	Porter Song, *Marta*	Flotow	
1223	Don Juan's Serenade	Tschaikowsky	

HAMILTON EARLE
BLACK LABEL, G&T. LONDON, 1903

			R.P.M.
2–2835	Myself when young, *In a Persian Garden*	Lehmann	73
2–2840	Deep in the heart of a Rose	Landon Ronald	
2–2867	Hear me ye winds and waves, *Scipio*	Handel	
02012	Air of Jupiter, *Philemon et Baucis*	Gounod	
02013	Vision fugitive, *Herodiade*	Massenet	
02014	After	Elgar	

PIERRE GAILHARD

FONOTIPIA. PARIS, 1903

39092	La Paloma	Yradier
39093	Hollah Matelots, *L'Africaine*	Meyerbeer

1904

39229	Serenata, *Faust*	Gounod
39230	Serenade, *Faust*	Gounod

MARCEL JOURNET

BLACK AND SILVER, COLUMBIA. 1905

3109	Infelice, *Ernani*	Verdi
3133	Vi ravviso, *Sonnambula*	Bellini
3134	Chanson des Peupliers, *Doria*	Machado
3135	Stances, *Lakma*	Delibes
3136	Vallons de l'Helvetie	Adam

RED LABEL, VICTOR-G&T. 1905

			R.P.M.
3-32518	Chanson des peupliers, *Doria*	Machado	78
3-42550	King's Prayer, *Lohengrin*	Wagner	
2-52515	Canzone del Porter, *Marta*	Flotow	
3-32668	Dans un delire, *Joconde*	Nicolo	
053093	Infelice, *Ernani*	Wagner	
032021	Ton doux regard, *Lakme*	Delibes	
032034	Les Boeufs	Dupont	
032035	Ella giammai, *Don Carlos*	Verdi	
032036	Serenade, *Faust*	Gounod	

1906

2-52516	Vecchia zimara, *La Boheme*	Puccini
3-32680	Le veau d'or, *Faust*	Gounod
042130	O du mein holder Abernstern, *Tannhauser*	Wagner
032036	Serenade, *Faust*	Gounod
032037	Les Deux Grenadiers	Schumann
032038	La Marseillaise	de l'Isle

1907

3-32685	Chanson de la Puce, *Damnation de Faust*	Berlioz
3-32686	Voici des Roses, *Damnation de Faust*	Berlioz
3-32687	Serenade, *Damnation de Faust*	Berlioz

ORESTS LUPPI

FONOTIPIA. MILAN, 1903

39062	Si donna infame, *Gioconda* (with Petri)	Ponchielli
39070	Ah del tebro, *Norma*	Bellini

1906

39732	Duet, *Ruy Blas*, Pt. 1 (with Martinez Patti)	Marchetti
39733	Duet, *Ruy Blas*, Pt. 2 (with Martinez Patti)	Marchetti
39738	Esci! a te, scegli, *Ernani* (with Martinez Patti)	Verdi
39739	Solingo, errante e misero, *Ernani* (with Martinez Patti)	Verdi
39799	Come protegge, *Ruy Blas* (with Corradetti)	Marchetti
39800	Ne ad un Bazan convien, *Ruy Blas* (with Corradetti)	Marchetti

See also under Russ, Bonci, Magini-Coletti, Sammarco, Petri and Garbin

1904

39138	Il lacerato spirito, *Simone Boccanegra*	Verdi
39139	Tu che fai l'addormentata, *Faust*	Gounod
39203	Infelice, *Ernani*	Verdi
39204	Ave Signor, *Mefistofele*	Boito
39205	La Calunnia, *Barbiere di Siviglia*	Rossini
39206	Ecco il mondo, *Mefistofele*	Boito
39273	Dio dell'or, *Faust*	Gounod
39311	Rammenta i lieta di, *Faust*	Gounod
39314	Vergin bella ed adorate, *Mephisto*	Carelli
39320	Do sposa, *Salvator rosa*	Gomez
39412	Madamina, *Don Giovanni*	Mozart
39413	Nella bionda, *Don Giovanni*	Mozart
39433	Dispersa s'en va, *Huguenots*	Meyerbeer
39376	Del mondo disingani, *Forza del Destino* (with Corradetti)	Verdi
39478	Leggiadre rondinelle, *Mignon* (with Ferraris)	Thomas
39479	Sofferto hai tu, *Mignon* (with Ferraris)	Thomas
39588	De Confutatis, *Requiem Mass*	Verdi
39589	Pro peccatis, *Stabat Mater*	Rossini

WATKIN MILLS
ODEON. LONDON, 1907

			R.P.M.
44759	Where e'er ye walk, *Semele*	Handel	72
44761	Is not his word like a Fire? *Elijah*	Mendelsohn	74
44795	The Lord worketh wonders, *Judas Maccabeus*	Handel	74
44796	Why do the Nations? *Messiah*	Handel	74
44682	There is a green hill	Gounod	
44812	Still is the Night	Abt	

POL PLANCON
INTERNATIONAL ZONOPHONE, SUCCESSIVELY ON
BLACK, ORANGE AND LIGHT BLUE LABELS.
PARIS, 1902

2061	Piff paff, *Huguenots*	Meyerbeer
2062	Serenade, *Faust*	Gounod
2062	Toreador Song, *Carmen*	Bizet
2065	Les Rameaux	Faure

RED LABEL, G&T. LONDON, 1902

			R.P.M.
2-2660	Air de Capulet, *Romeo et Juliette*	Gounod	72-75
2-2661	Piff-Paff, *Huguenots*	Meyerbeer	
2-2662	Les deux Grenadiers	Schumann	
2-2663	Serenade, *Faust*	Gounod	
2-2664	Air du Tambour-Major, *Le Caid*	Thomas	
2-2665	Les Rameaux	Faure	
2-2666	Au bruit des lourdes, *Philemon et Baucis*	Gounod	
2-2667	Air du Toreador, *Carmen*	Bizet	
2-2668	Ronde du Veau d'or, *Faust*	Gounod	
2-2717	Embarquez-vous	Godard	

1903

2–32909	Le Soupir	Bemberg
2–32910	Au Pays bleu	Chaminade
2–32911	Le Lazzarone	Ferrari
2–32918	En Route	Schumann

VICTOR-G&T. U.S.A., 1904

52070	Pro peccatis, *Stabat Mater*	Rossini
3–32179	Serenade, *Damnation de Faust*	Berlioz

RED LABEL, VICTOR-G&T
Recorded December, 1903

3–32661	Noel	Adam	78
3–32678	Serenade, *Damnation de Faust*	Berlioz
032019	Air du Tambour-Major, *Le Caid*	Thomas
032024	Vi ravviso, *La Sonnambula*	Bellini
032025	Les Rameaux	Faure

Recorded January, 1904

3–32644	Serenade, *Faust*	Gounod
3–32664	Air de Capulet, *Romeo et Juliette*	Gounod
52070	Pro Peccatis, *Stabat Mater*	Rossini
032018	Le Lac	Niedermeyer
032026	Les Deux Grenadiers	Schumann

Recorded February, 1904

3–32662	Embarquez-vous	Godard
3–32663	Air, Le Chalet	Adam
3–32665	Le veau d'or, *Faust*	Gounod

1905

032022	Le Vallon	Gounod
032023	Le Cor	Flegier
032029	Air du Laboureur, *Les Saisons*	Haydn
032027	Jesus de Nazareth	Gounod
032028	Le Lazzarone (Ferrari) and *Le Filibustier*	Georges
052090	Invocazione, *Flauto Magico*	Mozart
052117	Qui 'sdegno, *Flauto Magico*	Mozart
3–32590	Le Soupir	Bemberg
3–32591	Chant du Chasseur, *Pardon de Ploermel*	Meyerbeer
3–32592	Credo	Faure
3–32667	Si tu veux, *Mignon*	Massenet
3–32677	Couplets de Vulcain, *Philemon et Baucis*	Gounod

The recordings of 1906 consisted of repetitions, and
need not be re-stated here.

1907

2–52585	Canzone del porter, *Marta*	Flotow
3–32692	Chanson de la puce, *Damnation de Faust*	Berlioz
032064	Elle ne m'aime pas, *Don Carlos*	Verdi
032065	Air du Tambour-Major, *Le Caid*	Thomas
032066	Voici des Roses, *Damnation de Faust*	Berlioz

PINK LABEL, 1908

032077	Nonne qui reposez, *Robert le Diable*	Meyerbeer
032078	O jours hereux, *L'Etoile du Nord*	Meyerbeer
052217	Berceuse, *Mignon*	Thomas
052118	Pro Peccatis, *Stabat Mater*	Rossini

This concluded Plancon's recording.